D0026580

MORAL CONCEPTS

Edited by

JOEL FEINBERG

OXFORD UNIVERSITY PRESS

WILLIAM MADISON RANDALL LIBRARY UNC AT WILMINGTON

Oxford University Press, Walton Street, Oxford OX2 6DP

London Glasgow New York Toronto
Delhi Bombay Calcutta Madras Karachi
Kuala Lumpur Singapore Hong Kong Tokyo
Nairobi Dar es Salaam Cape Town
Melbourne Auckland

and associates in
Beirut Berlin Ibadan Mexico City Nicosia

ISBN 0 19 875012 9

© *Oxford University Press 1969*

First impression 1969
Reprinted 1982

All rights reserved. No part of this publication may be reproduced, stored in a retrieval system, or transmitted, in any form or by any means, electronic, mechanical, photocopying, recording, or otherwise, without the prior permission of Oxford University Press

This book is sold subject to the condition that it shall not, by way of trade or otherwise, be lent, re-sold, hired out, or otherwise circulated without the publisher's prior consent in any form of binding or cover other than that in which it is published and without a similar condition including this condition being imposed on the subsequent purchaser

Printed in Hong Kong

BJ21
.F4

CONTENTS

221483

vi CONTENTS

ively human tendencies and powers. Enjoyment, of course, is not to be sneered at; but it comes most reliably to those who aim at something else. Pleasure is a kind of added dividend, a by-product of the 'unimpeded exercise of a faculty', like the purr of a well-tuned motor (but not like its exhaust fumes). Similarly it is not pain and unpleasantness that the wise man guards against, but rather being blocked in his natural growth, a condition which is incidentally but perhaps not necessarily painful. Self-realization can be called happiness providing only that it is not con- fused thereby with mere enjoyment. A stunted oak tree is not 'in a happy state for an oak tree' even though the issue of enjoyment in its case can hardly arise. And so, this disagreement over ultimate goals led to emerging schools of thought: Hedonism (championing pleasure) and Eudaemonism (championing fulfilment), each armed with doctrines, arguments, and rejoinders.

Inquiries concerning the ideals of personal excellence also generated rival doctrines. Even before the dawn of formal philosophizing the Greeks had developed a rough and ready conception of an ideal person who combined virtues of a physical, aesthetic, moral, and intellectual kind. This 'four-square man'[1] had pre-eminently the virtues of the athlete and warrior—strength, co-ordination, endurance, resoluteness, and courage. His 'aesthetic virtues', notably what came to be called 'temper- ance', were largely a matter of style: especially did he avoid vulgarity and self-display, and his manner was free of *hubris*—self-importance or pomposity. His chief moral virtue consisted in minding his own business and respecting his neighbours' property; and his intellectual virtues in- cluded skills at arts and crafts, rhetoric and politics, even science and philosophy. By the time of Socrates, this conception had evolved into that of the 'four cardinal virtues'—courage, temperance, justice, and wisdom. In the ideal man the four kinds of excellence were blended and balanced all in proper proportion.

So much was part of the general background of moral philosophy in Greece; but there was still plenty of room for disagreement. Was it pos- sible to have any one cardinal virtue without having them all? Could the wise man, for example, be a coward? Is one of the four virtues more fundamental than the others? Could the four perhaps be reduced to one? And how was each virtue to be analysed? In what did true courage or wisdom consist? Common as disagreements were among the proposed answers to these questions, the disagreements that generated schools of

---

[1] The following account is drawn from C. M. Bowra, *The Greek Experience* (London: New English Library, and New York: New American Library, 1947), pp. 98 ff.

INTRODUCTION

LIKE THE sages and sophists who preceded them, the earliest moral philosophers were primarily devoted to two sorts of tasks: recommending life goals and specifying ideals of personal excellence. Men of affairs, in their reflective moments, turned to men called wise to learn the secret of the good life—of ultimate purposes and the goods most worth having; and sometimes, though probably much less often, they inquired about the traits of character most worth cultivating—the sorts of persons most worth being.

The leading conceptions of ultimate goods and personal ideals then are surely among the most important members of the class of 'moral concepts'. And these conceptions were not slow in suggesting themselves. Money and reputation could hardly be the things most worth having since their value is only instrumental; and many other valuable possessions, experiences, and activities are valued only in so far as they are enjoyed. This suggested to many thinkers in antiquity as well as modern times that it is only enjoyment as such that is valuable for its own sake, and that the good life therefore is the one that is most full of fun and free of pain and frustration. But battlelines quickly formed over this contention. Some, like Plato's successor in the Academy, Speusippus, and in modern times, Schopenhauer, held that pleasantness of experience could hardly be a positive good at all, since it is in its very nature a negative and illusory thing. The pain of hunger is a positive thing; but the 'pleasure' of eating, they argued, is merely the absence of pain. Replenishment, so to speak, brings us up to a centre line which is as high as we can get before 'deficiency' sets in again and we fall to the negative part of the scale. Others rejected hedonism on the ground that there is nothing distinctly human about pleasure, that a pampered pig or contented cow, on this theory, lives a better life than any human being who knows the slightest anxiety, disappointment, or grief; or on the ground that hedonism would rate the passive pleasures of a well-supplied opium addict as high or higher than the mixed pleasures and pains of the man of action.

Our ultimate goal, according to the Aristotelian critics of hedonism, is not mere enjoyment but rather a kind of *fulfilment*. The good life is that which actualizes our governing biological propensities, our distinct-

thought were largely of another kind. In times of stress and insecurity when communities depend upon the vigilance and toughness of the military class, the martial virtues are the most esteemed ones, and 'virtue' itself, as its etymology suggests, is nothing more nor less than manliness. But Roman republics tend to turn into Roman empires, and among the leisured, the martial virtues are a bore, and the softer, amiable ones are most esteemed. Thus, there have ever been

. . . two types of excellence . . . in the world. There have ever been stern, upright, self-controlled and courageous men, actuated by a pure sense of duty, capable of high efforts of self-sacrifice, somewhat intolerant of the frailties of others, somewhat hard and unsympathizing in the ordinary intercourse of society, but rising to heroic grandeur as the storm lowered on their path, and more ready to relinquish life than the course they believed to be true. There have also always been men of easy tempers and of amiable disposition, gentle, benevolent, and pliant, cordial friends and forgiving enemies, selfish at heart yet ever ready, when it is possible, to unite their gratifications with those of others; averse to all enthusiasm, mysticism, utopias, and superstition, with little depth of character or capacity for self-sacrifice, but admirably fitted to impart and to receive enjoyment, and to render the course of life easy and harmonious. The first are by nature Stoics, and the second, Epicureans.[1]

The good man on the one conception is very like the good soldier: tough, disciplined, reliable. On the other conception, he is more like the good friend, the comrade, the crony. The one is hard, the other gentle; the one more likely to be admired, the other to be liked. Perhaps the most striking difference between them is the supreme importance in the one, and absence in the other, of the sense of *duty*. Indeed the stoic conception of excellence is inseparable from the idea of duty. One's life is a drama, and one's place is one's role. The duties of one's station or role define that station or role itself. To know what it is to be a father or son, cobbler or cook, emperor or slave, is precisely to know a set of duties. And the whole of virtue is to discharge those duties as well as one can. That the 'moral concept' of duty is in turn capable of generating puzzles and disagreements hardly needs demonstrating. Anyone occupies dozens of roles whose defining duties can on occasion conflict. How can these roles be ranked in importance and how can the conflicts between duties be resolved? Does it make sense to speak of the duties of a man as such? If so, how does one learn what *they* are?

Not only did rival schools emerge from the efforts to make coherent statements of ultimate goods and ideals of excellence, they also arose over the question of how the goods are related to the ideals. It is a

[1] W. E. H. Lecky, *A History of European Morals*, Vol. I (London: D. Appleton & Co., 1927), p. 172.

truism that a man's ultimate good is to be 'well-off' (or to live well, or be in a happy state, etc.), however well-off-ness is to be understood; but suppose that being well-off can be bought at the price of personal excellence. Would it be a reasonable bargain? Which in the last analysis is the more important: to have the goods most worth having or to be the sort of person most worth being? Perhaps no question agitated the Greeks as much as this one. The question was much less likely to arise in connection with some virtues than with others. Some forms of excellence are highly developed knacks or skills; and in general, the *capable* man has a better chance, other things being equal, of faring well. But if this weren't true, many sceptics wondered, if courage and temperance, endurance and fortitude, did not help a man flourish, then what would be the point of cultivating them? After all, they are in themselves just so much trouble. But it is what we have come to call 'moral excellence' or Virtue (in a modern sense) that most frequently occasioned the problem. By and large it pays to be honest and upright; but in particular cases we may have to choose between that form of excellence called integrity, on the one hand, and being well or better off, on the other. Again schools of thought emerged. Some held that all conflict between virtue and well-being is illusory; that properly understood, what is good for my character is good for my interest, and vice versa. Others held that a man can be too virtuous for his own good; while still others maintained that the moral virtues, at least, and in particular, integrity, are themselves goods, in fact the most precious goods any man can 'possess', and superior even to happiness itself.

In the elaboration of such ethical doctrines, familiar ethical concepts —'goals', 'goods', 'excellence', 'virtues', 'pleasure', 'pain', 'happiness', 'duty', 'prudence', 'courage', 'integrity'—become the foci of argument and the prizes of controversy; and these everyday concepts, in turn, become sharpened and refashioned by theory. There comes a time, in fact very early in the game, when intelligent argument over rival doctrines must be postponed and critical attention directed instead to the crucial moral concepts themselves. For several reasons it is necessary to analyse these concepts objectively—quite apart from the context of any theory and with no aim at ideological axe-grinding. First of all, the acceptability of some proposed goal or ideal often seems to depend on what is meant by the word that expresses it. Is pleasure the highest good for man? Well, that surely depends on what we mean by 'pleasure'. Is 'pleasure' the name of a certain quality of bodily sensation, so that continuous sensuous titillation is the necessary means to its maximization? Or is pleasure simply the satisfaction that comes when we get what we desire, whatever we desire?

If the latter, how can we account for the disappointingly unsatisfying character of some 'satisfactions'? Is pleasure a 'positive' thing or simply the privation of pain? Do those chronic cigarette smokers who are unhappily resigned to their habit 'enjoy' smoking? Does the masochist derive pleasure from his pain? In what way then is pleasure the 'opposite' of pain? These examples show not only that deciding on the suitability of a proposed ideal requires getting clear about just what it is and what it commits us to, but also that clarity of conception is required if we are to speak coherently and avoid paradox.

I have in this book selected specimens of the analysis of particular moral concepts drawn from the recent work of leading British and American philosophers. The topics can be placed in three more or less overlapping categories. The first group includes 'pleasure' and 'happiness', the leading candidates, historically speaking, for the status of supreme goods or ultimate goals. The second, somewhat more motley group includes concepts employed in the specification of ideals of excellence, for example, 'duties', 'supererogation', 'rules', certain of those ideals themselves—'prudence', 'courage', 'proper self-regard', 'conscientiousness'—and also ways of falling short of the ideals, notably 'moral ignorance' and 'moral weakness'. Finally, a third category is reserved for an elusive notion that is fundamental to Judeo-Christian ethics, to Kantian philosophy, and to modern democratic liberalism, namely that 'infinite worth' of the individual human person that is said to be the basis of human rights.

Gilbert Ryle's treatment of the idea of pleasure has already become a new starting place for the philosophical discussion of that venerable concept. There is little doubt now that a new beginning was long overdue. For two centuries English-speaking philosophers have debated the hedonism of the classical utilitarians; but even among the enemies of hedonism there has been little close analysis of the concept of pleasure itself, with the consequence that there has been a widespread uncritical acceptance of Bentham's own conception of pleasure. The Benthamite analysis[1] has a number of elements. First of all, although Bentham sometimes speaks of pleasure and pain as 'kinds of sensations', he formally defines them, simply, as 'interesting perceptions'. It is therefore unlikely that Bentham held the precise but implausible view that all pleasures and pains simply are sensations. More likely he believed that pleasures and pains are discriminably agreeable or disagreeable aspects of 'perceptions' of all kinds, not only of simple sensations but also of various cogni-

[1] Jeremy Bentham, *An Introduction to the Principles of Morals and Legislation*, chapters iii-v *et passim*.

tive states, such as awareness, expectation, and recollection. Still his discussion of these complex matters is to the modern reader neither clear nor consistent; and there seems little doubt that both he and many of his followers often spoke as if there were one distinct experience of joy which, whatever its cause or object, can be introspectively discriminated and separately identified as 'pleasure' (and similarly for 'pain'). When we speak of activities or experiences which 'give' pleasure, the activity or experience, on this view, is one thing, and the pleasure is a separate sensation or feeling that accompanies or is caused by it.

Another important Benthamite doctrine (made even more of by J. S. Mill) was that there are intellectual and spiritual pleasures as well as bodily ones, these consisting in mental glows not localizable at any place in the body. Moreover, it was held that pleasure and pain are located at opposite ends of a common scale, or as Professor Ryle paraphrased the doctrine, 'the role of the concept of *pleasure* is the precise counterpart of the role of the concept of *pain*, as that of *north* is the counterpart of that of *south* . . .'[1] Finally, each quantitative 'dimension' of pleasure and pain (intensity, duration, etc.) is itself, according to Bentham, in principle measurable; and furthermore, these various quantitative aspects are mutually commensurable, so that it is possible, in theory, to speak of a total amount of pleasure or pain all told. According to Bentham we could, with more advanced techniques, not only derive such sum totals for individuals, but also speak of determinate net aggregates of pleasure or pain for groups.

At one place or another in his writings Professor Ryle has contested all of these doctrines. In the paper included here he specifically rejects the view that the enjoyment we get from an activity is something (a sensation, or an 'interesting perception', or whatever) distinct from the activity itself. 'Ryle maintains', as one commentator puts it, 'that when I enjoy some activity, e.g. playing golf, then it is the golf itself that I enjoy, not the sensations that I get from playing golf. For if there were a sensation arising from the golf, it would only serve as a distraction from the game itself, and to say that I enjoy a game of golf is precisely to say that I am not easily distractable and not in fact distracted during the game.'[2] To enjoy an activity, for Ryle, is to be engrossed in it, although this cannot be the whole of the matter since some forms of total engrossment (e.g. a continuously unsuccessful poker game) are not very enjoyable. Ryle claims only that attending to, or giving one's mind

---

[1] Gilbert Ryle, *Dilemmas* (Cambridge University Press: 1954), p. 57.
[2] A. R. Manser, 'Pleasure', *Proceedings of the Aristotelian Society*, N.S. Vol. LXI (1960-1), p. 224.

to, is the *genus* of which enjoying is one species. Some might contend, however, that it is not the sole genus in which the 'polymorphous' concept of enjoyment can fit. A soldier friend during the war once told me that whenever he had leave from his hated duties (cleaning garbage cans under conditions of severe discipline) he would constantly remind himself during his freedom that he was enjoying himself and this always intensified the enjoyment. He would tell himself at regular intervals while watching the ballet or a sports match—'I am now having fun; I will soon be at work longing for such a moment as this', and this distracting but 'interesting perception' always gave him a special thrill that mingled with and gave flavour to his enjoyment of the events he was observing. But even if Ryle is right about what it is to enjoy a walk or a game of golf, his analysis hardly seems to do justice to the pleasure one gets from sucking a lemon drop, which seems to be a matter primarily of savouring the gustatory sensations that accompany the activity. It is plain that finding one large genus for the analysis of all our enjoyment-idioms as they apply to the multifarious things we are said to enjoy will be no easy task.

Whatever the nature and value of pleasure, if there is one kind of thing which is certainly *evil*, most of us would say, that thing is pain. Still, as R. M. Hare points out, while the majority vote of philosophers concurs with this judgement, it is by no means unanimous. The ancient Stoics held not only that it is within every man's power to be completely free of frustration and disappointment ('mental pain') but also that physical pain itself needn't be a disagreeable or troublesome thing to the wise man who has cultivated the proper attitude towards it; and it was an Epicurean philosopher who boasted that he could be happy on the rack. Professor Hare in his paper in this volume argues that it is *logically* possible for a person not to dislike his painful sensations even while they are hurting, indeed even to find the hurt enjoyable. Whether these extraordinary reactions to pain ever occur, Hare argues, is an empirical question; but he finds some grounds in the recent literature of physiological psychology for thinking that they do.

Anthony Kenny examines the notion of happiness, which in the western philosophical tradition has often been held to be one and the same thing as a 'supreme good for man'. In modern English when we call a man happy we often mean no more than that he is in (or tends to be in) high spirits or a good mood;[1] but there is a long tradition

---

[1] W. D. Ross wrote that the English word 'happiness' suggests 'a state of feeling differing from pleasure, if at all, only by its suggestion of a greater permanence, depth, and serenity'. *Aristotle* (London: Methuen & Co., 1966), p. 190.

of philosophical usage which contrasts happiness with pleasure or enjoyment. Aristotle's word *eudaemonia*, usually translated as 'happiness', literally meant 'watched over by a good angel' or, as we would say, 'blessed'. In ordinary Greek it meant 'good fortune'. Perhaps 'well-being', 'faring well', or 'being well-off' are close to its sense, but they are probably insufficiently dynamic. 'Living well', 'really living', 'living to the hilt' perhaps come closer to catching its flavour. At any rate, if this is what happiness is, it is plain that it cannot be the same thing as the passive enjoyment of pleasant sensations. It is perhaps not quite self-evident that happiness, so conceived, is the highest good; but for Aristotle it was a mere truism that *eudaemonia* is the supreme end. The interesting question was—'In what does *eudaemonia* consist?'

Kenny quite naturally begins his discussion with Aristotle and the idea of a 'supreme good' that is identical with happiness. His interpretation exonerates Aristotle from the common charge that he held there to be a single end that all men seek in all their actions. In the course of this discussion Kenny brings to bear on the question several useful modern distinctions: happiness as a goal vs. happiness as an achieved state; happiness as a dominant end-among-other ends vs. happiness as a derivative or inclusive end; happiness as contentment vs. happiness as richness or fullness of life. The latter distinction is especially interesting. Both 'contentment' and 'fullness', Kenny plausibly suggests, are part of our concept of happiness, and they can pull in opposite ways. (J. S. Mill's theory of value was a valiant but hopeless attempt to ride both these horses in opposite directions at the same time.) It seems that on all the major theories of the ultimate human goods there is a basic and incorrigible *surdity*. If we hold that there is an irreducible plurality of goods (e.g. G. E. Moore's 'personal affections' and 'aesthetic enjoyment', or W. D. Ross's 'pleasure', 'virtue', 'knowledge', and 'just apportionment') then there is no way of telling how to choose between them when they conflict. We can say that amounts of knowledge being equal, then the more pleasure the better, and vice versa; but this does not tell us whether a fatally ill young man is better off knowing the unhappy truth or believing a reassuring lie. And if we find that it is conducibility to pleasure in the end that makes all good things good, new and equally inescapable pluralities emerge. How are we to weight the various quantitative dimensions of pleasures and pains when *they* conflict? Should we be romantic hedonists and prefer one hour of extremely intense pleasure to four hours of moderately intense pleasure, or conservative hedonists willing to forego the ephemeral ecstasies and transports for more durable but less exciting joys? If there is only one standard of value and that is pleasure, there is no rational way of making such decisions. And now, if Kenny is right, the same sorts of dilemmas confront the champions of 'a supreme good or happiness'. One of the morals of this is, I think, that increasing one's own good can never be a mere matter of calculation, like increasing one's money.

One of the traditional enterprises of moral philosophers has been to catalogue the 'duties of men', and if these can be reduced to some relatively simple formula, to affirm what is 'the whole duty of man'. On this conception, fidelity to duty is the supreme moral virtue. C. H. Whiteley distinguishes between the ordinary everyday senses of 'duty' and 'obligation' in which those terms refer to *commitments* derived from institutional rules, promises, and the occupancy of offices and social roles, on the one hand, and what has come to be the technical 'philosopher's sense' of 'duty' as 'the right thing to do, all things considered', on the other hand. One of the consequences of making duty the central and most comprehensive moral concept, the basis of all personal excellence and the organizing idea of the moral life, is that forms of virtue unrelated to commitment (e.g. spontaneous benevolence) and forms of right action that are beyond duty or simply irrelevant to duty are excluded altogether from the scope of morality. But if these traits and actions are analysed in terms of duty in the broad philosopher's sense, then there is a high danger that there will be some trading back and forth on the two conceptions of duty, with the result that commendable conduct that is totally alien to commitment will be understood as the discharging of commitments of a special and mysterious kind; and dealings between free and independent persons will be reinterpreted as rule-governed transactions between special office-holders in an all-embracing 'moral institution'.

One common way of institutionalizing moral concepts is to take those familiar legal and institutional regulations that control conduct by enjoining some actions and forbidding others as models for interpreting all moral principles and excellences. Such rules naturally divide all actions into three categories: the required, the permitted, and the forbidden. Those actions enjoined by the rules are duties and these are the only actions that have moral merit; permitted actions are merely 'all right'; forbidden actions are wrong. J. O. Urmson points out that this threefold classification, assumed by a surprising number of moral philosophers, prevents us from making distinctions we commonly make and would be loathe to give up. In particular it provides no pigeon-hole for the accommodation of heroic and saintly deeds, those actions which may present themselves as duties to those who perform them, but are in fact far in excess of anything that any moral rules could plausibly require.

The historical interest of Urmson's essay consists in the fact that he has mustered hardheaded, secular, 'utilitarian' reasons in support of a doctrine which has long had a place in Roman Catholic teachings and which was quite explicitly rejected by Luther. The early church fathers distinguished between *praecepta*, or commandments of God, disobedience to which is sin, and the *consilia evangelica* issued by Christ in the New Testament, which are in Tertullian's words 'advised rather than commanded'. The latter were discussed under three headings by Aquinas[1]—'Poverty, Chastity, and Obedience'—and included items of 'advice', mainly from the Sermon on the Mount, such as 'Love your enemies' (Matt. 5: 44) and 'Resist not evil' (Matt. 5: 39-41). As St. Thomas interprets these counsels of perfection, acting in accordance with them is not necessary for salvation, though they are instrumentalities for attaining that end 'better and more quickly'. Luther, on the other hand, held that the counsels were part of God's law, and denied that any infraction of law could be justified or that an inferior 'perfection' could be tolerated.[2]

How the Catholic doctrine is applied to casuistic questions is well illustrated by an editorial in a Catholic newspaper on the rights of the owner of a fall-out shelter to exclude his neighbours during a nuclear attack.

. . . a clear distinction must be maintained between the minimum requirements of morality, beyond which there is sin, and the ideal of the evangelical counsels given by Christ. To avoid sin one does not have to be heroic. One may turn the other cheek; one is not always obliged to do so. One may go the second mile; one does not sin if he does not. One can give away one's cloak; one may keep it without culpability. For even greater reason, the law of charity does not suspend the basic natural law, including in first place the law of self-preservation.

That is why under certain rigorous conditions one may repel an unjust attacker to save one's life, limbs, virtue, or necessities of life even to the point of killing him if necessary. On the other hand, an individual may for a higher motive sacrifice his life rather than repel or kill. He is free here. Christian perfection would urge him to sacrifice himself for the good of the

---

[1] *Summa Theologica*, ii. i., Qu. 108, art. 4 and Qu. 184, art. 3.

[2] For clear summaries of the differences between Luther and St. Thomas on this question see 'Consilia Evangelica' by Karl Thieme in *The New Schaff-Herzog Encyclopedia of Religious Knowledge*, ed. Samuel M. Jackson (Grand Rapids, Michigan: Baker Book House, 1949).

unjust aggressor. Christian moral theology would leave him free to defend himself without sin.[1]

Urmson agrees that a rational morality will pose ideals of self-denial and self-sacrifice as goals of aspiration while leaving an individual free to choose the less exacting path; but Urmson's reasons are not drawn from authorities or revealed texts. The function of a moral code, he tells us, is 'to serve human needs', and this is more efficiently done by a code that distinguishes ideals from basic duties. Without general performance of the code's minimal requirements, life would be a jungle; so in a sense, duties are more stringent and important than 'the higher flights of morality'. Moreover, to *require* everyone to do what only few could do would put the duty-imposing rules in disrepute. Again, a code requiring acts of saintliness and heroism, if generally followed, would lead to chaos, as millions would flock to be heroic at every opportunity, and get in each other's way. Too many cooks can spoil the moral broth. This could be prevented only by rules of unworkable complexity. Furthermore, if there were duties of perfection, Urmson argues, then each of us could demand self-sacrificing services from total strangers, and there would be no occasion afterwards for gratitude. If these are all conceded to be unhappy results, then the distinction between freely offered meritorious services and the acts demanded by duty can be seen to be a distinction with a ('utilitarian') point.

Hardly anyone would deny that the virtue of character variously called scrupulosity, probity, and conscientiousnesss is of very great moral importance. Most writers analyse this form of excellence in terms of motives. The man who acts on the motive called 'the sense of duty', says P. H. Nowell-Smith, is precisely the man who is called conscientious.[2] This may or may not be so, but it does seem clear that the conscientious man is to be distinguished from the merely 'dutiful' man, as A. C. Garnett might maintain, by the greater critical prowess and sensitivity of his conscience. C. D. Broad's account of conscientiousness avoids mention of duty, and refers instead to 'the desire to do what is right as such'. This, I think, is an improvement, except perhaps in so far as leads him to speak of degrees of rightness. The most interesting feature of Professor Broad's account is his conclusion that it is well-nigh impossible for a person to know (or for another to know about him) that one

---

[1] *The Providence* (Rhode Island) *Visitor*, 19 October 1961. I am grateful to Professor J. W. Lenz for calling this to my attention.

[2] *Ethics* (Harmondsworth: Pelican Books, 1954), p. 245.

of his actions (e.g. his refusal to serve in a war) truly is conscientious. Paradoxically, the truly conscientious man is likely to have the strongest doubts about the purity of his own conscientiousness. In another essay (a contribution to a symposium in the 1930s on 'Ought We to Fight for Our Country in the Next War?'[1]) Professor Broad finds still other considerations to trouble the conscience of the conscientious objector whose livelihood depends on the protection of those of his countrymen who *are* fighting:

Plaintly there is a *prima facie* obligation not to put yourself in this situation of one-sided dependence on what you must regard as the wrong actions of people who are less virtuous or less enlightened than yourself. This complication would be avoided if the conscription law imposed the death penalty for refusal to undertake military or other war service. I am inclined to think that this ought to be done, and that really conscientious objectors to military service should welcome it.[2]

A willingness to die for one's moral convictions should strengthen an objector's confidence in his own conscientiousness, though if Broad's analysis is correct, there may well even yet be strong ground for doubts.

Conscientiousness was held by Kant to be the only motive of genuine moral worth, and it is held by ordinary citizens to be so worthy of respect that even in conditions of extreme danger there is surprisingly little resentment directed at conscientious objectors. Nowell-Smith suggested in his chapter on the subject[3] that conscientiousness may have had a better press than it deserves. Robespierre, he claimed, would have been a morally better man all told had he taken his deluded conscience a little *less* seriously. To this judgement Professor Garnett takes strong exception. It seems incredible to him that 'a man can be . . . a "better man" than he otherwise would be in performing an act even of sympathy and good will . . . which in the circumstances he regards as wrong'. One can easily feel the force of both sides in this controversy.[4] There is, I believe, a genuine moral paradox here, and one which requires for its resolution not merely a better understanding of the moral concepts 'conscience' and 'conscientiousness' but also of

---

[1] Included in *Ethics and the History of Philosophy* (London: Routledge & Kegan Paul, 1952), pp. 232-43.

[2] Ibid. p. 241.

[3] Op. cit., pp. 245-59.

[4] Nowell-Smith's view is similar to one Aristotle attributes to some unnamed sophists—that 'folly plus incontinence is a virtue' . . . 'For, they argue, a man who is both foolish and incontinent is led by his incontinence to do the opposite of what he thinks he ought to do, but he believes that good things are bad and that he ought not to do them. Ergo, he will do good and not bad things.' *Nich. Eth.* 46^a 25-30.

'moral worth'. What is it to be a morally good man as opposed to a man who is good in some other respect? Ambiguity sets snares all around this question. There are, first of all, both narrow and broad conceptions of moral worth paralleling in some ways, Whiteley's two conceptions of duty. In the narrow conception, a man has moral worth if he is honourable and upright, can be absolutely relied upon to honour his word, pay his debts, and obey those rules and authorities to which he finds himself subject. Trustworthiness, obedience, and loyalty, in this conception, are the distinctively moral virtues, and the morally good man is primarily contrasted with the betrayer, the liar, and the cheat. But a man can be 'good at' morality, conceived in this narrow way, and still not be much of a man. He might exude rectitude and yet be devoid of insight and sensitivity; he could be dour, self-righteous, egotistical, boring, humourless, insensitive, and unsympathetic. If so, he may be subject to low moral marks despite his rectitude, if we interpret his flaws as moral flaws. And why not? They are character flaws; and in the wider conception of moral worth, all traits of character, as opposed to traits of intellect, are relevant to the moral appraisal of a man. But there are dangers for this broad conception too. There are powerful, post-Aristotelian traditions that contrast the distinctively moral not merely with the intellectual but with all parts of a man's make-up not chargeable to, or subject to the direct control of, his will. A moral trait is one a person can be made to answer for; and we hesitate to hold a person to blame ultimately for being tasteless, unperceptive, cold, or humourless, since we find it hard to believe anyone would will or choose, even indirectly, to be any of these things.

If appraising the unconscientious Robespierre poses a paradox, there is still another paradox lurking behind it. No matter how we are to grade the man of deluded conscience who (luckily for us) does what he regards as wrong, we must understand in the first place, what seemed hardly intelligible to Plato and Aristotle, how a man—any man— could voluntarily do what 'in the circumstances he regards as wrong'. Donald Davidson is only speaking for common sense when he writes that he is absolutely certain that it sometimes happens that a person has 'an unclouded, unwavering judgement that [his] action is not for the best all things considered' and yet quite deliberately performs the action nevertheless. But he also claims to be speaking for common sense when he reports an apparent inconsistency between his belief in the occurrence of such actions and another apparent truism that 'in so far as a person acts intentionally he acts in the light of what he . . . judges to be the better course. How to cope with this apparent contradiction is the traditional problem of 'incontinence' or 'moral weakness' that so troubled Aristotle and Aquinas; but unlike many others who have tried to deal with it, Davidson generalizes the problem by declining to restrict incontinence to such 'special cases as being overcome by the beast in us, or of failing to heed the call of duty, or of succumbing to temptation'. There are apparent cases of voluntarily choosing the admittedly worse alternative that have nothing to do with temptation, or passion, or morality. 'Incontinence' in this general sense, Davidson tells us, is a special kind of conflict of reasons; and his explanation of 'how it is possible' incorporates a theory about the nature of practical reasoning.

The selection by W. D. Falk is part of a much larger essay on the status of self-regarding reasons in morality. In particular, Falk is concerned, in the larger essay, with the question of whether there can be a morality composed of moral precepts, commitments, and reasons of a wholly self-regarding kind, or whether morality by its very nature is social. If the latter alternative is correct, then it might yet be true of a man marooned on a desert island that he *ought* not to allow himself to become demoralized, or to ruin his health, or to neglect his talents, but this 'ought' would not be a distinctively moral 'ought' but perhaps only 'a mere matter of prudence or expediency'.

Now whether or not a purely self-regarding precept can ever properly be called a *moral* precept, Falk had argued earlier in his essay, can be a quite fruitless verbal question. There may be a 'cleft in the very concept' of the distinctively moral (moral as opposed to non-moral), since the concept 'may have grown from conflicting or only partially overlapping considerations . . . not fully reconciled in ordinary thinking'.[1] There are, according to Falk, at least three not fully reconciled criteria of the distinctively moral 'ought'. According to the first, it is an 'ought' whose grounds are social (other-regarding); according to the second, it has special force and stringency, and is stern, imposing, and onerous; according to the third, it is unqualified and categorical. Now the personal 'ought' (what one ought to do on his own account merely) does not satisfy the first criterion, and so it is not in that respect moral. But it doesn't follow, Falk insists, that it can't, on some occasions at least, satisfy the second and third criteria every bit as fully as a social 'ought' can. In any case, it is certainly false—and there is no gainsaying Falk on this point—that 'everything ones does for his own sake one does merely as a matter of prudence or expediency'. Sometimes one

[1] 'Morality and Self' in Castañeda and Nakhnikian, eds., *Morality and the Language of Conduct* (Detroit: Wayne State University Press, 1963), p. 33.

can be too prudent for one's own good; and a person sometimes owes it to himself to throw prudence to the winds and have the courage to shoulder a great risk. Falk then very carefully distinguishes the always self-regarding virtues of prudence and temperance from each other and from the sometimes wholly self-regarding virtue of courage. It may be fruitless to argue beyond a point whether these are genuinely 'moral' virtues; but the least misleading course is probably to agree with the ancients that they are.

The final group of essays switches the focus from persons as moral subjects to persons as moral objects, from the flaws and excellences of moral agents to the claims of moral 'patients' not to be mistreated. It was once a revolutionary idea that any person at all, no matter how lowly in status or deficient in merit, can make certain claims against everyone, that there are some human rights that are universal and unforfeitable. Now, however, most of us hold this view, and it has even come to be sanctioned by most national governments, East and West, and endorsed by international bodies including the United Nations itself. For all of this, the theory that there are rights held equally by all human beings has always troubled philosophers. It is natural to to imagine sceptics asking: 'Why *all* human beings and not just the deserving ones?' and 'Why *only* human beings and not some of the lower animals too?' In response to such challenges, philosophers have attempted to support the theory of human rights with a more fundamental theory of universal moral equality. There are certain rights that all men have because, no matter how they may differ in other ways, all men are equal in some one respect which is of supreme moral importance. But what is this respect? Some philosophers opt for certain natural capacities, no matter how fully realized, such as 'rationality', or for natural vulnerabilities such as the liability to pain and suffering. Others speak of distinctively moral or transcendental properties, a distinctively human 'worth', or 'dignity', or 'sacredness', attaching only to 'ends-in-themselves', and in turn, belonging to all and only human beings in virtue of the shared 'fatherhood of God', or 'simply because they are persons', or because of their 'common humanity'. None of this has proved very satisfactory. The proposed natural bases neither exclude differences in the strength of the claims different persons might make nor justify the exclusion of some animals; and the distinctively moral traits 'explain' only by renaming that which is to be explained.

John Rawls's essay is in part an effort to illuminate the obscure corners of the idea of moral equality, but his complicated and ambitious theory does more than this. The basis of a person's right to just treatment is his own capacity for a sense of justice, Rawls argues; and the sense of justice, in turn, requires for its explanation that its possessor be considered in his role as moral subject or agent. To have a sense of justice is in part to understand what justice is all about and in part to be capable of such full-fledged moral feelings as indignation, resentment, and remorse, which grow out of natural sentiments as conditioned by that understanding. It is a primary part of Rawls's purpose to sketch the natural history of that growth.

In an earlier essay, 'Justice as Fairness' (*Philosophical Review*, vol. 68, 1958), Rawls attempted to explain in a very general way what justice is all about. It is to this explanation that he refers when he mentions his 'analytic construction', or hypothetical model. The 'construction' is a kind of experiment in the imagination. We are asked to imagine a group of more or less self-interested and rational individuals each free to join or not join with all the others depending on whether they can agree on principles to be used in designing their common legal and social institutions. We are further to abstract from these individuals all knowledge of their physical and psychological strengths and disabilities and all other knowledge that would enable them to anticipate how they might fare in various hypothetical competitions with the others. If they should consider legalizing slavery in their new community, for example, none of them would have any information bearing on the likelihood of his becoming a slave or a master. Playing it safe, each might vote, as Rawls suggests, for the kind of social system that would best preserve his initial liberty, even on the assumption that 'his enemy were to assign him his place' in it.

The persons described in this 'construction' are already so abstract that they must be understood as mere fictions; but as such they can still be useful models for our understanding. What Rawls claimed in his earlier article about these abstract persons is that they would unanimously and necessarily vote to be governed by one particular set of principles, and that such a choice follows logically from their description as *rational* and normally *self-interested* persons. The construction then provides us with a model for understanding what many other philosophers have said, namely that the (correct) principles of justice are 'grounded' in or 'derived from' reason itself. The principles of justice themselves can be stated simply. One of them affirms that there will always be a presumption in favour of preserving the equal liberty of the 'original position', and the other states the conditions under which that presumption can be overridden, namely when departures from equality work out to *everyone's* advantage and when there is equality of opportunity to occupy offices of power and responsibility.

Gregory Vlastos, in the essay from which his contribution to this volume was taken, attempted to derive a theory of equal basic rights from a conception of underlying moral equality. This, of course, has been undertaken by many. What is especially valuable in Vlastos's essay is the clarity he gives the idea of a unique human worth, first by contrasting it with the idea of individual merits, and especially moral merits, which are, of course, possessed quite unequally by different men, and second by his translation of talk of human worth into talk about the equal intrinsic value of the 'well-being' and 'freedom' of all human beings. Bernard Williams approaches the same questions from a slightly different but equally fresh perspective. His essay is an effort to find solid ground between what he calls paradox and platitude in our ascriptions of equal worth to persons. In it he gives some body to the Kantian idea of a 'respect' that all persons deserve from their fellows; he gives an especially incisive analysis of the nature and limits of that 'equality of opportunity' that plays so large a role in political discourse; and in his contrast between the ideals of 'equality of respect' and 'equality of opportunity' he illustrates once more how 'noble and substantial ideals', when fully understood, tend to break into constituent claims that can be in conflict with one another. This causes us discomfort; but it is well worth that price if we learn more exactly what it is we are talking about when we talk about the things that are most important.

I

PLEASURE

GILBERT RYLE

WHAT SORT of a difference is the difference between taking a walk which one enjoys and taking a walk to which one is indifferent? (1) It might be suggested that it is, in genus if not in species, the sort of difference that there is between walking with a headache and walking without one; and that somewhat as one walker may recollect afterwards not only the ordinary acts and incidents of his walk, but also the steady or intermittent pains that he had had in his head while walking, so another walker who has enjoyed his walk might recall both the ordinary acts and incidents of his walk and also the steady pleasure or the intermittent pleasures that had been concomitant with the walk. It might even be suggested that as one walker may recollect that his headache had become specially acute just as he reached the canal, so another might recollect that his pleasure had become specially acute just as he reached the canal.

A person who made such a suggestion need not hold that to enjoy a walk is itself to have a special bodily sensation or series of bodily sensations concurrent with the walking. He might admit that while we can ask in which arm an agreeable or disagreeable tingle had been felt, we could not ask in which arm the agreeableness or disagreeableness of it had been felt. He might admit, too, that in the way in which pains yield to local or general anaesthetics, enjoyment and distaste are not the sorts of states or conditions for which anaesthetics are appropriate. But he might still suggest that pleasure is a non-bodily feeling, in supposedly the same generic sense of 'feeling' as pain is a bodily feeling. If sophisticated enough, he might suggest that pleasure is a specific, introspectible Erlebnis, where a headache is a specific bodily Erlebnis. Now a sensation or Erlebnis, like a tingle, may be agreeable, disagreeable or neutral. If enjoying and disliking were correctly co-classified with such Erlebnisse or feelings, one would expect,

From *Proceedings of the Aristotelian Society*, Supp. Vol. 28 (1954), pp. 135-46. Reprinted by courtesy of the Editor of the Aristotelian Society and the author.

by analogy, that one could similarly ask whether a person who had had the supposed pleasure-feeling or dislike-Erlebnis had liked or disliked having it. Enjoying or disliking a tingle would be, on this showing, having one bodily feeling plus one non-bodily feeling. Either, then, this non-bodily feeling is, in its turn, something that can be pleasant or unpleasant, which would require yet another, non-bodily feeling, . . . ; or the way or sense, if any, in which pleasure and distress are feelings is not in analogy with the way or sense in which tingles are feelings.

There are other places where the suggested analogy between pleasure and tingles collapses. If you report having a tingle in your arm, I can ask you to describe it. Is it rather like having an electric shock? Does it mount and subside like waves? Is it going on at this moment? But when you tell me how much you are enjoying the smell of peat smoke in my room, you cannot even construe the parallel questions about your enjoyment. Nor is your inability to answer due merely to the very important fact that in order to attend to my questions you have to stop attending to the smell, and so cannot still be enjoying it. You cannot answer my questions even in retrospect. There is no phenomenon to describe, except the smell of the peat smoke.

(2) The enjoyment of a walk might, however, be co-classified by some, not with feelings like tingles, but with feelings like wrath, amusement, alarm, and disappointment—which is a very different use of 'feeling'. It could be urged that though the walker would not naturally say that he had felt pleased all the time or had kept on feeling pleased, still he could quite naturally say such things as that he had felt as if he were walking on air, or that he had felt that he could go on for ever. These dicta, which would certainly suggest that he had enjoyed his walk, should, on this second view, be construed as reporting a passion or emotion, in that sense of those words in which a person who is scared, thrilled, tickled or surprised is in the grip of a more or less violent passion or emotion.

This second assimilation too collapses. The walker may enjoy his walk very much, but he is not, thereby, assailed or overcome by anything. A man may be too angry or surprised to think straight, but he cannot enjoy his walk too much to think straight. He can be perfectly calm while enjoying himself very much.

Panic, fury, and mirth can be transports, convulsions, or fits, but the enjoyment of the smell of peat smoke is not a paroxysm like these —not because it is very mild, where they are violent, but because it is not the sort of thing that can be resisted, whether successfully or unsuccessfully. It cannot be given way to either. It is not a gale or a squall, but nor is it even a capful of wind. There is no conquering it or being conquered by it, though there is certainly such a thing as conquering or being conquered by the habit of indulging in something or the temptation to indulge in it.

(3) There is the third, though surely not the last use of 'feeling' in which moods or frames of mind like depression, cheerfulness, irritability, and *insouciance* are often called 'feelings'. Typically, though not universally, a mood lasts some hours or even a day or two, like the weather. But the mood of irritability is unlike the emotion or passion of anger, not only in its typical duration and not only in being more like squally weather than like a squall, but also in not having a particular object. A man is angry with his dog or his tie, but his irritability has no particular object, except, what comes to the same thing, The Scheme of Things in General. To be irritable is to be predisposed to lose one's temper with no matter which particular object. A person in a cheerful or energetic mood is predisposed to enjoy, *inter alia*, any walk that he may take; but what he enjoys is this particular walk. His enjoyment of it is not the fact that he is predisposed to enjoy any occupations or activities. Moreover he enjoys his walk only while taking it, but he had felt cheerful or energetic, perhaps, ever since he got out of bed. So enjoying something is not the same sort of thing as being or feeling cheerful. On the contrary, the notion of being cheerful has to be explained in terms of the notion of pleasure, since to be cheerful is to be easy to please.

Sensations, emotional states, and moods can, in principle, all be clocked. We can often say roughly how long a tingle or a headache lasted, very roughly how long a fit of rage or amusement lasted, and extremely roughly how long a mood of depression or cheerfulness lasted. But pleasure does not lend itself to such clockings. The walker can, indeed, say that he enjoyed his walk until it began to rain, two hours after he started out; or the diner can say that he enjoyed, though decreasingly, every bite of Stilton Cheese that he took until satiety set in with the penultimate bite, and that this series of bites took about six minutes. But he cannot clock the duration of his enjoyment *against* the duration of the thing he enjoyed. He can, at best, divide the duration of the walk or meal into the parts which he enjoyed and the parts which he did not enjoy. The enjoyment of a walk is not a concomitant, e.g. an introspectible effect of the walking, such that there might be two histories, one the history of the walk, the other the history of its agreeableness to the walker. In particular there would be a glaring

absurdity in the suggestion that the enjoyment of a walk—might out-
last the walk—unless all that was intended was that the walker enjoyed
the walk and then enjoyed some after-effects or memories of the walk;
or that the walk had made him cheerful for some time afterwards.

Psychologists nowadays often avoid idioms which suggest that enjoying a walk is having a special feeling while one walks, by speaking
instead of the 'hedonic tone' of the walker. This new idiom, apart from
performing its one antiseptic function, does not by itself advance very
much our conceptual inquiry. It does not make clear what sort of a
thing pleasure is. Is the hedonic tone the sort of thing that could,
conceivably, be induced by drugs or hypnosis—as Dutch courage and
somnolence can be induced? Could a person be qualified by hedonic
tone, without his doing or having anything in particular to enjoy doing
or having? So let us try to make a more positive move of our own.

Sometimes I enjoy a smell, sometimes I dislike it, and very often
I am quite indifferent to it. But I could not enjoy it, dislike it or be
indifferent to it if I were totally oblivious or unaware of it. I cannot
say, in retrospect, that I liked the smell but did not notice it. I could,
of course, enjoy a complex of smells, views, cool air, and running water
without paying special heed to any one of them. But I could not have
enjoyed just that complex, while being totally oblivious of any one of
those components of it. This 'could not' is not a casual 'could not'. To
say that a person had enjoyed the music, though too preoccupied to
listen to it even as a background noise, would be to say something silly,
not to report a *lusus naturae*. Unnoticed things, like ozone in the air,
may certainly cause us to feel vigorous or cheerful. There may well be
such an unnoticed cause of our being predisposed to enjoy, *inter alia*,
the food and the music. But then we do not enjoy the ozone, but the
food and the music; and of these we cannot be both oblivious and
appreciative.

Similarly, when a person temporarily forgets his headache or tickle,
he must cease, for that period, to be distressed by it. Being distressed
by it entails not being oblivious of it. But just what is this connection
between enjoying and attending, or between being oblivious and being
undistressed? What, to begin with, is there to be said about the notions
of attention and oblivion themselves?

When we consider the notion of attending, a subject which we
consider far too seldom, we are apt to fancy that we have to do with
some nuclear, one-piece notion; as if, for example, all attending were
comparable with just switching on and aiming a torch in order to see
what is there whether we see it or not. But in real life we use a wide

variety of idioms for attending, most of which will not quite or even nearly do duty for one another. Some of these idioms correspond not too badly with the model of the torch-beam; others do not correspond with it at all.

For example, if at the prompting of someone else I come to notice a previously unnoticed smell, the way I become alive to the smell has some kinship with the way the hedgehog comes to be seen when the torch-beam is directed upon it. But then the way in which a strong smell so forces itself on my attention that I cannot *not* notice it is much more like a piece of barbed wire catching me than like an object being picked out by my exploring torch-beam.

When we describe someone as writing or driving carefully, we are describing him as attending to his task. But he is not, save *per accidens*, taking note of the things he is doing, since he is playing not an observer's part, but an agent's part. He is taking pains to avoid, among other things, ambiguities or collisions, where noticing a strong smell does not involve taking pains at all.

Consider some other differences between the functions of such idioms as those of noticing, heed, being careful, being vigilant, concentrating, taking interest, being absorbed, giving one's mind to something, and thinking what one is doing. When excited or bored, I may not think what I am saying; but to say this is to say less than that I am talking recklessly. I may be interested in something when it would be too severe to say that I am concentrating on it; and I may concentrate on something which fails to capture my interest. Attention is sometimes attracted, sometimes lent, sometimes paid, and sometimes exacted.

Philosophers and psychologists sometimes speak of 'acts' of attention. This idiom too is partially appropriate to certain contexts and quite inappropriate to others. When a person is actually bidden by someone else or by himself to attend, there is something which with some effort or reluctance he *does*. Where his attention had been wandering, it now settles; where he had been half-asleep, he is now wide awake; and this change he may bring about with a wrench. But the spectator at an exciting football match does not have to try to fasten or canalize his attention. To the question 'How many acts of attention did you perform?' his proper answer would be 'None'. For no wrenches had occurred. His attention was fixed on the game but he went through no operations of fixing it. The same man, listening to a lecture, might perform a hundred operations of fixing his attention and still fail to keep his mind on what was being said. Acts of attending occur when attending is difficult. But sometimes attending is easy; and sometimes it is difficult, sometimes impossible not to attend.

Even where it is appropriate to speak of acts of attention, the word 'act' carries very little of its ordinary luggage. In ordinary contexts we apply very multifarious criteria in determining what constitutes one act. Perhaps making one move in chess is performing one act; perhaps doing enough to warrant prosecution is performing one act; and perhaps getting from the beginning to the end of a speech without being side-tracked is one act. But a person who has, say, hummed a tune from beginning to end, not absent-mindedly but on purpose and with some application, has not performed two acts or accomplished two tasks, one of humming plus one of giving his mind to reproducing the tune; or, at any rate, he has not performed two acts in that sense of 'two acts' in which it would make sense to say that he might have done the second but omitted the first. Giving his mind to reproducing the tune is not doing something else, in the way in which a person sawing wood while humming is doing something else besides humming. We should say, rather, that a person who hums a tune with some concentration is humming in a different way from the way in which he hums automatically, for all that the difference might make no audible difference. It makes his humming a different sort of action, not a concomitance of separately performable actions.

I suggest that explicit talk about such things as heed, concentration, paying attention, care and so on occurs most commonly in instruction-situations and in accusation-situations, both of which are relatively small, though important sections of discourse. Elsewhere, even when talking about human beings, we tend to make relatively few explicit mentions of these things, not because it would be irrelevant, but because it would be redundant to do so. The notions are already built into the meanings of lots of the biographical and critical expressions which we use in talking to people and about them. In partly the same way we do not often need to make explicit mention of the special functions of parti-cular utensils and instruments; not because they have not got functions, but because the names of these utensils and instruments themselves generally tell us their functions. The gunsmith does not advertise 'Guns to shoot with'.

When, in our philosophizing, we do remember how notions of care, vigilance, interest and the like are built into the meanings of lots of our biographical and critical expressions, we may still be tempted to assimilate all of these notions to the two special notions that are cardinal for pedagogues and disciplinarians, of *studying* and *conforming*. We then find that our resultant account of the spectator's interest in an exciting game has a smell of unreality about it. For he is not taking pains to improve his wits, or dutifully abiding by any rules. He is attending, but not in either of these special modes of attention. Being excited or interested is not being sedulous; it is, more nearly, not-having-to-be-sedulous.

The general point that I am trying to make is that the notion of *attending* or *giving one's mind to* is a polymorphous notion. The special point that I am trying to make is that the notion of *enjoying* is one variety in this genus, or one member of this clan, i.e. that the reason why I cannot, in logic, enjoy what I am oblivious of is the same as the reason why I cannot, in logic, spray my currant-bushes without gardening.

Let us consider again the moderately specific notion of *interest*. To be, at a particular moment, interested in something is certainly to be giving one's mind to it, though one can give one's mind to a task, without being interested in it. The notions of *being fascinated, carried away, being wrapped up in, excited, absorbed, puzzled, intrigued*, and many congeners, clearly tie up closely, though in different ways, with the notion of interest. Now to say that someone has been enjoying a smell or a walk at least suggests and maybe even implies that he has been interested in the smell or in the exercise and the incidents of the walk—not that he gave his mind to them in, e.g., the sedulous way, but rather that his mind was taken up by them in a spontaneous way. This is, of course, not enough. Alarming, disgusting, and surprising things capture my attention without my having to fix my attention on them. So do pains and tickles.

I should like, at this stage to be able to answer these questions: What is it, in general, to give one's mind to something? What, more specifically, is it to give one's mind to something in the mode of being interested in it? What, finally, is it to give one's mind to something in that special dimension of interest which constitutes enjoyment? I cannot do this, but will throw out a few unscholastic remarks.

It will not, I think, be suggested that interest is either a separable process or activity or a peculiar feeling. Even if there are acts of attention, there are not acts of interest, or pangs of it either. *En passant*, it is just worth mentioning that a person might be, for a spell, wholly taken up with something, like a smell or a taste, though he would not claim that the smell or taste had been interesting—or of course boring either. We tend to reserve the adjective 'interesting' for what provokes hypotheses or even for what would provoke hypotheses in the best people. A connoisseur might find a wine interesting; the ordinary diner might describe it as piquant or attractive or just nice.

Think of the partly metaphorical force of the expressions 'absorbed' and 'occupied'. When the blotting-paper absorbs the ink, we picture the ink as unresisting and the blotting-paper as having the power. It thirstily imbibes every drop of the docile ink and will not give it up again. Somewhat similarly, when a child is absorbed in his game, he —every drop of him—is sucked up into the business of manipulating his clockwork trains. All his thoughts, all his talk, all his controllable muscular actions are those of his engine-drivers, signalmen, and station-masters. His game is, for the moment, his whole world. He does not coerce or marshal himself into playing, as, maybe, his conscripted father does. Else there would be some drop of him which was recalci-trant to the blotting-paper. Yet when we say that he is wholly absorbed in his game, we do not accept the entire parallel of the ink and the blotting-paper. For the blotting-paper has been one thing and the ink-blot another. But the game which absorbs the child is nothing but the child himself, playing trains. He, the player, has, for the moment, sucked up, without resistance, every drop of himself that might have been on other businesses, or on no business at all.

Or think of the notion of occupation. Victorious troops occupy a city; its police, administration, communications, and commerce are managed according to the policy or the whims of the victors. The citizens' public and private doings are subject to the permission and perhaps to the direction of their new masters. Yet there are different kinds of occupation. The city may be managed tyrannically, stiffly, amicably, paternally, or fraternally; and while the citizens may feel like slaves or helots or infants, they might feel like adolescents who are being shown how to be free; how to manage themselves. Somewhat so a person who is occupied in reading may feel oppressed; but he may feel merely shepherded, or advised, or partnered, or trusted, or left to his own devices. But here again, the parallel is only fragmentary, since here both the citizens and the occupying troops are the reader himself. He is under the control and he is the controller. It is his policy or his whim that directs and permits those doings of his own which, if he were unoccupied, would otherwise be without these directions and permissions—and therefore be quite different doings.

There is an important objection which could be made against both of these attempted illustrations. It could be said that I have in fact been sketching an elucidation of the notions of absorption and occupa-tion which fails for the reasons for which a *circulus in definiendo* ruins an attempted definition. To say that the child who is totally absorbed in a game has all his thoughts, conversation, and controllable muscular movements sucked up into the one activity of playing trains would be simply to say that being absorbed in A involves not being absorbed in B, C, or D. To say that a person who is occupied in reading brings and keeps all his doings under a unified control is only a long-winded way of saying that while he is engaged in reading, he is not engaged in bicycling or conversing; and these are truisms. I hope that I mean something less nugatory than this. A man who is not employed by one employer may not be employed by any other. He may be employable, but unemployed. Or he may be unemployable. Somewhat similarly, a person who is not taking an interest in A, need not be taking an interest in anything else. He may be inert, i.e. asleep or half-asleep. But he may not be inert and yet not be taking an interest in anything at all. He may be the victim of *ennui*, in which case he actively yawns, fidgets, wriggles, scratches, paces up and down, and whistles; yet he may do all of these things absent-mindedly or mechanically. He is restless but not employed; energetic but not occupied. He does plenty of things, but not on purpose, carefully with zeal or enjoyment. He is accomplishing nothing, for he is essaying nothing. He is merely responding to stimuli. The right thing to say would perhaps be that the child's game sucks up not all his thoughts, conversation, and controllable muscular movements but rather all his energies. These energies, when so sucked up, become the thinking, conversing, and manipulating that constitute his playing. But this notion of energies seems a rather suspicious character.

What is the point of pressing analogies or even plays upon words like these? One point is this. Where, as here, unpicturesque discourse still eludes us, the harm done by subjugation to one picture is partly repaired by deliberately ringing the changes on two or three. If they are appropriate at all, they are likely to be appropriate in different ways and therefore to keep us reminded of features which otherwise we might forget. The analogy of the blotting-paper may remind us of what the analogy of the torch-beam would, by itself, shut out of our heads, namely the facts—the conceptual facts—that there can be attending where there is no switching on of attention, and that there can be attending where there is no question of exploring or discerning. The analogy of the military occupation of a city may keep us in mind of the conceptual facts, which the other analogies do not bring out, that giving one's mind to something may but not need involve mutinousness, reluctance, or even dull acquiescence. One's mind may be given readily and it may be given with zest. Not all control is oppression. Sometimes it is release. Both the analogy of the blotting-paper and the analogy of the fraternal military occupation are meant to indicate, in a very unprofessional way, the conceptual region in which pleasure is located. But, at best, the real work remains to do.

II

PAIN AND EVIL

R. M. HARE

I

1. IT HAS been held by some philosophers in the past that pain is not
an evil, or not necessarily so.[1] In contrast with these ancient opinions,
we find some modern philosophers maintaining, not merely that pain
is an evil—an opinion with which most of us would agree—but that
this, or something like this, is true in virtue of the very meaning of
the word 'pain', and that it is therefore logically absurd to deny it.
In this paper I shall be concerned less with the question of whether
pain is, analytically, an evil, than with the preliminary questions of
whether it is logically possible to experience pain but not dislike it,
whether pain logically entails suffering, and the like. I shall leave
undiscussed the precise relations between disliking something and
thinking of it as an evil, and between being caused to suffer and undergoing an evil.

It must be noted, also, that the following sorts of cases are irrelevant
to the questions which I shall be discussing:

(1) Cases in which a person does not notice or attend to a pain
which he feels (or which he would feel if he attended to it) because
he is concentrating on something else (e.g. the game of football he
is playing);

(2) Cases in which a person, though he dislikes, in itself, the pain
which he has, accepts it willingly as a necessary condition for attaining something else which he values (e.g. sexual satisfaction or the
purgation of sin). It has been suggested that the masochist falls into
this class; I am not sure about this, but I shall for this reason leave
him out.

That is to say, I shall be discussing the question whether it is possible
for a person not to dislike *in itself* (or, analogously, not to be caused

[1] See, e.g., M. Antoninus, vi, 33.

From *Proceedings of the Aristotelian Society*, Supp. Vol. 38 (1964), pp. 91-106. Reprinted by courtesy of the Editor of the Aristotelian Society and the author.

to suffer, *pro tanto*, by) a pain to which he gives his full attention.

2. I will take, as an example of the thesis that pain has, analytically, to be disliked, the view of Professor Baier.[1] Baier's view is expounded by way of dissent from a statement of Professor Ryle's that "Pain is a sensation of a special sort, which we ordinarily dislike having."[2] Baier rejects the word 'ordinarily', as implying contingency. He thinks that the fact that we dislike pains is not a contingent fact; "whatever sorts of sensations we like and dislike, we only call pains those which we dislike. And if there are sensations which we ordinarily dislike but on some occasions like having, then we do not call them pains on those occasions on which we like having them."[3]

It is not clear from what Baier says whether he thinks that there is a distinct sensation or group of sensations called 'pain', different from, e.g. warmth, cold and pressure, or whether he thinks that 'pain' is simply a word we use of *any* sensation when, either because it has reached a certain intensity, or for some other reason, we dislike it. If he thinks the former, it will be difficult for him to answer the question, what we call this distinct sensation on those occasions, which he admits to exist, when we do not dislike it (since the description 'pain' is ruled out by his theory). If there is this distinct sensation, there is surely a place for a word to describe it without entailing dislike.[4] It is conceivable, indeed, that, since we almost universally dislike the sensation in question, we have not developed any word at all for describing it without implying dislike; but it is much more likely that we merely have not developed any *separate* word—i.e. that the word 'pain' itself is sometimes used to refer neutrally to this bare sensation, though sometimes, as no doubt Ryle also would admit, it is used in in such a way as to imply dislike. If this were so, the controversy between Baier and Ryle would begin to wear thin; for they might both be giving more or less correct accounts of different uses of the word 'pain'. Baier's account, however, suffers more from ambiguity than Ryle's

---

[1] *The Moral Point of View*, pp. 268 ff.
[2] *The Concept of Mind*, p. 109.
[3] Op. cit., p. 273.
[4] We shall see later that there are some narrower words (sometimes metaphorical) like 'pricking' and 'stinging' which are used of certain kinds of sensation which are certainly called 'pain' when they are intense enough to be disliked, but which there is a temptation to call 'pain' even when not disliked. These words, however, cannot be what we are looking for, since they would be inappropriate to other kinds of pain (e.g., pain caused by cold). On Baier's theory, interpreted in this first way, there ought to be a general word for the sensation which when we dislike it we call 'pain', but a word which can also be applied to it when we do not dislike it.

does; for we still have to consider the possibility that Baier thinks that there is no *distinct* sensation called 'pain', but that 'pain' is simply the name we give to any sensation when we dislike it. This view is less plausible. It has to meet the question of why, in that case, we do not call itches 'pains'—or sweltering heat, or cramps, or electric shocks, or the sensations which we have when tickled, or which we can give ourselves by gently massaging the funny bone, or by scraping our finger-nails down a blackboard. I must confess that the more I think about this subject, the more unpleasant sensations I seem to identify in my experience which are not pains. We have a phrase for the whole genus of these sensations, namely, 'unpleasant sensation'; but 'pain' seems to be a far narrower word than this.

It is true that often, when some sensation other than pain (e.g. warmth) becomes sufficiently intense, we start to feel pain; and it might be claimed that 'pain' means not '*any* disliked sensation' but, more narrowly, 'any of a limited number of sensations—including warmth, cold, and pressure—when disliked because above a certain intensity'. But even this will not do. For when we are touching something that is getting hotter, and the sensation of warmth turns to one of pain, and we say 'Now the sensation is painful', we do not mean the same as we would if we said that the sensation of warmth had got so intense that we disliked it. Neither logically nor phenomenologically is pain merely the upper end of the scales of intensity of the other sensations, coupled with dislike.

It seems, rather, that there is a phenomenologically distinct sensation or group of sensations which we have when we are in pain, and that there could be (whether there actually is or not) a word for this group of sensations which did not imply dislike. I say 'group of sensations' because burning pains, stinging pains, stabbing pains, aches, etc., are distinguishable from one another, although they clearly fall into a group which is bound together by more than the fact that they are all disliked. This phenomenologically distinct group of sensations, however, is almost universally disliked, and therefore it is convenient for us to have a word (such as 'pain' almost certainly is in one of its uses) which does imply dislike, but also is confined to this distinct group of sensations, and cannot be used of, for example, electric shocks, itches, or tickles. There is also a place for more general words or phrases which imply dislike, but are not restricted as to the sensation which is the object of the dislike. 'Unpleasant sensation' seems to be a phrase of this kind. Itches, tickles, electric shocks, etc., are unpleasant sensations, but they are not pains.

There are thus, in principle, at least three categories of words which we might use in speaking of our experiences when we are in pain. Our actual words may be expected to overflow from one of these categories into another, so that we shall often have to say that in one use a word falls into one category, while in another use it falls into a different category. This should not dismay us. The three categories are:

(1) Words which refer simply to the bare sensation, without implying dislike. I think that 'pain', in one of its uses, falls into this category, and would be so used more often if the occasions on which we have the sensation without disliking it were not so uncommon. This would seem to be the sense of the word to which Ryle refers.

(2) Words which refer to this same sensation, but in addition imply dislike, so that they cannot be used when the sensation is had but not disliked. If we used 'pain₁' and 'pain₂' for the word as used in the first and second categories respectively, we might say, without much distortion, that 'pain$_2$' meant 'pain$_1$ which is disliked', or 'pain$_1$ which is unpleasant'. 'Agony' and 'anguish' seem, in their literal senses, to fall into this category. If we speak of the 'agony' of a person who is not suffering intensely on account of one of the distinct group of sensations called 'pain', we do so in a metaphorical sense. The verb 'hurt' (intransitive), like 'pain' itself, seems to be used in both these first two categories, and, indeed, metaphorically in the third.

(3) Words which imply dislike, but can also be used of other things than pain in the literal sense. Such words are 'suffering', 'unpleasant', 'distress', and 'discomfort'. There will also, as we have seen, be found in this category metaphorical uses of words whose literal habitat is in one of the first two categories or both. For example, an unkind remark can hurt me.

3. Objection might be taken to the claim that there could be a 'bare sensation' of pain which was not disliked. What, it might be asked, would such an experience be like? Can we *imagine* such an experience? I think that I can not only imagine it, but have had it; but I shall return to this question later. Here I shall just make the obvious point that we cannot conclude, from the fact that something surpasses our imagination, that it cannot happen. I cannot myself imagine what the electric torture would be like; but that does not take away the possibility that it might be inflicted on me. It would be more relevant if it could be established that no *sense* could be given to the

expression 'experience which is like pain except for not being disliked'. But that is precisely the question at issue, and this whole paper is an attempt to see what sense can be given to such an expression.

An analogy may help us to understand this question. Let us suppose that I have always disliked a certain degree of cold (for example, that which I experience when I dive into water of a certain temperature having up till then been lying in the shade in still air of a certain other temperature; the experimental conditions could be made more exact, but this will be enough for our purposes). I am assuming that the coldness of the water is not sufficient to produce actual pain. Now is it not perfectly possible to understand what it would be like for me to experience the same degree of cold, but not dislike it (not be caused any discomfort or distress)? Suppose, for example, that I do this diving act many times in the hope of getting not to mind this degree of cold; and that in the end I succeed. It is not necessary to suppose that there is any change in the degree of cold that I feel (even subjectively); there might be, but that would spoil the example. It may be merely that through habituation I stop minding my skin feeling like that. We do not even need to suppose any course of habituation. Whether I found the cold unpleasant or invigorating might depend on my general state of mind—on whether I was feeling depressed or elated.

In the case of cold, the vocabulary which we actually have contains an expression—'to feel cold' which does not imply dislike. Even in the case of cold, admittedly, dislike of the sensation above a certain intensity is so universal that it might be assumed that a person who said he felt cold *did* dislike it, although the word itself does not imply this. But nevertheless, 'I liked feeling cold' is perfectly comprehensible. Intense cold can be liked because invigorating—and this does not mean 'as a means to the end of being invigorated'. *A fortiori*, it can be not disliked. But our vocabulary might have been different—it is very important to distinguish the question 'What does our present vocabulary allow?' from the question 'How could it comprehensibly be modified?' We could, that is to say, have had a word for the feeling of cold which did, like 'pain' in some of its uses, imply dislike. Let us suppose that 'cold' itself was used in this way, and that dislike of cold was much more universal than in fact it is, so that uses of 'cold' in the other way, as not implying dislike, were comparatively rare. 'Cold' would then behave much as 'pain' does now, in respect of implying or not implying dislike (though, of course, there would be other differences).

The difference between the behaviour of our *actual* words 'cold' and 'pain' reflects a difference in how people commonly react to these two sensations; but—and this is really the nub—that does not mean that we are under any *logical* constraint to react to cold or pain in the way that we do. The constraints that we are under are contingent, though they too are readily explicable. There are good reasons why very few people get into a state in which they do not mind high intensities of pain. Nearly all causes of pain are also causes of harm to the organism; pain is, therefore, such a good warning device—and has indeed been developed as such—that we have acquired, partly by evolution and partly by learning, a very firm disposition to avoid pain; and this firm disposition is associated with a subjective feeling of dislike. This dislike is so universal that it is, as we have seen, reflected in our vocabulary; but that does not make it anything else but contingent that we have the dislike—there logically could be a person who did not dislike high intensities of the sensation. With our vocabulary as it is, he could say that he did not dislike the pain, using the word in the sense of 'pain$_1$' above; but unless such cases became common there would certainly be conceptual misunderstandings and difficulties owing to the possibility of confusion between the two senses of the word which I have labelled 'pain$_1$' and 'pain$_2$'. And this is what has actually happened in the experimental and clinical situations to which I shall refer below.

The reasons why our actual word 'cold' does not behave like our actual word 'pain', in the sense of 'pain$_2$', are readily understandable. People who do not mind, or who like, high intensities of cold, though uncommon, are not *so* uncommon. Probably nobody who breaks the ice to bathe at Christmas and enjoys it does so without a good deal of self-schooling; but we all know perfectly well that the thing can be done. With 'pain' it would be much more of an oddity. I have said that I would leave the masochist out, because there is a doubt whether his case is relevant. We must therefore look for clearer cases. There are, in fact, small degrees of pain which are by no means disliked by everybody. Most people could draw the point of a needle rather gently across their skin (as in acupuncture) and say truthfully that they could distinctly feel pain, but that they did not dislike it. Some might say that they would rather be without it than with it; but that would apply to a great many sensations about which no philosopher, to my knowledge, takes the line that some do with pain. Most people would rather be without a feeling of giddiness (though children often induce it in themselves out of interest); but nobody says that no sense can be given to the sentence 'I feel giddy, but do not dislike it'.

With some diffidence in the use of this technical term, we might say that the 'threshold' of dislike of pain is usually somewhat above the threshold of pain itself (that is, of the pain$_1$-sensation).[1] Now let us suppose that we have a pain which is only just above the threshold of dislike. May I not, by habituation, come *not* to dislike this—to raise the threshold of dislike? We do not, perhaps, have to be heroes to achieve this much. But in any case, it is not necessary actually to achieve it. It is sufficient—indeed more than sufficient—to imagine what it would be like to achieve it; and this I find perfectly easy. Indeed, even imagination is, for the reason given above, not necessary. It is sufficient if I could understand what would be meant by somebody who claimed to have achieved this very minor feat. And this I can certainly do. But if I can do it in this marginal case, I do not see how it can be impossible to *understand*, though it may be difficult to *believe*, a man who says that, by practice, he has got into a state in which he does not dislike lying on a bed of nails, although he has exactly the same experiences, apart from the dislike, that I would have if I lay on a bed of nails. The case is analogous to that of a man who claims to be able to jump, unaided, twenty feet into the air, whereas I can only jump three feet into the air. I understand him, but I do not readily believe him. That in the 'bed of nails' case there would be a logical bar to demonstrating conclusively that the feat had been performed (he might just be *very* good at concealing his dislike) does not seem to me to be relevant.

I have put this whole argument in terms of the word 'dislike'. I think that it could have been put equally well in terms of the words 'discomfort', or 'suffering', or 'unpleasant'. I have heard it said that it is logically impossible for a man who is experiencing intense pain not to be suffering, because suffering just *is* intense pain. This is clearly wrong, not only for the irrelevant reason that there are other ways of suffering than by experiencing intense pain (tickling or stifling, for example, will do); but because, by an analogous argument to the preceding, it would become clear that we could understand my *faqir* on his bed of nails if he said that he was experiencing intense pain, but not suffering, not finding it unpleasant, and undergoing no discomfort.

4. I have discussed the problem so far with reference to our common experience. While looking for more exact accounts of the distinction between pain, considered as a bare sensation, and pain, considered as entailing dislike, I have read a good deal of physiological literature, though not, I fear, enough to be sure that I have understood the very

---

[1] See C. A. Keele, in *The Assessment of Pain in Man and Animals*, ed. Keele and Smith (1962), p. 41. Many of the other papers in this symposium are of considerable philosophical interest, especially that by R. Smith. I return to Keele's work below.

difficult physiological issues about which there is at the moment so much controversy going on. I will, however, select two physiological topics which I think have a very close bearing on our philosophical problem, and do my best to summarize what the physiologists say about them.

An attempt has been made, which is of great philosophical interest, to record the precise verbal descriptions given by experimental subjects of their experience when subjected to varying amounts of pain.[1] These verbal descriptions can be supplemented by one physiologist's account of his own experiences, and what he is disposed to say about them, and also by the records of the movements of an indicator moved by the subjects to correspond with their subjective experiences. The indicator scale was marked: No pain: slight: moderate: severe: very severe.'

Two contrasting features are very noticeable in the reports of these experiments. The first is a definite tendency, which supports the view of Baier, for subjects to confine the description 'pain' to experiences which they found unpleasant. For sensations (induced by putting various chemicals on an exposed blister base) which were not so intense as to be unpleasant, they used words like 'stinging' and 'pricking' (Smith, pp. 38–40). The other feature, which, on the contrary, supports Ryle's view, is the suggestion that the quality of the sensation below the level of unpleasantness is "continuous in most ways" with that above; Keele (p. 30) says, "the element of unpleasantness seems to be superimposed on a sensation which runs through the whole range". The 'continuity' of the sensation was to some extent borne out (for anyone but a philosopher) by the fact that, when the movements of the indicator recording the subjective intensity of the sensation were plotted against the amounts of the chemical in the solution applied to the blister (on a logarithmic scale), a very good correlation resulted.

Keele, attacking the conceptual difficulty in what seems a very sensible way, says, "It is simplest . . . to speak of a sensation of cutaneous pain which may range from the barest detectable level" (he has said earlier, on p. 30, that the sensation may be neutral or even pleasing) "to an intolerable unpleasant experience. If the word pain is used to characterize this sensation throughout its whole scale it would be convenient to have some qualifying word to describe that part of the scale in which the sensation is usually not unpleasant. Phrases such as 'non-painful pain' and 'sub-threshold pain' are clearly not applicable." He proposes the technical terms 'metaesthesia' for the lower part of the scale and 'algaesthesia' for the higher, unpleasant part. Some such technical vocabulary

[1] C. A. Keele and R. Smith, op. cit.

is obviously required, since the ordinary word 'pain' has given rise to confusion because of its ambiguity, already noticed. Keele goes on: "It must, however, be emphasized that the borderline between the metaesthetic and algaesthetic ranges of pain is variable and hard to define, but of the reality of the distinction between these two ranges of pain there can be no doubt."

While, as philosophers, we might cavil at some of this, I think that we should be content with the broad lines of this suggestion. The upshot is that there are two ranges of intensity of a certain sensation, the boundary between which is indefinite and variable; there is a tendency, but only a tendency, in ordinary subjects to reserve the word 'pain' for the higher, unpleasant, range, but an opposing tendency, stronger among the experimenters themselves, but perfectly comprehensible to anyone, to use the word 'pain' of the whole range, pleasant, neutral, or unpleasant. Once the phenomena are recognized—as they perhaps cannot be without more careful attention than the average man or even the average philosopher gives to the matter—we do not need to attach too much importance to the terminology, provided that it is consistently used; we shall have no difficulty in describing the phenomena whichever terminology we adopt.

5. The other physiological topic which I think it worth while to introduce (though with the greatest diffidence) is that of lobotomy. There is, as is well known, an operation to the frontal lobes of the brain which markedly alters what physiologists and psychologists call the 'pain-reaction'. Unfortunately this term is highly ambiguous, and before we can discuss the effects of the operation we shall have to sort out its different senses. We may distinguish, within the general class of reactions to pain, the following:

(1) Experiences:
   (a) The felt dislike of the pain;
   (b) The felt desire to be rid of the pain; some people might equate this with (a);
   (c) The felt desire or inclination to do some particular thing in order to be rid of the pain: e.g., to try to prevent the surgeon moving a painful limb;
   (d) Various after-effects such as fear of the painful event happening again.

(2) Behaviour:
   (e) Various automatic reactions or reflexes such as wincing, crying

out, etc. We do not need to discuss whether these are innate or learnt, but it is important that they can be inhibited.

(f) Voluntary 'pain-terminating' behaviour—i.e., doing particular things in order to be rid of the pain.

(g) Verbal behaviour of various sorts related to the pain: e.g., saying 'I am in pain' or 'that hurts' or 'that hurt frightfully'.

(h) Various behavioural after-effects such as the avoidance of the pain-producing situation, together with other manifestations of fear, neurotic symptoms, etc.

This classification is crude and almost certainly not exhaustive; and well-known philosophical problems arise concerning the relation between some items (e.g., as to whether (c) is, or involves, a disposition to do (f)). But it is detailed enough to show how careful we have to be when we read in case-reports that, for example, after lobotomy a patient's whole reaction to pain was altered. In particular, it appears that, contrary to what we might expect, (c) and (f) do not always go together; some lobotomized patients have a tendency to wince and cry out more than before (possibly because the operation has diminished the inhibition against these reflexes), but their reactions classified under (f) and (h) are diminished.[1] Among the 'experiences' classified under (1), it seems fairly clear that those mentioned under (d) can be markedly reduced by lobotomy, although the patients say that the pain is as intense as before; and this would seem to apply also to those mentioned under (c). Patients who have had the operation are said to be no longer bothered or troubled by the pain of their disease; and they co-operate better with the surgeon even when he is doing painful things to them. It seems natural to suppose that if the reactions under (c) are reduced, so also are those under (b); and, if those under (b) are reduced, it is hard to deny that those under (a) are reduced too (how could I dislike the pain just as much as before, but have a smaller desire to be rid of it?).

But the descriptions in the literature are not easy for a philosopher to unravel, because 'pain' and similar words are used indiscriminately by surgeons and patients, sometimes in the sense of 'pain₁' above, and sometimes in the sense of 'pain₂'. I am tempted to say that until some philosopher with a precise grasp of the distinctions involved actually has this operation done to him, it is unlikely that we shall be certain exactly what happens to the patient's dislike of the pain. For what it is worth, however, one surgeon says "In a sense, frontal lobotomy is not surgical

[1] For refs. see Hall, K. R., 'Studies of Cutaneous Pain', *Brit. J. Psychol.*, 44 (1953), pp. 289 f.

treatment for the relief of pain, but rather surgical treatment for the relief of suffering"[1] and another says "Psycho-surgery alters the subject's reaction to pain without materially changing his ability to feel pain."[2] It is therefore not improbable that this operation can reduce suffering, distress, and dislike without reducing the intensity of the pain-sensation. But whether it can or not, the suggestion that it can is a perfectly comprehensible one, and that is all that, as philosophers, we need. If we can understand what it would be for the suffering to be reduced while the sensation remained the same, we can surely understand also what it would be for the suffering or the distress or dislike to be altogether removed without any diminution in the pain-sensation. We may say, therefore, that the reports about this operation, obscure as they are, to some extent bear out the conclusions which we have already reached from examination of more normal experiences. We can also find in the reports examples of the conceptual difficulties which, if the word 'pain' has the two-faced character that I have claimed, we should expect.

Before leaving the subject of lobotomy, I will venture to make a tentative suggestion. One of the things that are most noticeable about these patients is that they in general stop being concerned about things; many of their other evaluations seem to go by the board or get reduced besides their dislike of pain. Thus one patient's son said of him, "It would make no difference to Dad whether I told him I had won a thousand pounds, or that I was going outside to shoot myself."[3] This, of course, entails a profound personality change, which has made surgeons very reluctant to use this operation except as a last resort. This lack of concern might be associated—I have not come across any clear evidence of this— with a shortening of the time-span over which the patient has fears or desires for the future. That could explain why patients who have had the operation to relieve a painful incurable disease cease to fear the onset of the attacks of pain. Now if the 'timespan of concern', as we may call it, were *sufficiently* shortened, would we be able to have any desires or concerns at all—since desire is always a desire for some future state (though this future state may be the continuance or discontinuance of a present state)? Is it not therefore logically possible for a patient to stop having any desires (to become quite apathetic, or in other words, not to like or dislike anything; for I cannot dislike something without, *pro tanto*, wanting it to stop, though of course I may want other things

[1] Koskoff, in comment on Dynes and Poppen, *Am. Med. Ass. J.*, 140 (1949), pp. 15 ff.
[2] W. Freeman and J. W. Watts, *Lancet* (1946), p. 955.
[3] M. Falconer, *Ass. Res. Nervous and Mental Disease*, vol. 27, 709.

more)? But if so, is it not logically possible for him to retain his sensations, and in particular the sensation of pain, with undiminished intensity, while ceasing to have any affective attitudes towards them?

It may be asked whether there are any *drugs* which, as lobotomy has been said to do, could relieve suffering without diminishing the intensity of the pain-sensation. Pharmacologists evidently disagree about the answer to this question.[1] But it is certainly logically possible that such a drug should be invented; and we have in our common experience of alcohol something which comes near to what we are looking for. Before anaesthetics proper came into use, surgeons used to give their patients whisky before operations; as anybody may verify, this does not diminish substantially the intensity of the pain-sensation, but may make it a great deal easier to bear. In *King Lear*, Edmund says, as he slashes his arm (in this case, admittedly, for an ulterior purpose), "I have seen drunkards do more than this in sport" (II, 1); and it does not have to be assumed that the drunkards feel any less of the pain-sensation than sober men—only that they do not mind it so much.

6. It may be objected at this point that, if it were logically possible not to dislike pains, and therefore not to display the manifestations of dislike, such as withdrawal of limbs from the painful stimulus, children could never learn the use of the word 'pain'. For, it might be said, we can only learn these words because, when we are young, our elders see us displaying these manifestations, and say 'Does it hurt?', 'Have you got a pain?', etc. A philosopher might seek to prove thus that there is an analytic connection between having a pain and manifestations of dislike. But the argument is ineffective; for the teaching procedure would work perfectly well if the connection between pain and the manifestations of dislike were not analytic but contingent, provided that cases of pain without the manifestations, or *vice versa*, were rare. For me to succeed in teaching children the use of the word 'pain', it is sufficient for me correctly to *guess*, on one or two occasions, that they are in pain because they are doing what normally manifests dislike of pain; it is not necessary for me to be certain (let alone logically certain) that if they are doing these things they are in pain, or that if they were in pain they would be doing these things.

From the fact that certain contingent circumstances have in general to obtain before a certain word can come into use (even if this fact is itself logically demonstrable) it by no means follows that these same contingent circumstances are logical conditions of the word's correct use on a particular occasion, or determine what its *meaning* is on that

[1] For references, see H. K. Beecher, *Measurement of Subjective Responses* (1959).

or other occasions. Thus 'pain' might be the name of a completely private experience (a word which could be legitimately used whatever was happening overtly) even though the word could not have come into use unless, normally, these private experiences were correlated with overt occurrences. This point is of some methodological importance, but there is no time to pursue it.

7. In conclusion, let me satisfy the demands of honesty by declaring the axe which I have been grinding in this paper—though I fancy that its edge will have become visible to most people by now. There are those who seek to impugn the distinction between descriptive and evaluative judgements; and one of the arguments that I have heard used in this controversy is the following. To say that I am in intense pain is to state a fact; I cannot truly deny, if I have a certain distinct experience, that I am in intense pain. Therefore, it is claimed, the statement 'I am in intense pain' satisfies the conditions for being called 'descriptive'. But on the other hand, I cannot be in intense pain without thinking it bad, or disliking it, or suffering; to think something bad, however, or to dislike it, or to suffer because of it, is already to be making an evaluation. And (the argument goes on) since all of this is true in virtue of the meaning of the word 'pain', 'I am in intense pain' seems also to satisfy the conditions for being called an evaluative judgement. Therefore, it is concluded, the distinction breaks down.

The answer that I would give to this argument will, I hope, be clear from the foregoing discussion. There may be a use of the word 'pain' such that it is analytic to say that a man who is in intense pain is suffering, or having something bad happen to him; or that a man who experiences pain always dislikes it. But if this is so, it may be only because 'pain' in this use is a complex word, implying *both* the existence of a certain distinct sensation, *and* suffering, etc. The argument does not rule out the possibility of a man having the very same experience except for the absence of the suffering. And if he did, there would be nothing to prevent him calling the experience which he had 'pain' in the sense of my 'pain₁', or, if this be objected to, using some other word. Let us, in order to avoid verbal dispute, use 'ø' for this other word.

Let it be admitted that, if a man is having the sensation ø, he cannot truly deny that he is having it. And let it be admitted, further, that if he is disliking the sensation, he cannot truly deny that he is disliking it (and similarly with suffering). This is the case, even if to dislike something is to make an evaluation; for if I am evaluating something in a certain way, I cannot truly deny that that is what I am doing. Let it be admitted, even, that on any particular occasion, if I do dislike the sensation ø, there is nothing I can do about it. This would not prevent disliking something from being a kind of evaluation; for there are many evaluations that are not psychologically *ad lib*. If I were flogged with a cat of nine tails, I should certainly dislike it, constituted as I am. But all this is not enough to establish the case of the philosophers whom I am now considering; for they want to make a logical, and not merely a psychological connection, however inescapable, between experiencing the sensation ø and disliking it, suffering, etc.

If it be once allowed that, as I have been trying to establish, it is logically possible to have the sensation ø without disliking it, to have it intensely without suffering, and so on, the argument falls down. If I have the sensation called 'ø', all that I can be compelled logically to admit is that I have the sensation called 'ø'. Logic cannot make me suffer. That I shall nearly always suffer when I experience intensely the sensation called 'ø' is a well-established contingent truth. To try to make it more is to succumb to one of the oldest temptations in philosophy: the temptation to try to prove synthetic conclusions by logical considerations alone.

III

HAPPINESS

Anthony Kenny

'From the dawn of philosophy,' wrote Mill, 'the question concerning the *summum bonum*, or, what is the same thing, concerning the foundation of morality, has been accounted the main problem in speculative thought and has occupied the most gifted intellects.' For some time the most gifted intellects have been averse to putting questions concerning the foundation of morality in terms of the *summum bonum*. But recently there has been some sign of a return of interest in the notion of a supreme good or happiness. We might instance the chapter on 'The Good of Man' in von Wright's *Varieties of Goodness* (1963), B. A. O. Williams, 'Aristotle on the Good' (*Ph. Q.*, Oct. 1962), W. F. R. Hardie, 'The Final Good in Aristotle's Ethics' (*Philos.*, Oct. 1965).

The notion of a supreme good is, I shall later argue, only one of the elements which have contributed to the formation of our concept of happiness. None the less, I shall follow the authors I have mentioned in taking my start from the discussion of this topic by Aristotle.

Aristotle defined the supreme good (*tagathon kai to ariston*) as 'an end of action which is desired for its own sake, while everything else is desired for the sake of it' (*E.N.* 1094a19). Prima facie, one can interpret the contention that there is a supreme good in three ways. One may take it as a logical truth, as an empirical observation, or as a moral imperative. Someone who says that there is a supreme good, in Aristotle's sense, may mean that as a matter of logical truth there is a single end which is aimed at in every choice of a human being. He may mean, on the other hand, that every man does as a matter of contingent fact have a single aim in every one of his choices. Or, finally, he may mean that every man should, under pain of being unreasonable or immoral, aim at a single end in each of his choices. Writers on the *summum bonum* do not always make clear which of these alternatives they have in mind.

From *Proceedings of the Aristotelian Society*, Vol. 66 (1965-6), pp. 93-102. Reprinted by courtesy of the Editor of the Aristotelian Society and the author.

Moreover, each of these alternatives is itself ambiguous. Is the 'single end' in question an end which is, or ought to be, common to every choice of every man? Or is it merely an end which governs every choice of each particular man, but which perhaps differs from man to man? The first of the foregoing alternatives, for instance, may be taken in two ways. It may be a strong thesis to the effect that it is a logical truth that every man, in every choice, aims at a single end which is common to all choices of all men. Or it may be the weaker thesis that each man, in each of his choices, pursues a single end, but one which is perhaps proper to himself.

Aristotle is sometimes thought to have presented the doctrine of the supreme good in a form which is equivalent to the stronger of the two logical theses just distinguished. It does seem to be a necessary truth that one cannot choose everything for the sake of something else: chains of reasoning about means and ends must come to a halt somewhere. Aristotle alludes to this truth on the first page of the *Nicomachean Ethics* (1094a18).

'If, then, there is some end of the things we do, which we desire for its own sake (everything else being desired for the sake of this), and if we do not choose everything for the sake of something else (for at that rate the process would go on to infinity, so that our desire would be empty and vain), clearly this must be the good and the chief good.' (Tr. Ross.)

This passage has been taken to contain a (fallacious) proof of the existence of a single supreme end of action. Thus Geach writes, 'It is clear that Aristotle thinks himself entitled to pass from "Every series whose successive terms stand in the relation *chosen for the sake of* has a last term" to "There is something that is the last term of every series whose successive terms stand in the relation *chosen for the sake of*" ' (*Journal of the Philosophical Association,* v, 1958, p. 112). Such a transition is clearly fallacious. Every road leads somewhere: it does not follow that there is somewhere—e.g., Rome—to which all roads lead.

To convict Aristotle of this fallacy one must assume that he is offering the second if-clause 'we do not choose everything for the sake of something else' as a reason for the hypothesis in the first if-clause 'there is some end of the things we do which we desire for its own sake'. But this, Williams argues, it is not necessary to do: the second hypothesis may be a consequence of, not a reason for, the first. Von Wright and Hardie agree with Williams in acquitting Aristotle of the fallacy attributed to him by Geach. Von Wright points out that if Aristotle here accepts the conclusion that there is one and only one end of all chains of practical reasoning, then he contradicts himself. Clearly, happiness, for Aristotle, is at least *one* supreme end. But 'Aristotle also admits that there are ends, other than happiness, which we pursue for their own sake. He mentions pleasure and honour among them' (*The Varieties of Goodness*, p. 89, citing *E.N.*, 1097b1-2). Aristotle seems, then, guiltless of the fallacy attributed to him, though it entrapped some of his followers, notably Aquinas (*S.T.*, Ia IIae, I, 4–6).

It seems, in fact, to be false that it is logically necessary that there should be some one end which a man pursues in each of his choices. It might be thought that if we made our end vague and general enough, we might avoid this conclusion. To act voluntarily is to act because one wants to, either because one wants the action for its own sake, or because one wants something to be gained by the action. Therefore, it might be argued, there is some one end which we pursue whenever we act voluntarily, namely the satisfaction of our wants. But this argument is fallacious. If all that is being said is that when I act out of desire for x, then I am pursuing the satisfaction of my desire for x, it has not been established that I am pursuing a single end in all my actions; for there are as many different satisfactions as there are desires to satisfy. If, on the other hand, it is alleged that whenever a man acts he must be pursuing a goal which consists in the satisfaction of *all* his desires, then the theory, so far from being necessarily true, is not even empirically true. For it is perfectly possible not to have as a goal the satisfaction of all one's desires, and indeed positively to hope that not all one's desires will be satisfied. Russell, for instance, in *The Conquest of Happiness*, says 'to be without some of the things you want is an indispensable part of happiness'. In so far as Russell wants to be happy, he must, in conformity with his dictum, want to be without some of the things he wants.

There may seem to be a certain inconsistency here. It is akin to what logicians call ω-inconsistency—the sort of inconsistency which is illustrated by the sentence 'he was wearing a glove on one hand, and he was not wearing a glove on his left hand, and he was not wearing a glove on his right hand'. In persons, if not in systems, ω-inconsistency seems to me no bad thing. Modesty seems to demand that we should hold ω-inconsistent beliefs: e.g., that we should believe that some of our beliefs are false. Only a man who knows himself infallible could have reasonable confidence that all his beliefs were true. Similarly, patience seems to demand that we should have ω-inconsistent desires: at least that we should be willing that some of our desires should be dissatisfied. But whether or not such ω-inconsistency in desires is desirable, it is certainly possible. If so, it cannot be a logical truth that in everything we do we seek a single aim of total satisfaction.

Williams has argued that Aristotle accepted the thesis that whatever is pursued for a single aim, not on the basis of the fallacious argument about chains of practical reasoning, but on the basis of the considerations about function in 1097b25 ff. This account of Aristotle's argument seems to me mistaken. It is tendentious to translate '*ergon*' as *function*; we need not credit Aristotle with believing that men serve a purpose. If we translate '*ergon*' as *characteristic activity*, then the burden of the passage is as follows. Where an *F* has a characteristic activity, ø-ing, then a good *F* is an *F* which øs well. Different classes of men, and different parts of a man, each have their characteristic activity. Presumably, then, man has a characteristic activity: this must be an activity of the rational soul, else it would be common to animals and plants and so not characteristic of man as such. The characteristic activity of the good man, therefore, will be the good activity of the rational soul. Therefore, the good for man (*to anthropinon agathon*) will be the activity of the soul in accordance with excellence.

The surprising step in this argument is the identification of the good for man with the characteristic activity of the good man. Surely, we feel inclined to object, what is good for sculptors, e.g., adequate remuneration and good living conditions) is quite different from what the good sculptor does (e.g., sculpt well). But presumably Aristotle would reply that this merely showed the difference between what was good for sculptors *qua* men and what was good for them *qua* sculptors. What it is good for a man, *qua* man, to do is what the good man in fact does *qua* good man. But what the good man does is what all men *should* do: nothing follows about what all men *do*. The argument from the *ergon* of man, then, cannot show that, as a matter of fact or logic, all men pursue whatever they pursue for the sake of happiness.

Even as a matter of fact, Aristotle did not believe that men seek a single end in all their actions. The incontinent man who is described in book seven, pursues pleasure in some of his actions, though the end he sets for his life is other than pleasure. However, we are told that the incontinent man does not *choose* to seek pleasure, so perhaps, it might be argued, Aristotle would support the weaker thesis that whatever is *chosen* is chosen for the sake of happiness. But even this thesis is ruled out by the passage at 1097a34 which Williams himself quotes. There we are told that while happiness is always chosen for its own sake and never for the sake of anything else, honour and pleasure and reason and virtue are chosen both for their own sake and for the sake of happiness. This seems to refute Williams' claim that Aristotle accepted the thesis $\exists y \forall x\, (Px \rightarrow Pxy)$ where '*Px*' is to be interpreted as '*x* is pursued' and '*Pxy*' as '*x* is pursued for the sake of *y*'. However, Williams' predicate letters are ambiguous, as he realizes. He asks whether it is a sufficient condition of the truth of '*Pa*' that a is at some time pursued by somebody. One might have thought it more natural to take '*Pa*' to refer to some particular occasion of pursuit. Williams refuses to resolve the ambiguity. The difficulties, he says, 'lie not so much in the formalization of Aristotle's discussion by means of the predicate "*P*" as in Aristotle's discussion itself' (loc. cit. p. 290). But Aristotle's text at this point does not appear ambiguous. He says that happiness is *never* chosen for anything but itself, whereas other things are chosen for the sake of happiness. It is clear that he means not that on some particular occasion honour and pleasure are chosen both for their own sakes and for the sake of happiness, but that on some occasions they are chosen for their own sakes, and on other occasions for the sake of happiness.

We can distinguish between two ways of taking Williams' formula. We may take it as saying that on each occasion when something is pursued, it is pursued for the sake of some one thing, namely, happiness. Or we may take it as saying that if something is ever pursued, then it is pursued on at least one occasion for the sake of happiness. Taken in the first way, the formula, as we have seen, would be rejected by Aristotle: pleasure is sometimes pursued for its own sake. I do not see that Aristotle gives us enough information for us to decide what truth-value he would assign to the formula taken in its second sense. Might there not be some things—perhaps, say, some of the perversions listed in Book VII, ch. 5—which were sometimes pursued for the sake of pleasure, and never pursued when pleasure was being pursued for the sake of happiness (as by the intemperate man) but only pursued when pleasure was being pursued for its own sake (as by the incontinent man)? There would then be some things which were pursued but never pursued for the sake of happiness. I do not see that Aristotle is committed to ruling out this possibility.

The suggestion that all actions have a single end is one which Aristotle several times considers, but never opts for. At 1097b23 he says that if there is a single end of everything that is done, then this will be *to prakton agathon*, but if there be more than one such end, then it will be these. He at once goes on to say 'there is obviously more than one end', and to exclude from consideration those ends which are not *teleia*, i.e., things such as flutes, wealth, etc., which are always sought in virtue of some other end. But it is not even the case that there is only one *teleion* end: there are some things which are sought both for themselves, and for another end.

In the *Eudemian Ethics* Aristotle says, 'Everyone who has the power

to live according to his own choice should dwell on these points and set
up for himself some object for the good life to aim at, whether honour
or reputation or wealth or culture, by reference to which he will do all
that he does, since not to have one's life organized in view of some end
is a sign of great folly' (1214b6 ff., quoted Hardie, p. 277). The fact that
this is made as a recommendation shows that what is recommended is
not something that is already the case in the behaviour of all men.

It is not true, either in logic or in fact or in Aristotelian doctrine, that
all men seek happiness in all they do. Is it even true that all men seek
happiness? Here it is useful to follow Hardie in distinguishing between
a dominant and an inclusive end. If happiness is thought of as a dominant end, then it is the object of a single prime desire: say, for money,
or for philosophy. If it is thought of as an inclusive end, then the desire
for happiness is the desire for the orderly and harmonious gratification
of a number of independent desires. It seems clear that not everyone has
a single dominant aim in life: it is surely possible to lead a life consisting
of the successive pursuit of a number of unrelated aims of equal importance. If by happiness we mean something sought as a dominant aim, it
seems to be untrue that all men seek happiness.

What of happiness considered as an inclusive aim? It may well be
argued that a being who did not plan his life at all, and had absolutely
no principles by which he ordered the pursuit of his desires, would be
something less than human. But not every inclusive plan of life is a
plan for the pursuit of happiness. A man may map out his life in the
service of someone else's happiness or for the furtherance of some cause,
perhaps devoting his efforts to the pursuit of some end which it may be
possible to realize only after his death. Notoriously, such selfless dedica-
tion is sometimes the upshot of the wreck of a man's own hopes: he is
crossed in love, or loses his family, or sees the collapse of the institutions
for which he has worked. '*I* shall never be happy again,' he may think,
'but at least I can work for the happiness of others, or seek truth, or help
bring about the millennium.' Someone in such a position *has* sought
happiness, and so would not be a counter-example to the thesis that all
men (at some time or other) seek happiness. But selflessness is not always
like this: people may be trained from childhood to pursue an ideal such
as the service of the Party, or obedience to God, without this necessarily
being presented to them as a means to their own happiness in this life
or in another life. A daughter, from the first moment at which she is of
an age to manage her own life, may forgo the prospect of marriage and
congenial company and creative work in order to nurse a bedridden
parent. It is unconvincing to say that such people are seeking their own

happiness in so far as they are doing what they want to do. Happiness, considered as an inclusive goal, may include constitutive elements of many different kinds; but not *every* long-term goal consistently pursued is capable of constituting an ideal of happiness. In the cases I have considered happiness is renounced in favour of some other goal; but it is possible to renounce happiness for other reasons also, e.g., because the only possible way to achieve one's own happiness may involve the breaking of a promise. In such a case, we might say, the agent must have the long-term goal of acting virtuously: but this would be a goal in a different way from happiness, a goal identified with a certain kind of action, and not a goal to be secured by action.

Aristotle, who considers happiness only in the dominant sense, does not make even the modest claim that everyone seeks happiness. He certainly says that all agree that happiness is the purpose of ethics, and that it is the highest of practical goods. But there is no reason why he should think that everybody practises ethics, or pursues the highest good. All he needs to presume, and all that he does presume, is that all of his lecture audiences are in search of happiness.

Later, Aristotle seeks to show that happiness is identical with philosophic contemplation. Even if he were right about this, it would not, of course, follow that all who seek happiness seek philosophic contemplation. Aquinas, adapting Aristotle, denied that the search for happiness involved any awareness of God. 'Admittedly, man is by nature aware of what by nature he desires, and he desires by nature a happiness which is to be found only in God. But this is not, simply speaking, awareness that there is a God, any more than to be aware of someone approaching is to be aware of Peter, even though it should be Peter approaching: many in fact believe the ultimate good which will make us happy to be riches or pleasure, or some such thing.' This is the phenomenon familiar to logicians as referential opacity.

In books one and ten of the *Nicomanchean Ethics* Aristotle behaves like the director of a marriage bureau, trying to match his client's description of his ideal partner. In the first book he lists the properties which men believe to be essential to happiness, and in the tenth book he seeks to show that philosophical contemplation, and it alone, possesses to the full these essential qualities. Aristotle's belief that the pursuit of happiness must be the pursuit of a single dominant aim, and his account of the nature of philosophy, seem to be both so seriously mistaken as to make unprofitable a discussion of his arguments that happiness consists in *theoria*. But the properties which he assigns to happiness in the first book are of great interest. They emerge largely negatively from his arguments against inadequate conceptions of happiness.

Aristotle starts from the traditional theme of the three ways of life—
the apolaustic, the political, and the theoretic. It is wrong, he says, to
think that the life of pleasure is the happy life, for this is brutish. Happiness, then, is to be regarded as a peculiarly human thing. Later on, he
expressly denies that animals can be happy, and says that if children are
called happy it is only for the hope of happiness which is in them. In
English there are idioms in which it is natural to ascribe happiness to
animals, but it seems clear that they do not pursue long-term, high-order
goals of the kind we have been discussing. But there seems no reason
why the pursuit of happiness might not include the pursuit of some
things such as health and good food which are benefits which could be
enjoyed also by irrational animals. Man differs from other animals in his
concern for the absent and the future, and this naturally affects his
enjoyment of and attitude to animal goods. Men, unlike animals, suffer
from boredom, and human welfare must include some degree of intellectual stimulation and interest. Human happiness, therefore, could not
consist wholly in participation of benefits which human beings have in
common with non-human animals. But it does not follow, as Aristotle
thought, that is must consist wholly in some activity which they do not
share at all with other animals.

It seems odd to us that Aristotle should consider happiness an activity
at all. He argues that happiness cannot be identical with virtue because
it is possible for a man who has virtue to sleep or be idle throughout his
whole life, or to suffer great misfortune, and no one would call such a
man happy. But surely, if a man spends his whole life in bed and never
does any virtuous actions, then it seems at least equally odd to call him
virtuous. Happiness seems, like virtue, to be a long-term state rather
than a particular activity or career; and if, unlike virtue, it is a state which
is vulnerable to misfortune, this is not because it is an activity which is
interrupted by misfortune.

Aristotle mentions two other properties of happiness: it must be perfect (*teleion*) and it must be self-sufficient (*autarkes*). Happiness is the
most perfect thing: this is something we have already considered, namely,
the fact that happiness, unlike wealth and pleasure and reason, is
chosen only for its own sake. But there is a difficulty here, for when
Aristotle speaks at 1097b2 of honour, pleasure and reason, it looks as if
he has in mind once again the three kinds of life. But later he is to
identify the life of happiness with the theoretic life. It is odd, then, that
nous should appear here as something distinct from happiness, and
therefore not most perfect, when in book ten the theoretic life is going

to be praised as most perfect. Perhaps this is just an example of something familiar in recent philosophy, that what appears under one description as a means may appear under another description as an end; as the killing of an enemy may be done *for* revenge and yet be itself the revenge.

The self-sufficiency of happiness, Aristotle says, does not consist in its being a life for a hermit, but rather in its being an activity which by itself, and without anything else, makes life choice-worthy and complete. Of course, other goods added to happiness will add up to something more choice-worthy. This last remark makes it clear that Aristotle did not consider happiness an inclusive state made up of independent goods.

So far we have considered happiness as a goal pursued. So considered, it appears as a long-term, inclusive, comparatively self-regarding goal. Happiness as a realized state cannot be simply identified with the achievement of such a goal; for notoriously a man in pursuit of happiness may realize all the specific goals he has planned and yet not be happy. Happiness as realized appears to be a state of mind, or perhaps rather a state of will: it appears to be akin to contentment and satisfaction, and might perhaps be described as an attitude, were it not that an attitude seems to be something which can be adopted at will in a way in which happiness cannot. Happiness in this sense might seem to be the satisfaction of one's major desires coupled with the belief that such satisfaction is likely to endure. The difficulty in such a definition arises with the word 'major': what is a major desire? It does not seem that we can say that every desire which occupies a great part of an agent's attention and efforts is a major desire in this context; for we might be reluctant to call a man happy whose only concern was to procure heroin, even if he was in a position to obtain regular and safe supplies. On the other hand it does not seem that we can decide *a priori* what a man's major desires must be by considerations of the major needs and concerns of human beings in general. For it seems that a man may be happy in sacrificing his own welfare: many martyrs have died proclaiming their happiness. The pursuit of altruistic goals, I have argued, cannot be called the pursuit of happiness; but the achievement of altruistic goals may bring happiness as a kind of epiphenomenon.

In assessing happiness we have regard not only to the satisfaction of desires, but also to the nature of the desires themselves. The notions of contentment and of richness of life are in part independent, and this leads to paradox in the concept of happiness, which involves both. Plato and Mill sought to combine the two notions, by claiming that those who had experience of both inferior and superior pleasures would be contented only with the superior pleasures of a rich intellectual life. This, if true, might show the felicity of Socrates satisfied, but will not prove that Socrates dissatisfied is happier than a fool satisfied. The greater a person's education and sensitivity, the greater his capacity for the 'higher' pleasures and therefore for a richer life; yet increase in education and sensitivity brings with it increase in the number of desires, and a corresponding lesser likelihood of their satisfaction. Instruction and emancipation in one way favour happiness, and in another militate against it. To increase a person's chances of happiness, in the sense of fulness of life, is *eo ipso* to decrease his chances of happiness, in the sense of satisfaction of desire. Thus in the pursuit of happiness, no less than in the creation of a world, there lurks a problem of evil.

IV

ON DUTIES

C. H. WHITELEY

CONSIDER THE following propositions:

(1) A man can have a duty to pursue the interest of others, but no duty to pursue his own interest, as such.

(2) An action can be a duty irrespective of its consequences, and one can know it to be a duty without knowing what its consequences will be.

(3) Duties are apprehended by reason alone; in discovering what they are, no reference to emotion, desire, or liking is relevant.

(4) Duties may conflict.

(5) Many actions are morally indifferent; a man may have no duty either to do them or to refrain from doing them.

(6) Any action which is a duty for a man in a given situation would also be a duty for another man in a similar situation.

(7) If an action is my duty, I am morally responsible for doing it; if I do it I acquire merit, and if I fail to do it I incur demerit and am liable to punishment.

(8) A man can have no duty which he is not capable of recognizing as his duty.

(9) Only a rational being can have a duty, and he can have it only towards another rational being.

All these propositions have been asserted by some moral philosophers, and denied by others. There is a tendency for those who accept some of them to accept the others also (Kant, for instance, accepted most of them). Together they make up a coherent point of view, corresponding fairly closely to what is often understood by 'intuitionism'. I shall maintain that all these propositions are true, and most of them obviously true, if the word 'duty' is used in its commonest sense; but that this sense is not the sense in which the word is generally used in philosophical discussion. The conflict which leads some philosophers to assert, and others to deny, the above propositions, owes something to an unclearness

From *Proceedings of the Aristotelian Society*, Vol. 53 (1952-3), pp. 97-104. Reprinted by courtesy of the Editor of the Aristotelian Society and the author.

in the use of the word 'duty' and its approximate synonym 'obligation'.

In moral philosophy, 'duty' and 'obligation' are normally used in a sense in which 'my duty' or 'what I am obliged to do' is equivalent to 'the right thing to do', 'the best thing to do', 'what a virtuous man would do'. In this sense, to declare what a man's duty is in a given situation is to make a definitive recommendation as to what he should do, taking all the circumstances into account. It would be absurd to say that the right thing for a man to do was not his duty, or that something other than his duty was a better action than his duty.

But this sense of the words 'duty' and 'obligation' is not their usual sense in common speech. The ordinary sense is that in which we speak of 'the duties of a professor', of a policeman being 'on point duty', of 'putting a person under an obligation', of 'discharging one's obligations'. In this sense, a duty or obligation is a consequence of a contract or undertaking, either explicit or implicit. My duty is that which I am engaged or committed to do, and which other people can therefore expect and require me to do. I have a duty to keep a promise, because I have bound myself thereto. I have a duty to render certain services to my wife, my employer, my clients, my constituents, which I need not render to other persons, because I have taken upon myself the status of a husband, an employee, a consultant, a delegate, and thereby committed myself to the performance of the tasks pertaining to such a status. I have a duty to speak the truth if by offering information I have thereby made myself responsible for its accuracy (the extent of this responsibility varies according to the conventions of the situation; they are not the same in an Oriental bazaar or a session of diplomats as in a judicial inquiry or a Government White Paper). I have a duty to conform to the rules of the society to which I belong, in so far as I give others to expect that I shall do so, and in so far as I take advantage of the reciprocal conformity of other members. If we may distinguish between the *customs* of a society, as what its members generally do, and its *conventions*, as what its members are generally expected to do, then nobody calls an action a duty because (like shaving the beard or taking tea with the afternoon meal) it is customary, unless it is also conventional.

Now, if the terms 'duty' and 'obligation' are understood in this ordinary sense, in which a duty is a function of a trust-relationship, my nine propositions are all true.

(1) A man can have no duty to pursue his own interest. For he cannot make bargains with himself, give himself promises, or call himself to account. The sort of situation which most nearly answers to this description is where a man, taking up the attitude of an external censor, resolves

to live up to a certain standard; and then, if he 'lets himself down', he may feel much the same as though he had let someone else down. But we should not say that a man had a duty to keep such undertakings made to himself as if they had been made to someone else; we should say he had a perfect right to change his mind.

(2) An action is determined as a duty in virtue of some past commitment. It can therefore be known to be a duty without knowledge of any of its consequences apart from those involved in the fulfilling of the commitment, and such consequences cannot make any difference to its being a duty. Doing one's duty does not necessarily involve producing or trying to produce any good.

(3) To understand the nature and extent of my commitments, there may be need of reasoning. But there is no need for emotions, desires, or preferences, and no such feelings or inclinations can contribute towards answering the question What have I rendered myself bound to do?

(4) It is possible in principle, and it often happens in practice, that different commitments have been undertaken which in a particular situation are incompatible with each other. In such a case there is a conflict of duties.

(5) It cannot be a duty to do, or not to do, an action, unless that action is covered by some commitment. It is possible in principle, and often happens in practice, that many actions are not subject to any obligation, and that in some situations a man has no duty to do anything.

(6) The ground of my duty is always a specific feature of the situation, namely, a trust-relation between myself and some other person or persons. Other men might enter into a similar relation, and their duties would then be the same as mine. Often, indeed, the ground of obligation is a general rule which applies to all members of the community of which it is a rule.

(7) If I am committed to an action, then those to whom I am committed are entitled to require of me the performance of that action. If I fail to perform it, they are entitled to demand an explanation; and in case of harm arising through my default, they are entitled to demand compensation or penalty in return. That is, in engaging myself to do an action, I also make myself answerable and liable to penalty if I fail to perform it. It cannot, however, be said that the fulfilment of a duty entitles me to claim a reward, unless the duty was undertaken in consideration of such reward. To say 'I only did my duty' is often to renounce any claim to a reward.

(8) A man cannot commit himself without knowing that he does so (though he may, of course, commit himself without fully realizing the

extent of his commitment). Consequently, if I am incapable of recognizing that an action is my duty, I cannot have committed myself to it, and it cannot therefore be my duty. Of course, I may be capable of recognizing an action as a duty, and through negligence or passion omit to recognize it on a particular occasion.

(9) The only kind of creature who can have a duty is one who is able to undertake a commitment. To do this, he must have sufficient intelligence to understand a trust-situation; and he must also have sufficient control over his passions to be able at one time to guarantee his actions at a later time. Whoever fulfils these conditions is properly called a 'rational being'. Thus infants, idiots, and animals have no duties. Conversely, one can give an undertaking only to another rational being who is capable of understanding the commitment, of relying on it, and of demanding its fulfilment. Thus we have no duties towards infants, idiots, and animals, though we may have duties towards third parties in respect of them. If it seems paradoxical to deny that we have duties towards insufficiently rational human beings, this may be because we think of them as potentially rational—the relationship between an infant and its parents gradually develops into one of mutual trust.

If, however, the words 'duty' and 'obligation' are understood in the sense usual in moral philosophy, in which 'duty' is equivalent to 'the right thing' or 'the best thing to do', and 'doing one's duty' is equivalent to 'living virtuously', then my nine propositions are at least disputable and, I think, false.

(1) We do sometimes think that the best thing for a man to do is something which is to his own advantage, and that it is best because it is to his own advantage; we urge him to do it, and blame him for 'neglecting his own good' if he does not.

(2) While we think that the existence of a commitment to do an action is a good reason for doing it, we do not think that it is a conclusive reason. We all allow that there are occasions on which, to procure a great good or to avert a great evil, contracts should be broken, undertakings ignored. Thus we cannot rule out any expected good or evil consequences of an action as having no bearing on its rightness.

(3) Historical inquiry and logical deduction will tell a man what his commitments are. They will not tell him whether it is better to honour them or to repudiate them. Could a being without emotions, desires, and tastes, incapable of appreciation or abhorrence, judge one action to be worth doing rather than another? It is not easy to suppose so.

(4) In any given situation, there can be but one action which is right and best. Hence, in the philosophical sense of 'duty', the expression

'conflict of duties' is nonsense. (Of course, one can say that two or more actions might be equally good or right; but then there would be no duty to do either of them rather than the other.)

(5) Similarly, there are always some alternative courses of action which are better than others. Hence, no choice is morally indifferent, since one might always have done either something better or something worse.

(6) The right thing for a man to do in a given situation, taking into account the whole situation, is not necessarily the sort of action which it would be right for another person to perform in any other actual or possible situation. The duties required of husbands towards their wives by law, convention, and the marriage contract are the same for all husbands and wives in the same cultural community. But the manner in which I ought to behave towards my wife depends on the unique character of our personalities and the relations between us, and is not necessarily the manner in which any other individual husband ought to behave towards his wife. Of course, you can say that anybody in *precisely* the same situation ought to behave in precisely the same way; but this assertion is entirely empty.

(7) A man is responsible, and liable to penalties, for failing to do that which he is committed to do. He is not, in general, responsible or liable to penalty, for failing to do the best thing that he could have done. He is not responsible for doing more than he has undertaken to do, though he may be praised and rewarded if he does so. I am answerable to my creditors if I fail to pay my debts. But I am answerable to no one if I fail to contribute any of my means to charitable objects, though it may be right that I should do so.

(8) The right action is the right action, whether I am capable of recognizing it or not.

(9) Infants, idiots, and animals are capable of doing the right or the wrong thing, of behaving well or badly. Also, one may behave towards them in a right and good way, or in a wrong and bad way.

I have been arguing that 'my duty', and 'what I ought to do', or 'what it is right to do' or 'what it is best to do', are not in general equivalent expressions; and that many well-known opinions in moral philosophy are plausible only if it is assumed that they are equivalent. To assume this equivalence, to pose the main question of moral philosophy as an inquiry into the duties of men, is already to be half-committed to a particular view of morally good conduct. According to this view, morality is not the completion of a pattern, nor the attainment of an end, but the fulfilling of commitments. Morality is a reciprocal affair, in which men make concessions to each other's interests; a moral issue arises only

when one man's interest collides with another's. Right conduct is that
which is required of a man in order to maintain an equilibrium between
receipts and contributions, claims and counter-claims. Moral philosophy
then becomes an analysis of the conditions of a contract- or trust-relationship. It concerns itself only with the fully deliberate, 'rational' actions
of men. It dismisses as valueless or irrelevant all impulses, sentiments, and
interests except the deliberate performance of duty for duty's sake, the
resolve not to betray the trust of those to whom one is committed. The
notions of moral responsibility, merit, and guilt are in place in this
context; and so is the notion of the equal worth of all moral agents,
not as equal in their achievements, but as equal in their capacity to fulfil
their different commitments. Such a view of the nature of right conduct
is not uncommon; especially, perhaps, in those communities in which
contractual relations are comparatively important and the range of responsibility of the independent individual is comparatively wide.

There is also an important religious influence contributing to the
identification of 'doing right' with 'doing one's duty'. If a man comes to
believe that, in view of the greatness of God's favours granted or to
come, he has towards God an obligation which is not limited to the
performance of specific services, but which requires that he should do
the best thing possible on all occasions, if he thinks that God requires of
him obedience to the injunction 'Be ye perfect', then for him all virtuous
behaviour can also be regarded as a duty towards God, and the distinction between the right and the obligatory disappears. In fact, the moral
philosophies whose key terms are Duty and Obligation, in contrast to
those whose key terms are Good and Virtue and Happiness, usually
have a Christian background of ideas.

There is, then, a widespread tendency to confine 'moral' questions to
questions of 'duty' in the ordinary sense; that is, questions of the fulfilling
of commitments to other persons. But this restriction is unsatisfactory.
We must ask ourselves what commitments it is right for us to undertake; under what circumstances a commitment may be neglected in order
to bring about a good or avert an evil; which of two commitments should
be preferred in circumstances in which they conflict (if we are to decide
between them, it must be on other grounds than that we are committed
to them, for the property of being-a-commitment does not admit of
degrees). And we want to classify these questions also as 'moral' questions.

Yet there is a difficulty here. The field of 'duty' is capable of a reasonably clear demarcation; and the demands of others for the fulfilment of
our commitments present themselves with a peculiar compulsiveness

which serves to mark off the 'sense of duty' from other motives to action. Thus, if morality is confined to the doing of 'duties', questions of morality can be adequately distinguished from questions of taste or of expediency. But, if we abandon this restriction, if we count amongst 'moral' considerations some which do not involve commitments to others, the distinction is much more puzzling. 'Duty' and 'obligation' have their own proper context. But 'right' and 'good' spread over the whole area of human preferences, with no evident distinction of moral from non-moral senses. Is *'virtù'* in Machiavelli an ethical term, and is his eulogy of Cesare Borgia a moral judgement? The question whether I shall spend my surplus cash on a car or on works of art, the question whether the nation shall spend its resources on guns or butter, may involve no commitments to anybody: are they moral questions or not?

If we say No, holding to the restricted notion of morality whereby 'duty' as 'commitment' is identified with 'duty' as 'what ought to be done', then we must accept the consequence that doing one's duty is not the whole of the Good Life. Morality in this narrow sense is not autonomous or self-justifying. It is a consequence of the decision to undertake commitments for reasons which must in part lie outside morality. The question 'Why should I do my duty?' is then a sensible question, and can be answered in terms of the reasons for which men do make and keep agreements. And the question 'What moral system is the best?' is also a sensible question, and must be answered in terms of considerations which are not 'moral' on this narrower interpretation of 'moral'.

If, on the other hand, we adopt a broader interpretation of 'morality', such that the justification of our conventions and commitments is itself a moral issue, then we shall have great difficulty in marking off any set of considerations as distinctively moral. I am inclined to think that, if we abandon the restriction of 'morality' to the observance of commitments, we shall find ourselves obliged in ethical thinking to take account of *all* the reasons men may have for preferring one course of action to another.

V

SAINTS AND HEROES

J. O. URMSON

MORAL PHILOSOPHERS tend to discriminate, explicitly or implicitly, three types of action from the point of view of moral worth. First, they recognize actions that are a duty, or obligatory, or that we ought to perform, treating these terms as approximately synonymous; second, they recognize actions that are right in so far as they are permissible from a moral standpoint and not ruled out by moral considerations, but that are not morally required of us, like the lead of this or that card at bridge; third, they recognize actions that are wrong, that we ought not to do. Some moral philosophers, indeed, could hardly discriminate even these three types of action consistently with the rest of their philosophy; Moore, for example, could hardly recognize a class of morally indifferent actions, permissible but not enjoined, since it is to be presumed that good or ill of some sort will result from the most trivial of our actions. But most moral philosophers recognize these three types of action and attempt to provide a moral theory that will make intelligible such a threefold classification.

To my mind this threefold classification, or any classification that is merely a variation on or elaboration of it, is totally inadequate to the facts of morality; any moral theory that leaves room only for such a classification will in consequence also be inadequate. My main task in this paper will be to show the inadequacy of such a classification by drawing attention to two of the types of action that most conspicuously lie outside such a classification; I shall go on to hazard some views on what sort of theory will most easily cope with the facts to which I draw attention, but the facts are here the primary interest.

We sometimes call a person a saint, or an action saintly, using the word 'saintly' in a purely moral sense with no religious implications; also we sometimes call a person a hero or an action heroic. It is too

From *Essays in Moral Philosophy*, ed. A. I. Melden (University of Washington Press, 1958), pp. 198-216. Reprinted by permission of the publisher and the author. © 1958 by the University of Washington Press.

clear to need argument that the words 'saint' and 'hero' are at least normally used in such a way as to be favourably evaluative; it would be impossible to claim that this evaluation is always moral, for clearly we sometimes call a person a saint when evaluating him religiously rather than morally and may call a person the hero of a game or athletic contest in which no moral qualities were displayed, but I shall take it that no formal argument is necessary to show that at least sometimes we use both words for moral evaluation.

If 'hero' and 'saint' can be words of moral evaluation, we may proceed to the attempt to make explicit the criteria that we implicitly employ for their use in moral contexts. It appears that we so use them in more than one type of situation, and that there is a close parallel between the ways in which the two terms 'hero' and 'saint' are used; we shall here notice three types of situation in which they are used which seem to be sufficiently different to merit distinction. As the first two types of situation to be noticed are ones that can be readily subsumed under the threefold classification mentioned above, it will be sufficient here to note them and pass on to the third type of situation, which, since it cannot be subsumed under that classification, is for the purposes of this paper the most interesting.

A person may be called a saint (1) if he does his duty regularly in contexts in which inclination, desire, or self-interest would lead most people not to do it, and does so as a result of exercising abnormal self-control; parallel to this a person may be called a hero (1) if he does his duty in contexts in which terror, fear, or a drive to self-preservation would lead most men not to do it, and does so by exercising abnormal self-control. Similarly for actions: an action may be called saintly (1) if it is a case of duty done by virtue of self-control in a context in which most men would be led astray by inclination or self-interest, and an action may be called heroic (1) if it is a case of duty done by virtue of self-control in a context in which most men would be led astray by fear or a drive for self-preservation. The only difference between the saintly and the heroic in this sort of situation is that the one involves resistance to desire and self-interest; the other, resistance to fear and self-preservation. This is quite a clear difference, though there may be marginal cases, or cases in which motives were mixed, in which it would be equally appropriate to call an action indifferently saintly or heroic. It is easy to give examples of both the heroic and the saintly as distinguished above: the unmarried daughter does the saintly deed of staying at home to tend her ailing and widowed father; the terrified doctor heroically stays by his patients in a plague-ridden city.

A person may be called a saint (2) if he does his duty in contexts in which inclination or self-interest would lead most men not to do it, not, as in the previous paragraph, by abnormal self-control, but without effort; parallel to this a person may be called a hero (2) if he does his duty in contexts in which fear would lead most men not to do it, and does so without effort. The corresponding accounts of a saintly (2) or heroic (2) action can easily be derived. Here we have the conspicuously virtuous deed, in the Aristotelian sense, as opposed to the conspicuously self-controlled, encratic deed of the previous paragraph. People thus purged of temptation or disciplined against fear may be rare, but Aristotle thought there could be such; there is a tendency today to think of such people as merely lucky or unimaginative, but Aristotle thought more highly of them than of people who need to exercise self-control.

It is clear that, in the two types of situation so far considered, we are dealing with actions that fall under the concept of duty. Roughly, we are calling a person saintly or heroic because he does his duty in such difficult contexts that most men would fail in them. Since for the purposes of this paper I am merely conceding that we do use the term 'saintly' and 'heroic' in these ways, it is unnecessary here to spend time arguing that we do so use them or in illustrating such uses. So used, the threefold classification of actions whose adequacy I wish to deny can clearly embrace them. I shall therefore pass immediately to a third use of the terms 'heroic' and 'saintly' which I am not merely willing to concede but obliged to establish.

I contend, then, that we may also call a person a saint (3) if he does actions that are far beyond the limits of his duty, whether by control of contrary inclination and interest or without effort; parallel to this we may call a person a hero (3) if he does actions that are far beyond the bounds of his duty, whether by control of natural fear or without effort. Such actions are saintly (3) or heroic (3). Here, as it seems to me, we have the hero or saint, heroic or saintly deed, *par excellence*; until now we have been considering but minor saints and heroes. We have considered the, certainly, heroic action of the doctor who does his duty by sticking to this patients in a plague-ridden city; we have now to consider the case of the doctor who, no differently situated from countless other doctors in other places, volunteers to join the depleted medical forces in that city. Previously, we were considering the soldier who heroically does his duty in the face of such dangers as would cause most to shirk—the sort of man who is rightly awarded the Military Medal in the British Army; we have now to consider the case of the soldier who does more than his superior officers would ever ask him to do—the man to whom, often posthumously, the Victoria Cross is awarded. Similarly, we have to turn from saintly self-discipline in the way of duty to the dedicated, self-effacing life in the service of others which is not even contemplated by the majority of upright, kind, and honest men, let alone expected of them.

Let us be clear that we are not now considering cases of natural affection, such as the sacrifice made by a mother for her child; such cases may be said with some justice not to fall under the concept of morality but to be admirable in some different way. Such cases as are here under consideration may be taken to be as little bound up with such emotions as affection as any moral action may be. We may consider an example of what is meant by 'heroism' (3) in more detail to bring this out.

We may imagine a squad of soldiers to be practising the throwing of live hand grenades; a grenade slips from the hand of one of them and rolls on the ground near the squad; one of them sacrifices his life by throwing himself on the grenade and protecting his comrades with his own body. It is quite unreasonable to suppose that such a man must be impelled by the sort of emotion that he might be impelled by if his best friend were in the squad; he might only just have joined the squad; it is clearly an action having moral status. But if the soldier had not thrown himself on the grenade would he have failed in his duty? Though clearly he is superior in some way to his comrades, can we possibly say that they failed in their duty by not trying to be the one who sacrificed himself? If he had not done so, could anyone have said to him, 'You ought to have thrown yourself on that grenade'? Could a superior have decently ordered him to do it? The answer to all these questions is plainly negative. We clearly have here a case of a moral action, a heroic action, which cannot be subsumed under the classification whose inadequacy we are exposing.

But someone may not be happy with this conclusion, and for more respectable reasons than a desire to save the traditional doctrine. He may reason as follows: in so far as that soldier had time to feel or think at all, he presumably felt that he ought to do that deed; he considered it the proper thing to do; he, if no one else, might have reproached himself for failing to do his duty if he had shirked the deed. So, it may be argued, if an act presents itself to us in the way this act may be supposed to have presented itself to this soldier, then it is our duty to do it; we have no option. This objection to my thesis clearly has some substance, but it involves a misconception of what is at issue. I have no desire to present the act of heroism as one that is naturally regarded as optional by the hero, as something he might or might not do; I concede that he might regard himself as being obliged to act as he does. But if he were to survive the action only a modesty so excessive as to appear false could make him say, 'I only did my duty,' for we know, and he knows, that he has done more than duty requires. Further, though he might say to himself that so to act was a duty, he could not say so even beforehand to anyone else, and no one else could ever say it. Subjectively, we may say, at the time of action, the deed presented itself as a duty, but it was not a duty.

Another illustration, this time of saintliness, may help. It is recorded by Bonaventura that after Francis of Assisi had finished preaching to the birds on a celebrated occasion his companions gathered around him to praise and admire. But Francis himself was not a bit pleased; he was full of self-reproach that he had hitherto failed in what he now considered to be his duty to preach to the feathered world. There is indeed no degree of saintliness that a suitable person may not come to consider it to be his duty to achieve. Yet there is a world of difference between this failure to have preached hitherto to the birds and a case of straightforward breach of duty, however venial. First, Francis could without absurdity reproach himself for his failure to do his duty, but it would be quite ridiculous for anyone else to do so, as one could have done if he had failed to keep his vows, for example. Second, it is not recorded that Francis ever reproached anyone else for failure to preach to the birds as a breach of duty. He could claim this action for himself as a duty and could perhaps have exhorted others to preach to the birds; but there could be no question of reproaches for not so acting.

To sum up on this point, then, it seems clear that there is no action, however quixotic, heroic, or saintly, which the agent may not regard himself as obliged to perform, as much as he may feel himself obliged to tell the truth and to keep his promises. Such actions do not present themselves as optional to the agent when he is deliberating; but, since he alone can call such an action of his a duty, and then only from the deliberative viewpoint, only for himself and not for others, and not even for himself as a piece of objective reporting, and since nobody else can call on him to perform such an act as they can call on him to tell the truth and to keep his promises, there is here a most important difference from the rock-bottom duties which are duties for all and from every point of view, and to which anyone may draw attention. Thus we need not deny the points made by our imaginary objector in order to substantiate the point that some acts of heroism and saintliness cannot be adequately subsumed under the concept of duty.

Let us then take it as established that we have to deal in ethics not with a simple trichotomy of duties, permissible actions, and wrong actions, or any substantially similar conceptual scheme, but with something more complicated. We have to add at least the complication of actions that are certainly of moral worth but that fall outside the notion of a duty and seem to go beyond it, actions worthy of being called heroic or saintly. It should indeed be noted that heroic and saintly actions are not the sole, but merely conspicuous, cases of actions that exceed the basic demands of duty; there can be cases of disinterested kindness and generosity, for example, that are clearly more than basic duty requires and yet hardly ask for the high titles, 'saintly' and 'heroic'. Indeed, every case of 'going the second mile' is a case in point, for it cannot be one's duty to go the second mile in the same basic sense as it is to go the first—otherwise it could be argued first that it is one's duty to go two miles and therefore that the spirit of the rule of the second mile requires that one go altogether four miles, and by repetition one could establish the need to go every time on an infinite journey. It is possible to go just beyond one's duty by being a little more generous, forbearing, helpful, or forgiving than fair dealing demands, or to go a very long way beyond the basic code of duties with the saint or the hero. When I here draw attention to the heroic and saintly deed, I do so merely in order to have conspicuous cases of a whole realm of actions that lie outside the trichotomy I have criticized and therefore, as I believe, outside the purview of most ethical theories.

Before considering the implications for ethics of the facts we have up to now been concerned to note, it might be of value to draw attention to a less exalted parallel to these facts. If we belong to a club there will be rules of the club, written or unwritten, calling upon us to fulfil certain basic requirements that are a condition of membership, and that may be said to be the duties of membership. It may perhaps be such a basic requirement that we pay a subscription. It will probably be indifferent whether we pay this subscription by cheque or in cash—both procedures will be 'right'—and almost certainly it will be quite indifferent what sort of hat we wear at the meetings. Here, then, we have conformity to rule which is the analogue of doing one's duty, breach of rule which is the analogue of wrong-doing, and a host of indifferent actions, in accordance with the traditional trichotomy. But among the rule-abiding members of such a club what differences there

can be! It is very likely that there will be one, or perhaps two or
three, to whose devotion and loyal service the success of the club is
due far more than to the activities of all the other members together;
these are the saints and the heroes of the clubs, who do more for them
by far than any member could possibly be asked to do, whose many
services could not possibly be demanded in the rules. Behind them
come a motley selection, varying from the keen to the lukewarm, whose
contributions vary in value and descend sometimes to almost nothing
beyond what the rules demand. The moral contribution of people to
society can vary in value in the same way.

So much, then, for the simple facts to which I have wished to draw
attention. They are simple facts and, unless I have misrepresented
them, they are facts of which we are all, in a way, perfectly well aware.
It would be absurd to suggest that moral philosophers have hitherto
been unaware of the existence of saints and heroes and have never
even alluded to them in their works. But it does seem that these facts
have been neglected in their general, systematic accounts of morality.
It is indeed easy to see that on some of the best-known theories there
is no room for such facts. If for Moore, and for most utilitarians, any
action is a duty that will produce the greatest possible good in the
circumstances, for them the most heroic self-sacrifice or saintly self-
forgetfulness will be duties on all fours with truth-telling and promise-
keeping. For Kant, beyond the counsels of prudence and the rules of
skill, there is only the categorical imperative of duty, and every duty
is equally and utterly binding on all men; it is true that he recognizes
the limiting case of the holy will, but the holy will is not a will that goes
beyond duty but a will that is beyond morality through being incapable of
acting except in accordance with the imperative. The nearest to an equivalent to a holy will in the cases we have been noting is the saintly will in
the second sense we distinguished—the will that effortlessly does its duty
when most would fail—but this is not a true parallel and in any case does
not fall within the class of moral actions that go beyond duty to which
our attention is primarily given. It is also true that Kant recognized
virtues and talents as having conditional value, but not moral value,
whereas the acts of heroism and saintliness we have considered have
full moral worth, and their value is as unconditional as anyone could
wish. Without committing ourselves to a scholarly examination of
Kant's ethical works, it is surely evident that Kant could not consistently do justice to the facts before us. Intuitionism seems to me so
obscurantist that I should not wish to prophesy what an intuitionist
might feel himself entitled to say; but those intuitionists with whose

works I am acquainted found their theories on an intuition of the fitting, the prima facie duty or the claim; the act that has this character to the highest degree at any time is a duty. While they recognize greater and lesser, stronger and weaker, claims, this is only in order to be able to deal with the problem of the conflict of duties; they assign no place to the act that, while not a duty, is of high moral importance.

Simple utilitarianism, Kantianism, and intuitionism, then, have no obvious theoretical niche for the saint and the hero. It is possible, no doubt, to revise these theories to accommodate the facts, but until so modified successfully they must surely be treated as unacceptable, and the modifications required might well detract from their plausibility. The intuitionists, for example, might lay claim to the intuition of a non-natural characteristic of saintliness, of heroism, of decency, of sportingness, and so on, but this would give to their theory still more the appearance of utilizing the advantages of theft over honest toil.

Thus as moral theorists we need to discover some theory that will allow for both absolute duties, which, in Mill's phrase, can be exacted from a man like a debt, to omit which is to do wrong and to deserve censure, and which may be embodied in formal rules or principles, and also for a range of actions which are of moral value and which an agent may feel called upon to perform, but which cannot be demanded and whose omission cannot be called wrong-doing. Traditional moral theories, I have suggested, fail to do this. It would be well beyond the scope of this paper, and probably beyond my capacity, to produce here and now a full moral theory designed to accommodate all these facts, including the facts of saintliness and heroism. But I do think that of all traditional theories utilitarianism can be most easily modified to accommodate the facts, and would like before ending this paper to bring forward some considerations tending to support this point of view.

Moore went to great pains to determine exactly the nature of the intrinsically good, and Mill to discover the *summum bonum*, Moore's aim being to explain thereby directly the rightness and wrongness of particular actions and Mill's to justify a set of moral principles in the light of which the rightness or wrongness of particular actions can be decided. But, though there can be very tricky problems of duty, they do not naturally present themselves as problems whose solution depends upon an exact determination of an ultimate end; while the moral principles that come most readily to mind—truth-telling;

promise-keeping; abstinence from murder, theft, and violence; and the like—make a nice discrimination of the supreme good seem irrelevant. We do not need to debate whether it is Moore's string of intrinsic goods or Mill's happiness that is achieved by conformity to such principles; it is enough to see that without them social life would be impossible and any life would indeed be solitary, poor, nasty, brutish, and short. Even self-interest (which some have seen as the sole foundation of morality) is sufficient ground to render it wise to preach, if not to practise, such principles. Such considerations as these, which are not novel, have led some utilitarians to treat avoidance of the *summum malum* rather than the achievement of the *summum bonum* as the foundation of morality. Yet to others this has seemed, with some justification, to assign to morality too ignoble a place.

But the facts we have been considering earlier in this paper are surely relevant at this point. It is absurd to ask just what ideal is being served by abstinence from murder; but on the other hand nobody could see in acts of heroism such as we have been considering a mere avoidance of anti-social behaviour. Here we have something more gracious, actions that need to be inspired by a positive ideal. If duty can, as Mill said, be exacted from persons as a debt, it is because duty is a minimum requirement for living together; the positive contribution of actions that go beyond duty could not be so exacted.

It may, however, be objected that this is a glorification of the higher flights of morality at the expense of duty, towards which an unduly cynical attitude is being taken. In so far as the suggestion is that we are forgetting how hard the way of duty may be and that doing one's duty can at times deserve to be called heroic and saintly, the answer is that we have mentioned this and acknowledge it; it is not forgotten but irrelevant to the point at issue, which is the place of duty in a moral classification of actions, not the problem of the worth of moral agents. But I may be taken to be acquiescing in a low and circumscribed view of duty which I may be advised to enlarge. We should, it may be said, hitch our wagons to the stars and not be content to say: you must do this and that as duties, and it would be very nice if you were to do these other things but we do not expect them of you. Is it perhaps only an imperfect conception of duty which finds it not to comprise the whole of morality? I want to examine this difficulty quite frankly, and to explain why I think that we properly recognize morality that goes beyond duty; for it seems to me incontestable that properly or improperly we do so.

No intelligent person will claim infallibility for his moral views.

But allowing for this one must claim that one's moral code is ideal so far as one can see; for to say, 'I recognize moral code A but see clearly that moral code B is superior to it' is but a way of saying that one recognizes moral code B but is only prepared to live up to moral code A. In some sense, then, everybody must be prepared to justify his moral code as ideal; but some philosophers have misunderstood this sense. Many philosophers have thought it necessary, if they were to defend their moral code as ideal, to try to show that it had a super-human, *a priori* validity. Kant, for example, tried to show that the moral principles he accepted were such as any rational being, whether man or angel, must inevitably accept; the reputedly empiricist Locke thought that it must be possible to work out a deductive justification of moral laws. In making such claims such philosophers have uninten-tionally done morality a disservice; for their failure to show that the moral code was ideal in the sense of being a rationally justifiable system independent of time, place, circumstance, and human nature has led many to conclude that there can be no justification of a moral code, that moral codes are a matter of taste or convention.

But morality, I take it, is something that should serve human needs, not something that incidentally sweeps man up with itself, and to show that a morality was ideal would be to show that it best served man— man as he is and as he can be expected to become, not man as he would be if he were perfectly rational or an incorporeal angel. Just as it would be fatuous to build our machines so that they would give the best results according to an abstract conception of mechanical prin-ciples, and is much more desirable to design them to withstand to some extent our ham-fistedness, ignorance, and carelessness, so our morality must be one that will work. In the only sense of 'ideal' that is of importance in action, it is part of the ideal that a moral code should actually help to contribute to human well-being, and a moral code that would work only for angels (for whom it would in any case be unnecesary) would be a far from ideal moral code for human beings. There is, indeed, a place for ideals that are practically unworkable in human affairs, as there is a place for the blueprint of a machine that will never go into production; but it is not the place of such ideals to serve as a basic code of duties.

If, then, we are aiming at a moral code that will best serve human needs, a code that is ideal in the sense that a world in which such a code is acknowledged will be a better place than a world in which some other sort of moral code is acknowledged, it seems that there are ample grounds why our code should distinguish between basic rules, summarily set forth in simple rules and binding on all, and the higher flights of morality of which saintliness and heroism are outstanding examples. These grounds I shall enumerate at once.

1. It is important to give a special status of urgency, and to exert exceptional pressure, in those matters in which compliance with the demands of morality by all is indispensable. An army without men of heroic valour would be impoverished, but without general attention to the duties laid down in military law it would become a mere rabble. Similarly, while life in a world without its saints and heroes would be impoverished, it would only be poor and not necessarily brutish or short as when basic duties are neglected.

2. If we are to exact basic duties like debts, and censure failure, such duties must be, in ordinary circumstances, within the capacity of the ordinary man. It would be silly for us to say to ourselves, our children and our fellow men, 'This and that you and everyone else must do', if the acts in question are such that manifestly but few could bring themselves to do them, though we may ourselves resolve to try to be of that few. To take a parallel from positive law, the prohibition laws asked too much of the American people and were consequently broken systematically; and as people got used to breaking the law a general lowering of respect for the law naturally followed; it no longer seemed that a law was something that everybody could be expected to obey. Similarly in Britain the gambling laws, some of which are utterly unpractical, have fallen into contempt as a body. So, if we were to represent the heroic act of sacrificing one's life for one's comrades as a basic duty, the effect would be to lower the degree of urgency and stringency that the notion of duty does in fact possess. The basic moral code must not be in part too far beyond the capacity of the ordinary men on ordinary occasions, or a general breakdown of compliance with the moral code would be an inevitable consequence; duty would seem to be something high and unattainable, and not for 'the likes of us'. Admirers of the Sermon on the Mount do not in practice, and could not, treat failure to turn the other cheek and to give one's cloak also as being on all fours with breaches of the Ten Commandments, however earnestly they themselves try to live a Christian life.

3. A moral code, if it is to be a code, must be formulable, and if it is to be a code to be observed it must be formulable in rules of manageable complexity. The ordinary man has to apply and interpret this code without recourse to a Supreme Court or House of Lords. But one can have such rules only in cases in which a type of action

that is reasonably easy to recognize is almost invariably desirable or undesirable, as killing is almost invariably undesirable and promise-keeping almost invariably desirable. Where no definite rule of manageable complexity can be justified, we cannot work on that moral plane on which types of action can be enjoined or condemned as duty or crime. It has no doubt often been the case that a person who has gone off to distant parts to nurse lepers has thereby done a deed of great moral worth. But such an action is not merely too far beyond average human capacity to be regarded as a duty, as was insisted in (2) above; it would be quite ridiculous for everyone, however circumstanced, to be expected to go off and nurse lepers. But it would be absurd to try to formulate complicated rules to determine in just what circumstances such an action is a duty. This same point can readily be applied to such less spectacular matters as excusing legitimate debts or nursing sick neighbours.

4. It is part of the notion of a duty that we have a right to demand compliance from others even when we are interested parties. I may demand that you keep your promises to me, tell me the truth, and do me no violence, and I may reproach you if you transgress. But however admirable the tending of strangers in sickness may be it is not a basic duty, and we are not entitled to reproach those to whom we are strangers if they do not tend us in sickness; nor can I tell you, if you fail to give me a cigarette when I have run out, that you have failed in your duty to me, however much you may subsequently reproach yourself for your meanness if you do so fail. A line must be drawn between what we can expect and demand from others and what we can merely hope for and receive with gratitude when we get it; duty falls on one side of this line, and other acts with moral value on the other, and rightly so.

5. In the case of basic moral duties we act to some extent under constraint. We have no choice but to apply pressure on each other to conform in these fundamental matters; here moral principles are like public laws rather than like private ideals. But free choice of the better course of action is always preferable to action under pressure, even when the pressure is but moral. When possible, therefore, it is better that pressure should not be applied and that there should be encouragement and commendation for performance rather than outright demands and censure in the event of non-performance. There are no doubt degrees in this matter. Some pressure may reasonably be brought to persuade a person to go some way beyond basic duty in the direction of kindliness and forbearance, to be not merely a just man but also

not too hard a man. But, while there is nothing whatever objection-
able in the idea of someone's being pressed to carry out such a basic
duty as promise-keeping, there is something horrifying in the thought
of pressure being brought on him to perform an act of heroism. Though
the man might feel himself morally called upon to do the deed, it
would be a moral outrage to apply pressure on him to do such a deed
as sacrificing his life for others.

These five points make it clear why I do not think that the
distinction of basic duty from other acts of moral worth, which I claim
to detect in ordinary moral thought, is a sign of the inferiority of our
everyday moral thinking to that of the general run of moral theorists.
It in no way involves anyone in acquiescing in a second best. No doubt
from the agent's point of view it is imperative that he should endeavour
to live up to the highest ideals of behaviour that he can think of,
and if an action falls within the ideal it is for him irrelevant whether
or not it is a duty or some more supererogatory act. But it simply
does not follow that the distinction is in every way unimportant, for
it is important that we should not demand ideal conduct from others
in the way in which we must demand basic morality from them, or
blame them equally for failures in all fields. It is not cynicism to make
the minimum positive demands upon one's fellow men; but to
characterize an act as a duty is so to demand it.

Thus we may regard the imperatives of duty as prohibiting behaviour
that is intolerable if men are to live together in society and demanding
the minimum of co-operation toward the same end; that is why we
have to treat compliance as compulsory and dereliction as liable to
public censure. We do not need to ask with Bentham whether pushpin
is as good as poetry, with Mill whether it is better to be Socrates dissatisfied or a fool satisfied, or with Moore whether a beautiful world
with no one to see it would have intrinsic worth; what is and what
is not tolerable in society depends on no such nice discrimination.
Utilitarians, when attempting to justify the main rules of duty in
terms of a *summum bonum*, have surely invoked many different types
of utilitarian justification, ranging from the avoidance of the intolerable
to the fulfilment of the last detail of a most rarefied ideal.

Thus I wish to suggest that utilitarianism can best accommodate
the facts to which I have drawn attention; but I have not wished to
support any particular view about the supreme good or the importance
of pleasure. By utilitarianism I mean only a theory that moral justification of actions must be in terms of results. We can be content to
say that duty is mainly concerned with the avoidance of intolerable

results, while other forms of moral behaviour have more positive aims.

To summarize, I have suggested that the trichotomy of duties, indifferent actions, and wrong-doing is inadequate. There are many kinds of action that involve going beyond duty proper, saintly and heroic actions being conspicuous examples of such kinds of action. It has been my main concern to note this point and to ask moral philosophers to theorize in a way that does not tacitly deny it, as most traditional theories have. But I have also been so rash as to suggest that we may look upon our duties as basic requirements to be universally demanded as providing the only tolerable basis of social life. The higher flights of morality can then be regarded as more positive contributions that go beyond what is universally to be exacted; but while not exacted publicly they are clearly equally pressing *in foro interno* on those who are not content merely to avoid the intolerable. Whether this should be called a version of utilitarianism, as I suggest, is a matter of small moment.

VI

CONSCIENCE AND CONSCIENTIOUS
ACTION

C. D. BROAD

THE QUESTION whether an action is conscientious or not is mainly
a question about the agent's motives in doing it. We must clear up
the notion of motive a little before we can give a satisfactory definition
of 'conscientious action'. Suppose that an agent is contemplating a
certain possible course of action in a given situation. He will have
various beliefs and expectations about its qualities, its relations, and
its consequences, e.g. he may believe that it would be unpleasant to
himself, that it would please his mother, and that it would be a breach
of a promise made to his father, and so on. Some of these beliefs and
expectations will attract him towards doing the action, some will repel
him from doing it, and others may leave him unmoved. I call any
belief about an action which attracts one towards doing it a 'motive-
component *for* the action', and any belief about it which repels one
from doing it a 'motive-component *against* the action'. Suppose that
a certain action is in fact chosen and performed. Then I say that the
agent's 'total motive *in* doing the action' was the resultant of all the
motive-components for doing it and all the motive-components against
doing it. And I say that he did it *'because of'* the former, and *'in
spite of'* the latter.

Now suppose that there were several components for doing a certain
action, and several against doing it, and that it was in fact done because
of the former and in spite of the latter. Let us call the former *a*, *b*,
and *c*, and the latter *u*, *v*, and *w*. Now consider, e.g. the component
a. We can ask ourselves the following question about it. Would *a*
have been sufficient, in the absence of *b* and *c*, to induce the agent
to do this action in spite of the components *u*, *v*, and *w* against doing

From *Ethics and the History of Philosophy* by C. D. Broad (Routledge & Kegan
Paul, 1952), pp. 256-62. First published in *Philosophy*, Vol. 15 (1940). Reprinted by
permission of the Editor of *Philosophy*, Routledge & Kegan Paul Ltd., and the
author.

it? Or did the component *a* need to be supplemented by *b* or by *c* or by both in order to overcome the influence of *u*, *v*, and *w*? If and only if the first alternative is true, we can say that *a* was 'a *sufficient* motive-component for doing the action'. Next we can raise the following question. Would *bc* have been sufficient, in the absence of *a*, to induce the agent to do the action in spite of the components *u*, *v*, and *w* against doing it? Or did *bc* need to be supplemented by *a* in order to overcome the influence of *u*, *v*, and *w*? If, and only if, the second alternative is true, we can say that *a* was 'a *necessary* motive-component for doing the action'. Lastly, suppose that *a* had been the only component for doing the action. Then we could say that 'the action was done *purely* from the motive *a*'.

We can now apply these general considerations to the particular case of conscientious action. An action is conscientious if the following conditions are fulfilled. (i) The agent has reflected on the situation, the action, and the alternatives to it, in order to discover what is the right course. In this reflection he has tried his utmost to learn the relevant facts and to give each its due weight, he has exercised his judgement on them to the best of his ability, and he has striven to allow for all sources of bias. (ii) He has decided that, on the factual and ethical information available to him, the action in question is probably the most right or the least wrong of all those which are open to him. (iii) His belief that the action has this moral characteristic, together with his desire to do what is right as such, was either (*a*) the *only* motive-component for doing it, or (*b*) a *sufficient and necessary* motive-component for doing it. If the first alternative is fulfilled, we can say that his action was '*purely* conscientious'. If the second is fulfilled, we can say that it was '*predominantly* conscientious'. The following would be an example of a predominantly conscientious action. Suppose that a person, after reflection, decides that the right action for him is to undertake military service. Suppose that the two motive-components which induce him to undertake this action, in spite of fear, love of comfort, etc., are his belief that it is right, together with his desire to do what is right as such, and his dislike of being thought cowardly by his friends. Then the action is predominantly conscientious if (*a*) his desire to do what is right, as such, *would* have sufficed to overcome his fear and his love of comfort even in the absence of his dislike of being thought cowardly, while (*b*) his dislike of being thought cowardly *would not* have sufficed to overcome those motive-components in the absence of his desire to do what is right, as such. In such a case we can say that the non-conscientious component for doing the action which the agent believes to be right is indeed present but is superfluous and insufficient. It would be absurd to call the action 'conscientious' merely because a superfluous and insufficient non-conscientious motive-component for doing it happened to co-exist with the sufficient and necessary conscientious motive-component for doing it.

We come now to a much more difficult and doubtful case. Suppose that the agent's belief that the action is right, together with his desire to do what is right as such, is sufficient, but not necessary, to induce him to do it, in spite of the components against doing it. This would be illustrated by our old example if we varied it in the following way. We must now suppose that the agent's dislike of being thought cowardly *would* have sufficed to overcome his fear and his love of comfort and *would* have induced him to choose the course of action which he believes to be right, even if his belief that it is right and his desire to do what is right, as such, had been absent. The situation may be described as follows. The non-conscientious motive-component for doing the action is still superfluous; but now we must say that the conscientious component for doing it is equally superfluous. Each is sufficient, and therefore neither individually is necessary; all that is necessary is that one or other of them should be present. If you confine your attention to the *sufficiency* of the conscientious motive-component, you will be inclined to say that the action *is* conscientious; if you attend only to the *superfluity* of this component, you will be inclined to say that it is *not* conscientious.

We pass now to another difficult and doubtful case. Suppose now that the agent's belief that the action is right, together with his desire to do what is right as such, is necessary but not sufficient to induce him to do it in spite of the components against doing it. This would be illustrated by the following modification of our old example. We must now suppose (*a*) that the agent's belief that it is right for him to undertake military service, together with his desire to do what is right as such, would not have sufficed, in the absence of his dislike of being thought cowardly, to overcome his fear and his love of comfort; and (*b*) that the latter motive-component, in the absence of the former, would also not have sufficed to overcome his fear and his love of comfort. Each of the two motive-components for doing the action is now necessary, and therefore neither of them individually is sufficient. If you confine your attention to the *indispensability* of the conscientious motive-component, you will be inclined to say that the action *is* conscientious; if you attend only to its *insufficiency*, you will be inclined to say that it is *not* conscientious.

I will group together purely and predominantly conscientious actions, in the sense defined above, under the name of '*fully* conscientious actions'; and I will group together the two doubtful cases, which we have just been discussing, under the name of '*semi-conscientious* actions'. The two kinds of these can then be distinguished as (i) actions in which the conscientious motive-component is sufficient but superfluous, and (ii) actions in which the conscientious motive-component is indispensable but inadequate.

If a person does an act which he believes to be less right or more wrong than some other act open to him at the time, he does it in spite of his desire to do what is right, as such. Any action of this kind may be called '*contra-conscientious*'.

It is plain that a great many of our deliberate actions are neither fully conscientious, nor semi-conscientious, nor contra-conscientious; for many are done without considering them and the alternatives to them from the standpoint of rightness and wrongness. Such actions may be called '*non-conscientious*'. A non-conscientious action may be such that, if the agent had considered it and the alternatives to it from the standpoint of rightness and wrongness, he would have judged it to be the most right or the least wrong of the alternatives open to him. And it may be that he would then have done it for that reason alone or for that reason combined with others which are superfluous and insufficient. If both these conditions are fulfilled, we may say that this non-conscientious action was '*potentially* conscientious'. In a similar way we could define the statement that a certain non-conscientious act was '*potentially* contra-conscientious'.

I have now completed the task of analysis and definition, and I will conclude my paper with a few remarks about conscientious action, as defined above. (1) There is a very important sense of 'ought' in which it is true to say that a person ought always to do that alternative which he believes, at the time when he has to act, to be the most right or the least wrong of all those that are open to him. (There are, undoubtedly, other senses of 'ought' in which this would not be true; but we are not concerned with them here.) For this sense of 'ought' to be applicable it does not matter how ignorant or deluded the agent may be about the relevant facts, how incompetent he may be to make reasonable inferences from them, nor how crazy or perverted his judgements about right and wrong, good and evil, may be. But, the more fully this is admitted, the more obvious does the following complementary fact become. The most right or the least wrong act open to other individuals or to a society in certain cases, may be to prevent a conscientious individual from doing certain acts which he ought, in this sense, to do, and to try to compel him to do certain acts which he ought, in this sense, to refrain from doing. Moreover, if other individuals or the authorities in a society honestly believe that the most right or the least wrong action open to them is to treat a certain conscientious individual in this way, then they *ought*, in the very same sense, to do so. What is sauce for the conscientious goose is sauce for the conscientious ganders who are his neighbours or his governors. This fact is often obscured because many people inadvertently or dishonestly confine their attention to cases, such as the trial of Socrates or of Christ, in which subsequent generations have held that the individual was, not only conscientious, but also correct in his ethical opinions, while the tribunal which condemned him was either not conscientious or was mistaken in its ethical opinions. It may be salutary for such persons to widen their purview by envisaging the case of a high-minded Indian civilian conscientiously securing the capture and execution of a high-minded Thug for conscientiously practising murder.

(2) It is sometimes said that, when an individual sets up his conscience against the general opinion of his society or of mankind, he is claiming 'moral infallibility'. If he knows his business, he is doing nothing of the kind. In order for it to be his duty, in the present sense, to do a certain alternative, all that is necessary is that he should think it *probable*, after considering the question to the best of his ability, that this alternative is more right or less wrong than any of the others which are open to him. Since he has to enact one of the alternatives, it does not matter in the least whether this probability is high or low. Nor does it matter whether the difference in rightness or wrongness is great or small. In considering the question, it is his duty to give full weight to the fact that most members of his society or most of the human race have formed a certain opinion about it. If he is a wise man, he will attach very great weight to this fact. But if, in spite of having done so, he comes to a contrary opinion, he ought, in the present sense, to act upon it, no matter how far short of complete conviction his opinion may fall.

(3) The last remark that I have to make is this. A *purely* conscientious action, in the sense defined above, must be a very rare event. It is hardly credible, e.g. that either undertaking or refusing military service could be a purely conscientious act, in that sense; for everyone fears death and wounds and everyone dislikes to be thought cowardly.

Now the definitions of 'predominantly conscientious' acts, and of

ACTION

CONSCIENTIOUS ACTION
79

the two kinds of 'semi-conscientious' acts, all have the following peculiarity. They all involve the notion of what *would* have happened if certain conditions had been other than they in fact were. This notion of the consequences of unfulfilled conditions always enters whenever the question of sufficiency and dispensability is raised. It follows that an individual can seldom be rationally justified in feeling a very strong conviction that an action of his was conscientious; for, in order to decide this question, he has to form an opinion as to how he would have acted in the *absence* of certain motive-components which were in fact *present*. It seems to me that *a fortiori* it must be almost impossible for anyone to decide rationally as to whether another person's action is conscientious or not.

If I am right in this, the Tribunals have been given a task which is, from the nature of the case, incapable of being satisfactorily performed. This, so far as it goes, is a strong ground against allowing exemption from military service on grounds of conscience and against setting up Tribunals at all. There are, no doubt, other reasons which point in the opposite direction; and Parliament has decided that, in the present state of public opinion in England, the balance of advantage is in favour of allowing exemption on such grounds, and has therefore set up Tribunals to consider claims. It only remains for us to watch with sympathy and interest the efforts of these well-meaning men to deal with questions to which God alone can know the answer.

VII

CONSCIENCE AND CONSCIENTIOUSNESS

A. Campbell Garnett

Professor Nowell-Smith tells a story of an Oxford don who thought it his duty to attend Common Room, and did so conscientiously, though his presence was a source of acute distress both to himself and others. This story is told in illustration of a discussion of the question whether conscientiousness is good without qualification. The philosopher's comment is 'He would have done better to stay at home', and he reinforces this view with the historical judgement that 'Robespierre would have been a better man (quite apart from the question of the harm he did) if he had given his conscience a thorough rest and indulged his taste for roses and sentimental verse'.[1] The harm, in these cases, he points out, seems to spring, in part at least, from the very conscientiousness of these people, and he concludes that we have no reason for accepting the principle of the supreme value of conscientiousness and that there is nothing either self-contradictory or even logically odd in the assertion 'You think that you ought to do A, but you would be a better man if you did B'.[2]

This judgement, it should be noted, is a *moral* evalution. 'Better man' here means 'ethically better'. It explicitly excludes 'better' in the sense of 'more useful or less harmful to society' in the reference to Robespierre. Further, it is not restricted to the mere right or wrong of overt acts, saying, for example, that Robespierre would have done less that is objectively wrong if he had attended to his roses more and his conscience less, for it is a judgement on the moral character of the *man*, not merely on that of his overt acts, and moral judgements upon a man must take account of every feature of his personality concerned in the performance of his acts, i.e., his motives, intentions, character, beliefs, abilities and so forth. What we have here, therefore, is the

From *Insight and Vision*, ed. K. Kolenda (Trinity University Press, 1966), pp. 71-83. Previously published in *Rice University Studies*, Vol. 51 (1965). Reprinted by permission of Trinity University Press, San Antonio, Texas, and the author.
[1] P. H. Nowell-Smith, *Ethics* (London 1954), p. 247.
[2] Ibid., p. 253.

contention that in some cases where conscientiousness would lead to more harm than good (as it may do in cases of mistaken moral judgements or other ignorance) a man may be a morally better man by stifling his conscience and doing what he believes he ought not to do. It is not claimed that this will always be true in such cases, and it is not denied that conscientiousness is to some degree a value. But it is denied that it is the only moral value, or a value with supreme authority above all others, or that it is an essential feature of all moral value.

These denials are not uncommon among contemporary moralists, but it should be noted that they constitute a rejection of the major tradition in moral philosophy, from Plato to the present day. They also conflict with the convictions of the common man expressed in such injunctions as 'Let your conscience be your guide', 'Do what you yourself believe to be right, not what others tell you', 'Act on your own convictions', 'Always act in accord with your own conscience', 'To thine own self be true'. Conscientiousness is firmness of purpose in seeking to do what is right, and to most people it seems to be the very essence of the moral life and a value or virtue in some sense 'higher' or more important than any other. Among philosophers this view is notably expressed in Joseph Butler's doctrine of the 'natural supremacy' of conscience and in Immanuel Kant's insistence that there is nothing good in itself, intrinsically good, save the good will, and that this consists in the will to do one's duty for duty's sake. There are, evidently, some complex issues and confusions involved in these sharply varying positions and to clarify them we shall need to begin with an examination of what is involved in conscience itself.

Analysis of Conscience

Conscience involves both a cognitive and an emotive or motivational element. The cognitive element consists in a set of moral judgements concerning the right or wrong of certain kinds of action or rules of conduct, however these have been formed. The emotive or motivational element consists of a tendency to experience emotions of a unique sort of approval of the doing of what is believed to be right and a similarly unique sort of disapproval of the doing of what is believed to be wrong. These feeling states, it is generally recognized, are noticeably different from those of mere liking or disliking and also from feelings of aesthetic approval and disapproval (or aesthetic appreciation) and from feelings of admiration and the reverse aroused by non-moral activities and skills. They can become particularly acute, moving and even distressing, in the negative and reflexive form of moral disapproval of one's own actions and motives, the sense of guilt and shame. In this form (indeed in both forms) they may have some notably irrational manifestations, but the sense of shame also has a very valuable function as an inhibitory motive upon the person who contemplates the possibility of doing what he believes to be wrong.

These are the commonly recognized aspects of conscience, and they frequently function quite uncritically. Because of this uncritical emotive reaction conscience all too frequently moves people to approve or disapprove actions and rules concerning which adequate reflection would lead to a very different verdict, and sometimes it afflicts people with a quite irrational sense of guilt. These deplorable effects of some manifestations of conscience are a large part of the reason for its devaluation in the judgement of many modern moralists. What these thinkers rightly deplore is the uncritical emotive reaction which the person who experiences it calls his conscience, particularly when the emotive element in it inhibits any critical activity of the cognitive element. But it is not necessary, and it is not usually the case, that the emotive element in conscience stifles the critical, and there is no justification for jumping to the conclusion that conscience should be ignored. For critical ethical thinking is itself usually conscientiousness, and conscience can be trained to be habitually critical.

For clarity of thinking on this question we need to distinguish between the critical and the traditional conscience. The latter is uncritical. Here the emotive element attaches to moral ideas accepted from the tradition without critical re-evaluation of them. Its strength lies in this perpetuation of tradition, but this is also the source of its errors. It is this blind by emotive perpetuation of an outgrown and mistaken tradition that contemporary critics of the supreme evaluation of conscience, for the most part, are concerned to deplore. And thus far they are right. But one would be unfair to such critics if one were not to recognize that their efforts to point out the errors of the tradition are usually also conscientious and are not merely the echoing of another tradition. Sometimes their critical ideas are boldly new and very commonly they are presented with persistent and painstaking care and in spite of personal cost. Nietzsche and Marx, Schweitzer and Gandhi, as well as Robespierre, were thoroughly conscientious men. Their ideas were new but were held with great emotive strength and tenacity. The same is true of the prophets of Israel and the great moral innovators of other religions. Indeed, the outstanding examples of conscientious men are not the mere sustainers of a tradition but the thinkers who try to improve the tradition.

This fact of the vitality of the critical conscience shows the superficiality of Freud's identification of it with the super-ego and of the explanation of it as an after-effect of early social conditioning, as put forward by many psychologists and sociologists, and uncritically adopted by many philosophers. On this view the moral judgements which tend to arouse spontaneous emotions of approval or disapproval, shame and guilt, are those which we learned to make in our childhood and which we then heard expressed by those around us accompanied by strong manifestations of moral approval and disapproval. The child, it is pointed out, must naturally assimilate the tendency to feel similar emotions whenever he himself makes a moral judgement, and this emotive tendency remains with him in adult life together with the tendency to frame and express such judgements. Conscience is then said to be simply the inward echo of the emotionally expressed judgements of our childhood social environment. This may be accepted as part of the explanation of the emotive element in the uncritical traditional conscience, but as an explanation of how men come to feel the way they do about the results of their own original critical thinking, and of the motivational drive conscientiously to do original critical ethical thinking, it is woefully inadequate.

It is not difficult to see how the cognitive element in conscience, the judgement of right and wrong, becomes critical. To some extent it must be so from the beginning. A favourite word in every child's vocabulary is 'Why?' And especially does he ask for reasons when told that he *ought* to do something he does not want to do. If moral injunctions are accepted as such on mere authority it is because it is implicitly believed that the authority *has* good reasons for issuing them, or else that the demand or example of this authority is in itself a sufficient reason for obedience or conformity, as with kings and deities. Apart from authority, reasons for moral rules have to be found in their relevance to the needs and security and peace of the community and the well-being of the person himself. But always, it is a distinguishing mark of a *moral* rule that it is one for which it is believed that reasons can be given. Critical thinking about moral rules is therefore stimulated whenever the reasons presented seem inadequate, beginning with the child's 'Why?' and whenever there is a conflict of rules.

This critical thinking at first accepts as its basic principles the sort of reasons customarily given for moral rules and injunctions—the traditions of the tribe, its peace, security, prosperity and honour, revelations from divine sources, and so forth. But at a higher level of critical thinking conflicts are found between these basic principles themselves, and man is directed to the philosophical task of thinking out the *most* basic of all principles—if any such can be found. The search may end in scepticism and confusion, but so long as the thinker is prepared to accept any reason at all as a reason why something 'ought' (in the ethical sense) to be done he also feels conscientiously constrained to do that which his search for reasons has led him to believe that he ought to do. Further, the experience of finding reasons for rejecting old views and accepting new ones impresses upon him the need and value of the search. Thus, so long as he recognizes any moral reasons at all he must recognize a duty of continued critical examination of moral ideas. The critical conscience thus becomes its own stimulus to further critical thinking. Conscience takes the form of the firm conviction, not merely that one ought to do what one believes one ought to do, still less that one ought to do without question what one has been taught one ought to do, but that one ought to think for oneself as to what one really ought to do and then act on one's own convictions. And the emotive drive is apt to attach itself as firmly to this last formulation of the cognitive element in conscience as ever it does to the other two.

Conscience, Love, and Personal Integrity

It is clear that the motivational element of conscience in its most developed form is not merely the continuing echo of approvals and disapprovals of specific rules and actions impressed upon us by the social environment of our childhood. Yet the emotive content is continuous through all the changes in the sort of action the contemplation of which arouses it. One can imagine a youth of the eighteenth century feeling strong moral approval of a man who challenges a dangerous opponent to a duel in defence of his wife's good name, and later, in his maturity, feeling similar moral approval of another man who faces social obloquy for his refusal to fight a duel in similar circumstances because he is opposed in principle to duelling. In both cases it is the manifestation of courage in defence of principle that calls forth the moral approval, but his judgement has changed as to the principle of action worthy of such defence. We see that what has changed is the specific sort of action that calls forth approval and disapproval, while what remains the same is the specific sort of reason that is held to be appropriate for judging an action to be worthy of approval or disapproval. And this we would find to be true in general (if we had space to demonstrate it) through the whole process of critical re-examination of moral judgement. Moral approval and disapproval attach to whatever we find to have reasons for approval. These reasons, in the course of thinking, become more and more specifically formulated and more and more highly generalized into abstract principles of moral judgement and they are only changed as change is seen to be needed to bring them into consistency with one another. Emotive unwillingness to accept some of the consequences of this process of ethical thinking sometimes inhibits and distorts it, but through it all the emotive drives of approval and disapproval tend to attach themselves to whatever lines of action are thought to be character-ized by the recognized reasons for such attitudes.

On account of the complexity of all their implications the exact and proper statement of these basic ethical principles is a matter of very great difficulty. Yet there is a degree of agreement as to general principle which is really remarkable considering the complexity of human conduct and the diversity of traditional moral judgement with which we start. Thus, there is almost universal agreement that the fact that an act may have bad consequences for some persons is a good reason for disapproving it, and the reverse if it would have good consequences. Similarly there are certain rules of justice that are generally recognized, such as that of impartiality in the distribution of goods and burdens, the keeping of contracts and promises, the making of reparations, and the equitable application of the law. Questions arise as to how far the duties of bene-ficence should go, as to what to do when principles conflict in practical application, as to whether all principles can be comprehended under some one principle, and so forth. But the general trend is clear. Moral approval and disapproval are moved by the thought of the effect of our actions upon the weal or woe of human beings. This is the root of con-science. If some conscientious thinkers, such as Nietzsche, seem to be an exception to this rule it is because they have developed unusual or paradoxical views of what really constitutes true human weal or woe, or how it can best be promoted.

This connection of conscience with reasons for action bearing on the effects of action on human well-being enables us to understand the distinctive feeling-tone of moral approval and disapproval—i.e. their difference from mere liking and disliking, and from other emotions such as the aesthetic, and from non-moral admiration and its reverse. The moral emotions are often mingled with these others, but they are also different. There is in them a distinct element of concern for human welfare which is gratified by what promotes it and distressed at any-thing that seems injurious. For this reason the moral emotions have often been identified with sympathy, but they are not mere passive feeling states. There is in them an element of active concern for human values with an impulse to give help where it seems needed. For this reason these emotions are responsive to judgements about the effects of human action, bringing forth a positive response of approval to that which seems helpful and the reverse towards the hurtful. For this reason also moral approval is a gratifying emotion, inducing a favourable reaction, while moral disapproval is apt to become a source of distress and an occasion for anger. For moral approval, we can now see, is a specification in action of the most deeply satisfying of all human emotions, that of love, in its most general form of expression.

Moral approval, then, is a development of the basic social interest of man as a social animal, it is an expression of the general sympathetic tendency of concern for human values with special attention to those depending on the orderly life of the group. It is an expression of the desire to create and maintain those values. Its conflict with other motives is therefore, a conflict of desires. But this particular conflict, the conflict of conscience (moral approvals and disapprovals) with other desires (temptations) is not just an ordinary conflict of desires. It is a conflict in which the integrity of the personality is peculiarly involved. In an ordinary conflict of desires, in which there is no moral issue, the best solution is for one of the desires to be completely set aside and fade into oblivion without regrets, the opposing interest being completely triumphant. And, for the integrity of the personality it does not matter which interest gives way. But if the conflict be between 'conscience' (the interests involved in moral approval and disapproval) and 'temptation' (some opposed interest or desire) then it does matter which triumphs. The integrity of personality is involved. It tends to dissolve as a person slips into the habit of doing things he believes to be wrong. He loses his self-respect and his firmness of purpose. For a time the sense of guilt depresses. Later it tends to be repressed. With these psychological repressions the personality tends to manifest either general weakness or the over-compensations which give a false impression of strength as they manifest themselves in irrational drives. The guilty conscience and the repressed conscience are at the root of most of the disorders of personality, whether the guilt itself be reasonably conceived or not.

It is evident, therefore, that the emotive or motivational element that manifests itself in conscience is rooted in conative tendencies or interests which are of basic importance in the life of man. This psychological conclusion has, in recent years, been strongly emphasized by a number of workers in the field of psychotherapy, notably by Erich Fromm, who argues strongly that only in what he calls the 'orientation of productive love'[1] can the personality of man develop continuously and with the integrity necessary for mental health. From this conclusion concerning the psychological need of this type of orientation Fromm also develops a most important theory of conscience. What we have distinguished as the uncritical (or traditional) and the critical conscience he distinguishes as the 'authoritarian' and the 'humanistic' conscience. The former he dismisses as the internalized voice of an external authority, but the latter, he maintains, is 'the reaction of our total personality to its proper functioning or disfunctioning. . . . Conscience is thus . . . the voice of our true selves which summons us . . . to live productively, to develop fully and harmoniously. . . . It is the guardian of our integrity.'[2]

If Fromm's psychological analysis of the growth and structure of personality is accurate in essentials, and if our account of the growth of the critical conscience out of the uncritical is also correct, then we must recognize that conscience at every stage is, as Fromm says of the 'humanistic' conscience, 'the reaction of our total personality to its total functioning', its 'voice' is the experience of the constraint of the personality as a whole, in its seeking of a growing creative expression with integrity or wholeness, upon the occasional and temporary impulses and desires which would tend to stultify its creativity and destroy its integrity. It is because doing what we believe we ought not is destructive of that integrity that conscience demands that we always act in accord with our own convictions; and it is because the fundamental orientation of human life is social and creative that ethical thinking tends, through the course of history, to clarify itself in the light of principles which tend to formulate moral judgements as expressions of impartial concern for human well-being.

The Authority of Conscience

It is time now to return to the question with which we started. Is it true that a man would sometimes be a better man (i.e. morally better) for refusing to obey his conscience rather than obeying it? It should be noted that the question is not whether the consequences to himself or to others might be better in general, but whether he would, himself, be a morally better man for acting in this way. This raises the question whether it is ever morally right to go against one's conscience. Is it ever right to do as you think you ought not to do? And this, again, is not the question whether conscience is always right in what it

[1] Eric Fromm, *Man for Himself* (New York, 1947), pp. 92-107.
[2] Ibid., pp. 158-60.

commands us to do, but whether it is ever right to disobey those commands, thus choosing to do what we believe to be wrong? The traditional answer is given by Joseph Butler in asserting the 'natural
supremacy' of conscience, which 'magisterially asserts itself and approves
and condemns'. 'Had it strength as it had right: had it power, as it had
manifest authority, it would absolutely govern the world'.[1] Against
this we have the contemporary challenge voiced by Nowell-Smith.

One serious objection to this modern challenge to the traditional view
is that it is necessarily futile and worse than futile, as a guiding principle of moral behaviour. It is futile because, though a man may believe
that *perhaps*, in some cases, it *may* be that he would be a better man
if he did not do what he believes he ought to do, he can never believe
this in any particular case, for that would be to believe that he ought
not to do this that he believes he ought to do, which is self-contradictory.
Thus this piece of ethical theory is so paradoxical that it can never
function as a guide to action. Further, it is worse than futile, for it
implies, not merely that moral judgement may be mistaken (and therefore needs critical examination) but that the very effort not to do wrong
may itself sometimes be wrong—that the conscientious effort to try to
find out what is really right and act firmly in accord with one's own
convictions, is sometimes wrong and we have no way of knowing
when it is wrong. From this state of mind the only reasonable reaction
is to abandon the ethical inquiry and the ethical endeavour and make
the easiest and most satisfactory adjustment we can to the mores of the
community and the practical exigencies of our personal situation.

The logical alternatives, therefore, are either to abandon the moral
standpoint entirely, or to affirm, with Butler, the moral authority of
every man's own conscience. The fact that judgements conscientiously
made may be in error does not imply that this assertion of the
sovereignty of the individual conscience must lead to either conflict or
chaos. It rather avoids conflict, for each person, in asserting the rights
of his own conscience, at the same time affirms the right of freedom
of conscience for others. And it avoids chaos because, laying the injunction upon us to exercise continuous critical examination of our own
moral judgements, it points us on the only possible way to consistency
and order in moral judgement, by finding our errors and rectifying
them. A community of people open-mindedly seeking the best formulation and reformulation of its moral rules, and abiding by its most
intelligent findings, is more likely to maintain order with progress than
one in which conscience operates in any other way, or in no way at all.

[1] Joseph Butler, *Five Sermons* (New York, 1950), p. 41.

We must conclude, then, that if one were to accept Nowell-Smith's critique of conscience one could not apply it to the decision of any moral questions in one's own conduct, and that its acceptance, if taken seriously, would be apt to have a deteriorating effect upon personal moral endeavour. But it is still possible to grant it theoretical credence and apply it to our evaluation of the moral value of the personality of others. This is what Nowell-Smith does in the cases of Robespierre and the Oxford don: Robespierre would have been a better man if he had indulged his taste for roses and sentimental verse rather than follow the demands of his conscience that he strive by whatever terrible means seemed necessary to carry through the programme of the revolution; and the Oxford don would have been a better man if he had allowed his personal distaste for Common Room society to overcome his sense of duty which required him to attend it.

This is a judgement on the moral quality of the man as affected by his act of choice. The choice with which we are concerned is not that of his decision as to whether A or B is the right thing to do but his decision as to whether he would do what he believed to be the right thing or follow his personal wishes to do something that he found much more agreeable to himself. The latter act is the one he would do if he had not given any consideration to the effect of his actions on other people, or the needs of the social structure of which he is a part, except so far as his own interests were involved, and, coming as it does after he has considered these things and formed a judgement as to what they require of him, it is a decision to set aside the results of this thoughtful examination of the possible consequences of his conduct and do the thing he personally wants to do and would have done if he had never given the matter any ethical thought at all. When the issue is thus clearly stated it is very difficult to see how any thoughtful person could judge the unconscientious following of inclination to be the act of a better man, or an act that tends to make a better man, than the careful thinking and active self-determination involved in conscientiousness. It seems evident that those who have expressed the view that the following of personal inclination is sometimes morally better than conscientiousness are confusing this issue with another to which we must next given attention.

Conscientiousness and Other Values

For Immanuel Kant there was nothing good in itself, good without qualification, except a good will, and a good will, he explains, is good, not because it is a will to produce some good, or even the greatest possible good, but simply by reason of the nature of its volition as a will to do one's duty, a will to do what is conceived as right. Thus, for Kant, an action only has *moral* worth if it is done from a sense of duty, not from any inclination, even that of an impartial desire to promote general human well-being. Kant does not deny that good-natured inclinations have value, but he insists that the will to do one's duty has incomparably higher value and that it alone is of distinctly moral value. Kant's position here is an extreme one. Conscientiousness is regarded not merely as an essential part of moral value but as the only true moral value and supreme among all values. Against this Nowell-Smith is not alone in protesting, and it is this rejection of the extravagant claim for conscientiousness as compared with other values, that seems to him to justify the notion that there are some occasions when some other value should be preferred and conscientiousness rejected.[1]

It is true, as Nowell-Smith says, that 'we normally think of moral worth as meaning the worth of any virtuous motive and we normally think of sympathy and benevolence as virtuous motives'.[2] It is also true, that, contrary to Kant, we normally judge a right action done out of sympathy and good will to be morally better than the same action would be if done solely from a sense of duty but without sympathy or good will.[3] These normal judgements I think we must fully endorse, but they do not involve the implication that a man can be morally justified (i.e. can be a 'better man' than he otherwise would be (in performing an act, even of sympathy and good will (let alone indulging an interest in roses), which, in the circumstances, he regards as wrong.

There is a story told by Mark Twain of two ladies who lied to protect a runaway slave even though believing it wrong to do so and fearing that they might suffer in hell for their sin. In such a case we see a conflict, not merely of conscience with desire, but of the uncritical or traditional conscience with the critical. The deeper level of conscience, which they might well have called their 'intuitions', urged the protection of the poor, frightened slave. They were not sufficiently capable of philosophical thinking to formulate a philosophical critique in support of their own deeper insights, so they remained superficially of the traditional opinion that their action was wrong. But their choice was actually a conscientious one, true to the deeper levels of conscience, and we tend to endorse their

[1] Nowell-Smith, *Ethics*, p. 245.
[2] Ibid., p. 246.
[3] Ibid., p. 259.

decision because it is endorsed by our consciences too. But this example (and others like it) is not a case of judging that the motives of love and sympathy were here better than conscientiousness, but of judging that the will to do good, seen as the very root of righteousness, is better than the will to conform to rules uncritically accepted as right. Such a judgement is far from the same as judging that the Oxford don would have been a morally better man for indulging his reluctance to attend Common Room than he would for conscientiously fulfilling what he believed to be his duty in the matter.

If we accept a teleological ethics then we recognize that the purpose of moral rules is to protect and promote the more important aspects of social well-being. We then see that the motives of love and sympathy, if sufficiently strong, enlightened and impartial, would achieve the purposes of moral rules better than the moral rules do, and would also achieve other good purposes beyond them. A world of saints would be a better world than a world of conscientious persons without mutual love and sympathy. Seeing this, though there are no saints, we endorse such elements of saintliness as there are (i.e., love and sympathy expressed in this enlightened and impartial way) and recognize them as morally good and as expressions of a better type of personality than one in which conscientiousness is found without these motives. But this recognition of the greater value of enlightened and impartial good will, or love, can never involve a rejection of conscientiousness in favour of such love, for such love includes and transcends all that conscientiousness stands for. Such love is the fulfilling of the law and the fulfilling, not the rejection, of the conscientiousness which supports the law. Thus, while a teleological ethics rejects Kant's apotheosis of the will to do one's duty as the only intrinsic moral value it does not lead to an endorsement of the view that we should sometimes judge a man as morally better for neglecting his conscience to indulge some other inclination. If, on the other hand, we were to accept a de-ontological ethics we should find that to speak of a conflict between conscientiousness and an enlightened and impartial love and sympathy (or any other good motive) as a conflict between different moral values involves a category mistake. For conscientiousness and other good motives, on this view, are not moral values in the same sense. An act of love is not made moral by the kind of consequences at which it aims. The only moral actions are those which intentionally adhere to intuitively discerned principles. So whatever value is attached to love and sympathy, it is not moral value. Moral value belongs alone to conscientiousness. Thus a man could never become morally better by rejecting the morally valuable motive of conscientiousness for some other motive to which only non-moral value is attached. This de-ontological theory Nowell-Smith, I think rightly, rejects, but it is well to see that it, too, involves a rejection of his theory of the comparison of conscientiousness with other moral values.

Returning to the teleological point of view, and reflecting on the de-ontologist's claim, we can perhaps see the reason for the basic confusions that haunt people's minds on this question of the relative value of conscientiousness and impartial good will, or love. Conscientiousness is uniquely a moral motive in that its end is morality itself, the keeping of moral rules. All other motives, if without conscientiousness, are at best non-moral (operating without concern for moral rules) or at worst immoral— consciously in opposition to them. This is true even of love and sympathy, simply as such. But if the teleological point of view is correct it is not true of love and sympathy *with a concern for impartiality*, for this latter is the very basis of moral rules and such love is of the essence of the moral life. Thus conscientiousness and impartial good will share together the unique character of being moral in the sense of being motivated by a concern for morality as such, the former for the rules which formulate it in lines of conduct, and the latter for the basic principle of impartial concern for human well-being in accordance with which the rules merely formulate the guiding lines. But this merely means that impartial good will is a motive characterized by the critical conscience, while conscientiousness without love, sympathy or good will is an operation of the traditional or uncritical conscience alone. Thus the motive that is of uniquely moral value and of supreme moral authority is love finding expression in the form of the critical conscience.

The main conclusions, therefore, of this paper may be summed up briefly thus: (1) Conscientiousness, if it be properly critical, is good without qualification, but an uncritical conscientiousness is not. (2) Since we cannot be saints we need to be conscientious, and this includes both the effort to find out what we really ought to do and the effort to do it to the best of our ability. (3) We should also cultivate the motive of impartial love or good will, for it functions as both an illuminating guide and support to our efforts to be conscientious and is itself of intrinsic moral value. (4) We can be righteous, and to that extent good, men merely by being conscientious, but we can be much better men by being not only conscientious but men in whom, without conflicting with conscience, the effort to be conscientious is made unnecessary by the outflow of spontaneous and impartial good will. These are very ordinary conclusions, but it takes clear thinking to keep them free from some very extraordinary objections.

VIII

HOW IS WEAKNESS OF THE WILL POSSIBLE?*

Donald Davidson

An agent's will is weak if he acts, and acts intentionally, counter to his own best judgement; in such cases we sometimes say he lacks the will power to do what he knows, or at any rate believes, would, everything considered, be better. It will be convenient to call actions of this kind incontinent actions, or to say that in doing them the agent acts incontinently. In using this terminology I depart from tradition, at least in making the class of incontinent actions larger than usual. But it is the larger class I want to discuss, and I believe it includes all of the actions some philosophers have called incontinent, and some of the actions many philosophers have called incontinent.

Let me explain how I have generalized the concept of incontinence compared with possible alternatives. It is often made a condition of an incontinent action that it be performed despite the agent's knowledge that another course of action is better. I count such actions incontinent, but the puzzle I shall discuss depends only on the attitude or belief of the agent, so it would restrict the field to no purpose to insist on knowledge. Knowledge also has an unneeded, and hence unwanted, flavour of the cognitive; my subject concerns evaluative judgements, whether they are analysed cognitively, prescriptively, or otherwise. So even the concept of belief is perhaps too special, and I shall speak of what the agent judges or holds.

If a man holds some course of action to be the best one, everything

Printed by permission of the author (not previously published). © Donald Davidson 1969.

* Drafts of this paper were read during 1967 at the Annual Oregon Colloquium in Philosophy, where I had the benefit of the careful comments of Donald G. Brown, and the Chapel Hill Colloquium in Philosophy, where I learned more than I was able to use from Gilbert Harman's skilful criticism. I am also indebted to Carl Hempel, Georg Kreisel, Patrick Suppes, and Irving Thalberg. Gregory Vlastos and Amalie Rorty courteously showed me papers they had written that referred to some of my ideas on incontinence.

My research was supported by the National Science Foundation.

considered, or the right one, or the thing he ought to do, and yet does something else, he acts incontinently. But I would also say he acts incontinently provided he holds some available course of action to be better on the whole than the one he takes; or that, as between some other course of action which he believes open to him and the action he performs, he judges that he ought to perform the other. In other words, comparative judgements suffice for incontinence. We may now characterize an action that reveals weakness of the will or incontinence:

D. In doing x an agent acts incontinently if and only if: (a) the agent does x intentionally; (b) the agent believes there is an alternative action y open to him; and (c) the agent judges that, all things considered, it would be better to do y than to do x.[1]

There seem to be incontinent actions in this sense. The difficulty is that their existence challenges another doctrine that has an air of self-evidence: that, in so far as a person acts intentionally he acts, as Aquinas puts it, in the light of some imagined good. This view does not, as it stands, directly contradict the claim that there are incontinent actions. But it is hard to deny that the considerations that recommend this view recommend also a relativized version: in so far as a person acts intentionally he acts in the light of what he imagines (judges) to be the better.

It will be useful to spell out this claim in the form of two principles. The first expresses the natural assumption about the relation between wanting or desiring something, and action. 'The primitive sign of wanting is trying to get', says Miss Anscombe in *Intention*.[2] Hampshire comes closer to exactly what I need when he writes, in *Freedom of the Individual*,[3] that 'A wants to do X' is equivalent to 'other things being

[1] In a useful article, G. Santas gives this account of incontinence: 'In a case of weakness a man does something that he knows or believes he should (ought) not do, or fails to do something that he knows or believes he should do, when the occasion and the opportunity for acting or refraining is present, and when it is in his power, in some significant sense, to act in accordance with his knowledge or belief.' ('Plato's *Protagoras* and Explanations of Weakness', *Philosophical Review*, LXXV (1966), p. 3.) Most of the differences between this description and mine are due to my deliberate deviation from the tradition. But there seem to me to be two minor errors in Santas' account. First, weakness of the will does not require that the alternative action actually be available, only that the agent think it is. What Santas is after, and correctly, is that the agent acts freely; but for this it is not necessary that the alternative the agent thinks better (or that he ought to do) be open to him. On the other hand (and this is the second point), Santas' criteria are not sufficient to guarantee that the agent acts intentionally, and this is, I think, essential to incontinence.
[2] G. E. M. Anscombe, *Intention* (Oxford, 1957), p. 67.
[3] S. Hampshire, *Freedom of the Individual* (New York, 1965), p. 36.

equal, he would do X, if he could'. Here I take (possibly contrary to Hampshire's intent) 'other things being equal' to mean, or anyway to allow, the interpretation, 'provided there is not something he wants more'. Given this interpretation, Hampshire's principle could perhaps be put:

P1. If an agent wants to do x more than he wants to do y and he believes himself free to do either x or y, then he will intentionally do x if he does either x or y intentionally.

The second principle connects judgements of what it is better to do with motivation or wanting:

P2. If an agent judges that it would be better to do x than to do y, then he wants to do x more than he wants to do y.

P1 and P2 together obviously entail that if an agent judges that it would be better for him to do x than to do y, and he believes himself to be free to do either x or y, then he will intentionally do x if he does either x or y intentionally. This conclusion, I suggest, appears to show that it is false that:

P3. There are incontinent actions.

Someone who is convinced that P1–P3 form an inconsistent triad, but who finds only one or two of the principles really persuasive, will have no difficulty deciding what to say. But for someone (like myself) to whom the principles expressed by P1–P3 seem self-evident, the problem posed by the apparent contradiction is acute enough to be called a paradox. I cannot agree with E. J. Lemmon when he writes, in an otherwise admirable article, 'Perhaps akrasia is one of the best examples of a pseudo-problem in philosophical literature: in view of its existence, if you find it a problem you have already made a philosophical mistake.'[1] If your assumptions lead to a contradiction, no doubt you have made a mistake, but since you can know you have made a mistake without knowing what the mistake is, your problem may be real.

The attempted solutions with which I am familiar to the problem created by the initial plausibility of P1–P3 assume that P1–P3 do really contradict one another. These attempts naturally end by giving up one or another of the principles. I am not very happy about P1–P3 as I have

[1] E. J. Lemmon, 'Moral Dilemmas', *Philosophical Review*, LXXI (1962), pp. 144-5.

stated them: perhaps it is easy to doubt whether they are true in just their present form (particularly P1 and P2). And reflecting on the ambiguities, or plurality of uses, of various critical words or phrases ('judge better', 'want', 'intentional') it is not surprising that philosophers have tried interpreting some key phrase as meaning one thing in one principle and meaning something else in another. But I am convinced that no amount of justified tinkering with P1–P3 will eliminate the underlying problem: the problem will survive new wording, refinement, and elimination of ambiguity. I shall mention a few of the standard moves, and try to discredit them, but endless ways of dealing with the problem will remain. My basic strategy is therefore not that of trying to make an airtight case for P1–P3, perhaps by working them into less exceptionable form. What I hope rather is to show that P1–P3 do not contradict one another, and therefore we do not have to give up any of them. At the same time I shall offer an explanation of why we are inclined to think P1–P3 lead to a contradiction; for if I am right, a common and important mistake explains our confusion, a mistake about the nature of practical reason.

I

Here are some of the ways in which philosophers have sought, or might seek, to cope with the problem of incontinence as I have stated it.

The sins of the leopard—lust, gluttony, avarice, and wrath—are the least serious sins for which we may be eternally damned, according to Dante. Dante has these sins, which he calls the sins of incontinence, punished in the second, third, fourth, and fifth circles of Hell. In a famous example, Dante describes the adulterous sin of Francesca da Rimini and Paolo Malatesta. Commentators show their cleverness by pointing out that even in telling her story Francesca reveals her weakness of character. Thus Charles Williams says, 'Dante so manages the description, he so heightens the excuse, that the excuse reveals itself as precisely the sin . . . the persistent parleying with the occasion of sin, the sweet prolonged laziness of love . . .'[1] Perhaps all this is true of Francesca, but it is not essential to incontinence, for the 'weakness' may be momentary, not a character trait: when we speak of 'weakness' we may merely express, without explaining, the fact that the agent did what he knew to be wrong. ('It was one page did it.') Aristotle even seems to imply that it is impossible to be habitually incontinent, on the grounds that habitual action involves a principle in accord with which

[1] C. Williams, *The Figure of Beatrice* (London, 1943), p. 118.

one acts, while the incontinent man acts against his principle. I suppose, then, that it is at least possible to perform isolated incontinent actions, and I shall discuss incontinence as a habit or vice only as the vice is construed as the vice of often or habitually performing incontinent actions.[1]

A man might hold it to be wrong, everything considered, for him to send a valentine to Marjorie Morningstar. Yet he might send a valentine to Marjorie Eveningstar, and do it intentionally, not knowing that Marjorie Eveningstar was identical with Marjorie Morningstar. We might want to say he did something he held to be wrong, but it would be misleading to say he intentionally did something he held to be wrong; and the case I illustrate is certainly not an example of an incontinent action. We must not, I hope it is clear, think that actions can be simply sorted into the incontinent and others. 'Incontinent', like 'intentional', 'voluntary', and 'deliberate', characterizes actions only as conceived in one way rather than another. In any serious analysis of the logical form of action sentences, such words must be construed, I think, as non-truth-functional sentential operators: 'It was incontinent of Francesca that . . .' and 'It was intentional of the agent that . . .' But for present purposes it is enough to avoid the mistake of overlooking the intentionality of these expressions.

Incontinence is often characterized in one of the following ways: the agent *intends* to do *y*, which he holds to be the best course, or a better course than doing *x*; nevertheless he does *x*. Or, the agent *decides* to do *y*, which he holds to be the best course, or a better course than doing *x*, and yet he does *x*. Or, the agent *chooses* *y* as the result of deliberation,[2] and yet does *x*, which he deems inferior to *y*. Each of these forms of behaviour is interesting, and given some provisos may be characterized as inconsistent, weak, vacillating, or irrational. Any of them might be a case of incontinence, as I have defined it. But as they stand, they are not necessarily cases of incontinence because none of them entails that at

[1] 'Incontinence is not strictly a vice . . . for incontinence acts against choice, vice in accord with it' (*Nic. Eth.* 1151a); 'vice is like dropsy and consumption, while incontinence is like epilepsy, vice being chronic, incontinence intermittent' (1150b). But Donne apparently describes the vice of incontinence in one of the Holy Sonnets:

> Oh, to vex me, contraries meet in one;
> Inconstancy unnaturally hath begot
> A constant habit; that when I would not
> I change in vows, and in devotion.

[2] Aristotle sometimes characterizes the incontinent man (the akrates) as 'abandoning his choice' (*Nic. Eth.*, 1151a) or 'abandoning the conclusion he has reached' (1145b); but also often along the lines suggested here: 'he does the thing he knows to be evil' (1145b) or 'he is convinced that he ought to do one thing and nevertheless does another thing' (1146b).

the time he acts the agent holds that another course of action would, all things considered, be better. And on the other hand, an action can be incontinent without the agent's ever having decided, chosen or intended to do what he judges best.

Principle 2 states a mild form of internalism. It says that a judgement of value must be reflected in wants (or desires or motives). This is not as strong as many forms of internalism: it does not, for example, say anything at all about the connection between the actual value of things (or the obligatory character of actions) and desires or motives. Nor does it, so far as I can see, involve us in any doctrine about what evaluative judgements mean. According to Hare, 'to draw attention to the close logical relations, on the one hand between wanting and thinking good, and on the other between wanting and doing something about getting what one wants, is to play into the hands of the prescriptivist; for it's to provide yet another link between thinking good and action'.[1] I confess I do not see how these 'close logical relations', which are given in one form by P1 and P2, support any particular theory about the meaning of evaluative sentences or terms. A possible source of confusion is revealed when Hare says '. . . if moral judgements were not prescriptive, there would be no problem about moral weakness; but there is a problem; therefore they are prescriptive' (p. 68). The confusion is between making a judgement, and the content of the judgement. It is P2 (or its ilk) that creates the problem, and P2 connects *making* a judgement with wanting and hence, *via* P1, with acting. But prescriptivism is a doctrine about the *content* or *meaning* of what is judged, and P2 says nothing about this. One could hold, for example, that to say one course of action is better than another is just to say that it will create more pleasure and yet maintain, as Mill perhaps did, that anyone who believes a certain course of action will create more pleasure than another (necessarily) wants it more. So I should like to deny that there is a simple connection between the problem of incontinence as I have posed it and any particular ethical theory.

Perhaps the most common way of dealing with the problem of incontinence is to reject P2. It seems obvious enough, after all, that we may think *x* better, yet want *y* more. P2 is even easier to question if it is stated in the form: if an agent thinks he ought (or is obligated) to do *x*, then he wants to do *x*; for of course we often don't want to do what we think we ought. Hare, if I understand him, accounts for some cases of incontinence in such a way; so, according to Santas, did Plato.[2]

[1] R. M. Hare, *Freedom and Reason* (Oxford, 1963), p. 71.
[2] G. Santas, 'The Socratic Paradoxes', *The Philosophical Review*, LXXIII (1964), pp. 147-64.

It is easy to interpret P2 in a way that makes it false, but it is harder to believe there is not a natural reading that makes it true. For against our tendency to agree that we often believe we ought to do something and yet don't want to, there is also the opposite tendency to say that if someone really (sincerely) believes he ought, then his belief must show itself in his behaviour (and hence, of course, in his inclination to act, or his desire). When we make a point of contrasting thinking we ought with wanting, this line continues, either we are using the phrase 'thinking we ought' to mean something like 'thinking it is what is required by the usual standards of the community' or we are restricting wanting to what is attractive on a purely selfish or personal basis. Such ways of defending P2, though I find them attractive, are hard to make conclusive without begging the present question. So I am inclined, in order to move ahead, to point out that a problem about incontinence will occur in some form as long as there is any word or phrase we can convincingly substitute for 'wants' in both P1 and P2.

Another common line to take with incontinence is to depict the akrates as overcome by passion or unstrung by emotion. 'I know indeed what evil I intend to do. But stronger than all my afterthoughts is my fury', rants Medea. Hare makes this the paradigm of all cases of weakness of the will where we cannot simply separate moral judgement and desire, and he adds that in such cases the agent is psychologically unable to do what he thinks he ought (*Freedom and Reason*, p. 77). Hare quotes Euripides' Medea when she says '. . . an unknown compulsion bears me, all reluctant, down', and St. Paul when he writes, 'The good which I want to do, I fail to do; but what I do is the wrong which is against my will; and if what I do is against my will, clearly it is no longer I who am the agent . . .' (*Romans* 7.) This line leads to the view that one never acts intentionally contrary to one's best judgement, and so denies P3; there are no incontinent actions in the sense we have defined.[1]

A related, but different, view is Aristotle's, that passion, lust, or pleasure distort judgement and so prevent an agent from forming a full-fledged judgement that his action is wrong. Though there is plenty of room for doubt as to precisely what Aristotle's view was, it is safe to say that he tried to solve our problem by distinguishing two senses in which a man may be said to know (or believe) that one thing is better than

---

[1] Aquinas is excellent on this point. He clearly distinguishes between actions performed from a strong emotion, such as fear, which he allows are involuntary to a certain extent and hence not truly incontinent, and actions performed from concupiscence, for example: here, he says 'concupiscence inclines the will to desire the object of concupiscence. Therefore the effect of concupiscence is to make something to be voluntary.' (*Summa Theologica*, Part II. Q.6.)

another; one sense makes P2 true, while the other sense is needed in the definition of incontinence. The flavour of this second sense is given by Aristotle's remark that the incontinent man has knowledge 'in the sense in which having knowledge does not mean knowing but only talking, as a drunken man may mutter the verses of Empedocles' (*Nic. Eth.*, 1147b).

Perhaps it is evident that there is a considerable range of actions, similar to incontinent actions in one respect or another, where we may speak of self-deception, insincerity, *mauvais foi*, hypocrisy, unconscious desires, motives and intentions, and so on.[1] There is in fact a very great temptation, in working on this subject, to play the amateur psychologist. We are dying to say: remember the enormous variety of ways a man can believe or hold something, or know it, or want something, or be afraid of it, or do something. We can act as if we knew something, and yet profoundly doubt it; we can act at the limit of our capacity and at the same time stand off like an observer and say to ourselves, 'What an odd thing to do.' We can desire things and tell ourselves we hate them. These half-states and contradictory states are common, and full of interest to the philosopher. No doubt they explain, or at least point to a way of describing without contradiction, many cases where we find ourselves talking of weakness of the will or of incontinence. But we ourselves show a certain weakness as philosophers if we do not go on to ask: does every case of incontinence involve one of the shadow-zones where we want both to apply, and to withhold, some mental predicate? Does it never happen that I have an unclouded, unwavering judgement that my action is not for the best, all things considered, and yet where the action I do perform has no hint of compulsion or of the compulsive? There is no proving such actions exist; but it seems to me absolutely certain that they do. And if this is so, no amount of attention to the subtle borderline bits of behaviour will resolve the central problem.[2]

Austin complains that in discussing the present topic, we are prone to '. . . collapse succumbing to temptation into losing control of ourselves . . .' He elaborates:

Plato, I suppose, and after him Aristotle, fastened this confusion upon us, as

---

[1] 'It is but a shallow haste which concludeth insincerity from what outsiders call inconsistency.' (George Eliot, *Middlemarch*.)

[2] 'Oh, tell me, who first declared, who first proclaimed, that man only does nasty things because he does not know his own real interests. . . . ? What is to be done with the millions of facts that bear witness that men, knowingly, that is fully understanding their real interests, have left them in the background and have rushed headlong on another path . . . compelled to this course by nobody and by nothing . . .' (Dostoevsky, *Notes from the underground*.)

bad in its day and way as the later, grotesque, confusion of moral weakness
with weakness of will. I am very partial to ice cream, and a bombe is served
divided into segments corresponding one to one with persons at High Table:
I am tempted to help myself to two segments and do, thus succumbing to
temptation and even conceivably (but why necessarily?) going against my
principles. But do I lose control of myself? Do I raven, do I snatch the morsels
from the dish and wolf them down, impervious to the consternation of my
colleagues? Not a bit of it. We often succumb to temptation with calm and
even with finesse.[1]

We succumb to temptation with calm; there are also plenty of cases where
we act against our better judgement and which cannot be described as
succumbing to temptation.

In the usual accounts of incontinence there are, it begins to appear,
two quite different themes that interweave and tend to get confused.
One is, that desire distracts us from the good, or forces us to the bad; the
other is that incontinent action always favours the beastly, selfish passion
over the call of duty and morality. That these two themes can be separa-
ted was emphasized by Plato both in the *Protagoras* and the *Philebus*
when he showed that the hedonist, on nothing but his own pleasure bent,
could as easily go against his own best judgement as anyone else. Mill
makes the same point, though presumably from a position more sympathetic to the hedonist: 'Men often, from infirmity of character, make
their election for the nearer good, though they know it to be the less
valuable; and this no less when the choice is between two bodily
pleasures than when it is between bodily and mental.' (*Utilitarianism*,
Chap. II.) Unfortunately, Mill goes on to spoil the effect of his point by
adding, 'They pursue sensual indulgences to the injury of health, though
perfectly aware that health is the greater good.'

As a first positive step in dealing with the problem of incontinence,
I propose to divorce that problem entirely from the moralist's concern
that our sense of the conventionally right may be lulled, dulled, or duped
by a lively pleasure. I have just relaxed in bed after a hard day when it
occurs to me that I have not brushed my teeth. Concern for my health
bids me rise and brush; sensual indulgence suggests I forget my teeth
for once. I weigh the alternatives in the light of the reasons: on the
one hand, my teeth are strong, and at my age decay is slow. It won't
matter much if I don't brush them. On the other hand, if I get up, it
will spoil my calm and may result in a bad night's sleep. Everything
considered I judge I would do better to stay in bed. Yet my feeling that

[1] J. L. Austin, 'A Plea for Excuses', reprinted in *Philosophical Papers* (Oxford,
1961), p. 146.

I ought to brush my teeth is too strong for me: wearily I leave my bed and brush my teeth. My act is clearly intentional, although against my better judgement, and so is incontinent.

There are numerous occasions when immediate pleasure yields to principle, politeness, or sense of duty and yet we judge (or know) that all things considered we should opt for pleasure. In approaching the problem of incontinence it is a good idea to dwell on the cases where morality simply doesn't enter the picture as one of the contestants for our favour —or if it does, it is on the wrong side. Then we shall not succumb to the temptation to reduce incontinence to such special cases as being overcome by the beast in us, or of failing to heed the call of duty, or of succumbing to temptation.[1]

II

Under sceptical scrutiny, P1 and P2 appear vulnerable enough, and yet tinkering with them yields no satisfactory account of how incontinence is possible. Part of the reason at least lies in the fact that P1 and P2 derive their force from a very persuasive view of the nature of intentional action and practical reasoning. When a person acts with an intention, the following seems to be a true, if rough and incomplete, description of what goes on: he sets a positive value on some state of affairs (an end, or the performance by himself of an action satisfying certain conditions); he believes (or knows or perceives) that an action, of a kind open to him to perform, will promote or produce or realize the valued state of affairs; and so he acts (that is, he acts *because* of his value or desire and his belief). Generalized and refined, this description has seemed to many philosophers, from Aristotle on, to promise to give an analysis of what it is to act with an intention; to illuminate how we explain an action by giving the reasons the agent had in acting; and to provide the beginning of an account of practical reasoning, i.e. reasoning about what to do, reasoning that leads to action.

[1] I know no clear case of a philosopher who recognizes that incontinence is not essentially a problem in moral philosophy, but a problem in the philosophy of action. Butler, in the *Sermons*, points out that 'Benevolence towards particular persons may be to a degree of weakness, and so be blamable', but here the note of self-indulgence sounds too loud. And Nowell-Smith, *Ethics* (London, 1954), pp. 243 ff., describes many cases of incontinence where we are overcome by conscience or duty: 'We might paradoxically, but not unfairly, say that in such a case it is difficult to resist the temptation to tell the truth. We are the slaves of our own consciences.' Slaves don't act freely; the case is again not clear.
Aristotle discusses the case of the man who, contrary to his own principle (and best judgement) pursues (too strongly) something noble and good (he cares too much for honour or his children), but he refuses to call this incontinence (*Nic. Eth.*, 1148).

In the simplest case, we imagine that the agent has a desire, for example, to know the time. He realizes that by looking at his watch he will satisfy his desire; so he looks at his watch. We can answer the question why he looked at his watch; we know the intention with which he did it. Following Aristotle, the desire may be conceived as a principle of action, and its natural propositional expression would here be something like 'It would be good for me to know the time' or, even more stiffly, 'Any act of mine that results in my knowing the time is desirable.' Such a principle Aristotle compares to the major premise in a syllogism. The propositional expression of the agent's belief would in this case be, 'Looking at my watch will result in my knowing the time': this corresponds to the minor premise. Subsuming the case under the rule, the agent performs the desirable action: he looks at his watch.

It seems that, given this desire and this belief, the agent is in a position to infer that looking at his watch is desirable, and in fact the making of such an inference is something it would be natural to describe as subsuming the case under the rule. But given this desire and this belief, the conditions are also satisfied that lead to (and hence explain) an intentional action, so Aristotle says that once a person has the desire and believes some action will satisfy it, *straightway he acts*. Since there is no distinguishing the conditions under which an agent is in a position to infer that an action he is free to perform is desirable from the conditions under which he acts, Aristotle apparently identifies drawing the inference and acting: he says, 'the conclusion is an action'. But of course this account of intentional action and practical reason contradicts the assumption that there are incontinent actions.

As long as we keep the general outline of Aristotle's theory before us, I think we cannot fail to realize that he can offer no satisfactory analysis of incontinent action. No doubt he can explain why, in borderline cases, we are tempted both to say an agent acted intentionally and that he knew better. But if we postulate a strong desire from which he acted, then on the theory, we also attribute to the agent a strong judgement that the action is desirable; and if we emphasize that the agent's ability to reason to the wrongness of his action was weakened or distorted, to that extent we show that he did not fully appreciate that what he was doing was undesirable.

It should not be supposed we can escape Aristotle's difficulty simply by giving up the doctrine that having the reasons for action always results in action. We might allow, for example, that a man can have a desire and believe an action will satisfy it, and yet fail to act, and add that it is only if the desire and belief cause him to act that we can speak of an intentional action.[1] On such a modified version of Aristotle's theory (if it really is a modification) we would still have to explain why in some cases the desire and belief caused an action, while in other cases they merely led to the judgement that a course of action was desirable.

The incontinent man believes it would be better on the whole to do something else, but he has a reason for what he does, for his action is intentional. We must therefore be able to abstract from his behaviour and state of mind a piece of practical reasoning the conclusion of which is, or would be if the conclusion were drawn from the premises, that the action actually performed is desirable. Aristotle tends to obscure this point by concentrating on cases where the incontinent man is motivated by a wild desire; but he recognizes that even the incontinent man behaves 'under the influence of rule and an opinion' (*Nic. Eth.*, 1147b; cf. 1102b).

Aquinas is far clearer on this important point than Aristotle. He says:

He that has knowledge of the universal is hindered, because of a passion, from reasoning in the light of that universal, so as to draw the conclusion; but he reasons in the light of another universal proposition suggested by the inclination of the passion, and draws his conclusion accordingly . . . Hence passion fetters the reason, and hinders it from thinking and concluding under the first proposition; so that while passion lasts, the reason argues and concludes under the second.[2]

An example, given by Aquinas, shows the plight of the incontinent man:

THE SIDE OF REASON	THE SIDE OF LUST
(M_1) No fornication is lawful	(M_2) Pleasure is to be pursued
(m_1) This is an act of fornication	(m_2) This act is pleasant
(C_1) This act is not lawful	(C_2) This act is to be pursued

We can make the point more poignantly, though here we go beyond Aristotle and Aquinas, if we construe principles and conclusions as comparative judgements concerning the merits of committing, or not committing, the act in question. The two conclusions (C_1) and (C_2) will then be (given some natural assumptions): It is better not to perform this act than to perform it, and, it is better to perform this act than not to perform it. And these are in flat contradiction on the assumption that better-than is asymmetric.

And now we must observe that *this picture of moral reasoning is not*

[1] For a version of this theory, see my 'Actions, Reasons, and Causes', *The Journal of Philosophy*, LX (1963), pp. 685-700.
[2] *Summa Theologica*, Part II, Q. 77, Art. 2, reply to objection 4. Aquinas quotes the apostle: 'I see another law in my members fighting against the law of my mind.'

*merely inadequate to account for incontinence; it cannot give a correct
account of simple cases of moral conflict.* By a case of moral conflict I
mean a case where there are good reasons both for performing an action
and for performing one that rules it out (perhaps refraining from the
action). There is conflict in this minimal sense whenever the agent is
aware of considerations that, taken alone, would lead to mutually incompatible actions; feelings of strife and anxiety are inessential embellish-
ments. Clearly enough, incontinence can exist only when there is conflict
in this sense, for the incontinent man holds one course to be better (for
a reason) and yet does something else (also for a reason). So we may set
aside what is special to incontinence for the moment, and consider conflict generally. The twin arguments of the previous paragraph depict not
only the plight of the incontinent man, but also of the righteous man
in the toils of temptation; one of them does the wrong thing and the
other the right, but both act in the face of competing claims.

The situation is common; life is crowded with examples: I ought to
do it because it will save a life, I ought not because it will be a lie; if
I do it, I will break my word to Lavinia, if I don't, I will break my
word to Lolita; and so on. Anyone may find himself in this fix, whether
he be upright or temporizing, weak-willed or strong. But then unless
we take the line that moral principles cannot conflict in application to
a case, we must give up the concept of the nature of practical reason we
have so far been assuming. For how can premises, all of which are
true (or acceptable), entail a contradiction?

It is astonishing that in contemporary moral philosophy this problem
has received little attention, and no satisfactory treatment. Those who
recognize the difficulty seem ready to accept one of two solutions: in
effect they allow only a single ultimate moral principle; or they rest
happy with the notion of a distinction between the prima facie desirable
(good, obligatory, etc.) and the absolutely desirable (good, obligatory,
etc.).[1] I shall not argue the point here, but I do not believe any version

---

[1] Examples of views that in effect allow only one ultimate moral principle: Kurt
Baier, in *The Moral Point of View* (Ithaca, 1958), holds that in cases of conflict between principles there are higher-order principles that tell which principles take
precedence; Singer, 'Moral Rules and Principles' in *Essays in Moral Philosophy*, ed.
A. Melden (Seattle, 1958), claims that moral principles cannot conflict; Hare, in
The Language of Morals (Oxford, 1952), argues there are no exceptions to acceptable
moral principles, for counter-examples to the principles we hold force us to alter the
principles. If ultimate principles never conflict or have counter-examples, we may
accept the conjunction of ultimate principles as our single principle, while if there
is a higher-order principle that resolves conflicts, we can obviously construct a single,
exceptionless, principle. And of course all outright utilitarians, rule or otherwise,
believe there is a single exceptionless moral principle.

of the 'single principle' solution, once its implications are understood, can be accepted: principles, or reasons for acting, are irreducibly multiple. On the other hand, it is not easy to see how to take advantage of the purported distinction between prima facie and absolute value. Suppose first that we try to think of 'prima facie' as an attributive adverb, helping to form such predicates as 'x is prima facie good, right, obligatory' or 'x is better, prima facie, than y'. To avoid our recent trouble, we must suppose that 'x is better, prima facie, than y' does not contradict 'y is better, prima facie, than x', and that 'x is prima facie right' does not contradict 'x is prima facie wrong'. But then the conclusion we can draw, in every case of conflict (and hence of incontinence) will be 'x is better, prima facie, than y, and y is better, prima facie, than x'. This comes down, as is clear from the structure practical reasoning would have on this assumption, to saying 'There is something to be said for, and something to be said against, doing so and so—and also for and against not doing it.' Probably this can be said about any action whatsoever; in any case it is hard to accept the idea that the sum of our moral wisdom concerning what to do in a given situation has this form. The situation I describe is not altered in any interesting way if 'prima facie' or 'prima facie obligatory' is treated as a (non-truth-functional) sentential operator rather than as a predicate. I shall return shortly to this problem; now let us reconsider incontinence.

The image we get of incontinence from Aristotle, Aquinas, and Hare is of a battle or struggle between two contestants. Each contestant is armed with his argument or principle. One side may be labelled 'passion' and the other 'reason'; they fight; one side wins, the wrong side, the side called 'passion' (or 'lust' or 'pleasure'). There is, however, a competing image (to be found in Plato, as well as in Butler and many others). It is adumbrated perhaps by Dante (who thinks he is following Aquinas and Aristotle) when he speaks of the incontinent man as one who 'lets desire pull reason from her throne' (*Inferno*, Canto v). Here there are three actors on the stage: reason, desire, and the one who lets desire get the upper hand. The third actor is perhaps named 'The Will' (or 'Conscience'). It is up to The Will to decide who wins the battle. If The Will is strong, he gives the palm to reason; if he is weak, he may allow pleasure or passion the upper hand.

This second image is, I suggest, superior to the first, absurd as we may find both. On the first story, not only can we not account for incontinence; it is not clear how we can ever blame the agent for what he does: his action merely reflects the outcome of a struggle within him. What could he do about it? And more important, the first image does not allow us to make sense of a conflict in one person's soul, for it leaves no room for the all-important process of weighing considerations.[1] In the second image, the agent's representative, The Will, can judge the strength of the arguments on both sides, can execute the decision, and take the rap. The only trouble is that we seem back where we started. For how can The Will judge one course of action better and yet choose the other?

It would be a mistake to think we have made no progress. For what these colourful gladiatorial and judicial metaphors ought now to suggest is that there is a piece of practical reasoning present in moral conflict, and hence in incontinence, which we have so far entirely neglected. What must be added to the picture is a new argument:

THE WILL (CONSCIENCE)

(M_3) M_1 and M_2

(m_3) m_1 and m_2

(C_3) This action is wrong

Clearly something like this third argument is necessary if an agent is to act rightly in the face of conflict, or incontinently. It is not enough to know the reasons on each side: he must know how they add up.[2] The incontinent man goes against his better judgement, and this surely is (C_3), which is based on all the considerations, and not (C_1) which fails to bring in the reasons on the other side. You could say we have discovered two quite different meanings of the phrase 'his better judgement'. It might mean, any judgement for the right side (reason, morality, family, country); or, the judgement based on all relevant considerations known to the actor. The first notion, I have argued, is really irrelevant to the analysis of incontinence.

But now we are brought up against our other problem, the form or nature of practical reasoning. For nothing could be more obvious than that our third 'practical syllogism' is no syllogism at all; the conclusion simply doesn't follow by logic from the premises. And introducing the third piece of reasoning doesn't solve the problem we had before anyway: we still have contradictory 'conclusions'. We could at this point try once more introducing 'prima facie' judiciously into suitable places: for example, into (M_1), (M_2), (C_1), and (C_2). We might then try to relate prima facie desirability to desirability sans phrase by making (C_1) and (C_2), thus interpreted, the data for (C_3). But this is an unpromising line.

[1] A more sophisticated account of conflict that seems to raise the same problem is Ryle's account in *The Concept of Mind* (London, 1949), pp. 93-5.

[2] My authority for how they do add up in this case is Aquinas: see the reference in footnote 2, page 104.

We can hardly expect to learn whether an action ought to be performed simply from the fact that it is both prima facie right and prima facie wrong.

The real source of difficulty is now apparent: if we are to have a coherent theory of practical reason, we must give up the idea that we can *detach* conclusions about what is desirable (or better) or obligatory from the principles that lend those conclusions colour. It is the tacit assumption that moral principles have the form of universalized conditionals that gives the trouble; once this assumption is made, nothing we can do with a prima facie operator in the conclusion will save things. The situation is, in this respect, like reasoning from probabilistic evidence. As Hempel has emphasized with great clarity,[1] we cannot reason from:

(M_4) If the barometer falls, it almost certainly will rain
(m_4) The barometer is falling

to the conclusion:

(C_4) It almost certainly will rain

since we may at the same time be equally justified in arguing:

(M_5) Red skies at night, it almost certainly won't rain
(m_5) The sky is red tonight
∴ (C_5) It almost certainly won't rain

The crucial blunder is interpreting (M_4) and (M_5) to allow detachment of a modal conclusion. A way to mend matters is to view the 'almost certainly' of (M_4) and (M_5) as modifying, not the conclusion, but the connective. Thus we might render (M_4), 'That the barometer falls probabilizes that it will rain'; in symbols, '$pr(Rx, Fx)$', where the variable ranges over areas of space-time that may be characterized by falling barometers or rain. If we let 'a' name the space and time of here and now, and 'Sx' mean that the early part of x is characterized by a red sky of evening, we may attempt to reconstruct the thought bungled above thus:

$pr(Rx,Fx)$ $pr(\sim Rx,Sx)$
Fa Sa
∴ $pr(Ra,pr(Rx,Fx)$ and $Fa)$ ∴$pr(\sim Ra,pr(\sim Rx,Sx)$ and $Sa)$

[1] Carl Hempel, *Aspects of Scientific Explanation* (New York, 1965). pp. 394-403.

If we want to predict the weather, we will take a special interest in:

$pr(\sim Ra,e)$ or $pr(Ra,e)$

where e is all the relevant evidence we have. But it is clear that we can infer neither of these from the two arguments that went before, even if e is simply the conjunction of their premises (and even if for our qualitative 'pr' we substitute a numerical measure of degree of support).

I propose to apply the pattern to practical reasoning in the obvious way. The central idea is that a moral principle, like 'Lying is (prima facie) wrong', cannot coherently be treated as a universally quantified conditional, but should be recognized to mean something like, 'That an act is a lie prima facie makes it wrong'; in symbols, '$pf(Wx,Lx)$'. The concept of the prima facie, as it is needed in moral philosophy, relates propositions. In logical grammar, 'prima facie' is not an operator on single sentences, much less on predicates of actions, but on pairs of sentences related as (expressing) moral judgement and ground. Here is how the piece of practical reasoning misrepresented by (M_1), (m_1) and (C_1) might look when reconstituted:

(M_6) $pf(x$ is better than y, x is a refraining from fornication and y is an act of fornication)
(m_6) a is a refraining from fornication and b is an act of fornication
$\therefore$ (C_6) $pf(a$ is better than b, (M_6) and $(m_6))$

Similarly, (M_2) and (m_2), when rewritten in the new mode, and labelled (M_7) and (m_7), will yield:

(C_7) $pf(b$ is better than a, (M_7) and $(m_7))$

A judgement in which we will take particular interest is:
(C_8) $pf(a$ is better than b, $e)$

where e is all the relevant considerations known to us, including at least (M_6), (m_6), (M_7) and (m_7).

Of course (C_8) does not follow logically from anything that went before, but in this respect moral reasoning seems no worse off than predicting the weather. In neither case do we know a general formula for computing how far or whether a conjunction of evidence statements supports a conclusion from how far or whether each conjunct supports it. There is no loss either, in this respect, in the strategy of relativizing moral judgements as here: we have no clue how to arrive at (C_8) from the reasons, but its faulty prototype (C_3) was in no better shape. There has, however, been a loss of relevance, for the conditionalization that keeps (C_6) from clashing with (C_7), and (C_8) from clashing with either, also insulates all three from action. Intentional action, I have argued in defending P1 and P2, is geared directly to unconditional judgements like 'It would be better to do a than to do b.' Reasoning that stops at conditional judgements such as (C_8) is practical only in its subject, not in its issue.

Practical reasoning does however often arrive at unconditional judgements that one action is better than another—otherwise there would be no such thing as acting on a reason. The minimal elements of such reasoning are these: the agent accepts some reason (or set of reasons) r, and holds that $pf(a$ is better than $b, r)$, and these constitute the reason why he judges that a is better than b. Under these conditions, the agent will do a if he does either a or b intentionally, and his reason for doing a rather than b will be identical with the reason why he judges a better than b.

This modified account of acting on a reason leaves P1 and P2 untouched, and Aristotle's remark that the conclusion (of a piece of practical reasoning) is an action remains cogent. But now there is no (logical) difficulty in the fact of incontinence, for the akrates is characterized as holding that, all things considered, it would be better to do b than to do a, even though he does a rather than b and with a reason. The logical difficulty has vanished because a judgement that a is better than b, all things considered, is a relational, or pf, judgement, and so cannot conflict logically with any unconditional judgement.

Possibly it will be granted that P1-P2, as interpreted here, do not yield a contradiction. But at the same time, a doubt may arise whether P3 is plausible, given this interpretation. For how is it possible for a man to judge that a is better than b, all things considered, and not judge that a is better than b?

One potential confusion is quickly set aside. 'a is better than b, all things (viz. all truths, moral and otherwise) considered' surely does entail 'a is better than b', and we do not want to explain incontinence as a simple logical blunder. The phrase 'all things considered' must, of course, refer only to things known, believed or held by the agent, the sum of his relevant principles, opinions, attitudes, and desires. Setting this straight may, however, seem only to emphasize the real difficulty. We want now to ask: how is it possible for a man to judge that a is better than b on the grounds that r, and yet not judge that a is better than b, when r is the sum of all that seems relevant to him? When we say that r contains all that seems relevant to the agent, don't we just mean that nothing has been omitted that influences his judgement that a is better than b?

Since what is central to the solution of the problem of incontinence proposed in this paper is the contrast between conditional (prima facie) evaluative judgements and evaluative judgements sans phrase, perhaps we can give a characterization of incontinence that avoids the troublesome 'all things considered'. A plausible modification of our original definition (D) of incontinence might label an action, x, as incontinent provided simply that the agent has a better reason for doing something else: he does x for a reason r, but he has a reason r^1 that includes r and more, on the basis of which he judges some alternative y to be better than x.[1] Of course it might also have been incontinent of him to have done y, since he may have had a better reason still for performing some third action z. Following this line, we might say that an action x is continent if x is done for a reason r, and there is no reason r' (that includes r), on the basis of which the agent judges some action better than x.

This shows we can make sense of incontinence without appeal to the idea of an agent's total wisdom, and the new formulation might in any case be considered an improvement on (D) since it allows (correctly, I think) that there are incontinent actions even when no judgement is made in the light of all the reasons. Still, we cannot rule out the case where a judgement is made in the light of all the reasons, so the underlying difficulty may be thought to remain.

In fact, however, the difficulty is not real. Every judgement is made in the light of all the reasons in this sense, that it is made in the presence of, and is conditioned by, that totality. But this does not mean that every judgement is reasonable, or thought to be so by the agent, on the basis of those reasons, nor that the judgement was reached from that basis by a process of reasoning. There is no paradox in supposing a person sometimes holds that all that he believes and values supports a certain course of action, when at the same time those same beliefs and values cause him to reject that course of action.[2] If r is someone's reason for holding that p, then his holding that r must be, I think, a cause of his holding that p. But, and this is what is crucial here, his holding that r may cause his holding that p without r being his reason; indeed, the agent may even think that r is a reason to reject p.

---

[1] We might want to rule out the case, allowed by this formulation, where the agent does what he has the best reason for doing, but does not do it for that reason.

[2] At this point my account of incontinence seems to me very close to Aristotle's. See G. E. M. Anscombe, 'Thought and Action in Aristotle', in *New Essays on Plato and Aristotle*, ed. R. Bambrough (London, 1965).

It is possible, then, to be incontinent, even if P1 and P2 are true; but where is the fault? The akrates does not, as is now clear, hold logically contradictory beliefs, nor is his failure necessarily a moral failure. What is wrong is that the incontinent man acts, and judges, irrationally, for this is surely what we must say of a man who goes against his own best judgement. Carnap and Hempel have argued that there is a principle which is no part of the logic of inductive (or statistical) reasoning, but is a directive the rational man will accept. It is the *requirement of total evidence for inductive reasoning*: give your credence to the hypothesis supported by all available relevant evidence.[1] There is, I suggest, an analogous principle the rational man will accept in applying practical reasoning: perform the action judged best on the basis of all available relevant reasons. It would be appropriate to call this the *principle of continence*. There may seem something queer in making the requirement of total evidence an imperative (can one tailor one's beliefs to order?), but there is no such awkwardness about the principle of continence. It exhorts us to actions we can perform if we want; it leaves the motives to us. What is hard is to acquire the virtue of continence, to make the principle of continence our own. But there is no reason in principle why it is any more difficult to become continent than to become chaste or brave. One gets a lively sense of the difficulties in St. Augustine's extraordinary prayer: 'Give me chastity and continence, only not yet' (*Confessions*, VIII, vii).

Why would anyone ever perform an action when he thought that, everything considered, another action would be better? If this is a request for a psychological explanation, then the answers will no doubt refer to the interesting phenomena familiar from most discussions of incontinence: self-deception, overpowering desires, lack of imagination, and the rest. But if the question is read, what is the agent's reason for doing *a* when he believes it would be better, all things considered, to do another thing, then the answer must be: for this, the agent has no reason. We perceive a creature as rational in so far as we are able to view his movements as part of a rational pattern comprising also thoughts, desires, emotions, and volitions. (In this we are much aided by the actions we conceive to be utterances.) Through faulty inference, incomplete evidence, lack of diligence, or flagging sympathy, we often enough fail to detect a pattern that is there. But in the case of incontinence, the attempt to read reason into behaviour is necessarily subject to a degree of frustration.

---

[1] See Hempel, op. cit., pp. 397-403 for important modifications, and further references.

What is special in incontinence is that the actor cannot understand him-self: he recognizes, in his own intentional behaviour, something essen-tially surd.

IX

PRUDENCE, TEMPERANCE, AND COURAGE

W. D. FALK

WHENEVER ONE remarks that clearly there are things which one ought to avoid or do if only for one's own sake, someone is sure to say, 'No doubt; but any such ought is only a precept of prudence or expediency.' It is a textbook cliché against Hobbes that his account of morality comes to just this. And this is said as if it were an obvious truth and enough to discredit all such precepts in one go. This assumes a great deal and settles nothing.

What it assumes is this: that everything that one ever does for one's own sake, one does as a matter of prudence *or* expediency; that there is no difference between these two; that morality always differs from prudence as a scent differs from a bad smell; and that everyone knows how so and why.

None of this will do.

In the first place, not everything done for oneself is done for reasons of prudence. That one ought to insure one's house, save for one's old age, not put all one's money into one venture, are precepts of prudence. But it is not a precept of prudence, though it may be a good precept, that some-one ought to undergo a dangerous operation as a long shot to restoring his health rather than linger under a disability forever after.

The point is that prudence is only one way of looking after oneself. To act prudently is to play safe, for near-certain gains at small risks. But some good things one cannot get in this way. To get them at all one has to gamble, taking the risk of not getting them even so, or of coming to harm in the process. If one values them enough, one will do better by oneself to throw prudence to the winds, to play for high stakes, knowing full well the risk and the price of failure. Explorers, artists, scientists,

Part 2 of 'Morality and Self' by W. D. Falk, from *Morality and the Language of Conduct*, ed. Hector-Neri Castañeda and George Nakhnikian (Wayne State University Press, 1963), pp. 34-39. Reprinted by permission of the publisher and the author.
© 1963 by Wayne State University Press, Detroit 2, Michigan. All rights reserved.

mountaineers are types who may serve themselves better by this course. So will most people at some juncture. Thus, if someone values security, then that he ought to save in order to be secure is a precept of prudence. But that someone ought to stick to his vocation when his heart is in it enough to make it worth risking security or health or life itself is not a precept of *prudence*, but of *courage*.

One says sometimes, 'I ought to save, as I *want* to be prudent', but sometimes 'as I *ought* to be prudent'. One may also decide that in one's own best interests one ought to be prudent rather than daring, or daring rather than prudent, as the case may be. Now, that one ought to do something as it would be prudent is a dictate of prudence. But that one really ought to be prudent, in one's own best interests, would not be a dictate of prudence again. One then ought to play safe in order to serve oneself *best* and not in order to serve oneself *safely*.

A dictate of prudence where one wants to be prudent but ought to be courageous in one's own best interests is a dictate of timidity. A dictate of courage, where one feels reckless but ought to be prudent, is a dictate of foolhardiness. Both will then plainly be morally imperfect precepts. But there is nothing obviously imperfect about a dictate of prudence where one ought to be prudent, or a dictate of courage where one ought to be daring. Such precepts seem near-moral enough to allow one to call the habit of acting on them a virtue. The Ancients considered both prudence and courage as moral virtues. Oddly enough, in our time, one is more ready to view courage on one's own behalf as a moral virtue than prudence. It needs the reminder that precepts of self-protection may be precepts of courage as well as of prudence for one to see that any precept of self-protection may have a moral flavour. I think that the dim view which we take of prudence corresponds to a belief that to be daring is harder than to be level-headed, a belief most likely justified within our own insurance-minded culture. But such belief would have seemed strange to Bishop Butler and the fashionable eighteenth-century gentlemen to whom he addressed himself. Prudence in Butler's time, as throughout the ancient world, was not yet the cheap commodity which it is with us; and the price of virtue varies with the market.

There are other precepts of self-protection which are not 'just a matter of prudence' either. That one ought not to take to drugs or drink, indulge oneself in one's sorrows, waste one's talents, commit suicide just in the despair of the moment, are precepts made of sterner stuff. One wants to say, 'Surely, it is more than just a matter of prudence that one ought to avoid these things.' And rightly so. The effect on oneself of taking to drugs or drink, or of any of the others, is not conjectural, but quite certain. To avoid them is therefore more than a matter of *taking no risks*. Sometimes, when one looks down a precipice, one feels drawn to jump. If one refrains, it will hardly be said of one, 'How prudent he is, he takes no chances.' The avoidance of excesses of all kinds in one's own best interests is in this class. The habit of avoiding them the Greeks called temperance, a virtue distinct from prudence.

Another error is to equate the prudent with the expedient, and, again, the expedient with everything that is for one's own good. To save may be prudent; but whether it is expedient or convenient to start now is another matter. With a lot of money to spare at the moment it will be expedient; otherwise it will not. But it may be prudent all the same. Again, one marries in the hope of finding happiness; but marriage in this hope is not a marriage of convenience. The point is that reasons of expediency are reasons of a special sort: reasons for doing something on the ground that it is incidentally at hand to serve one's purpose, or because it serves a purpose quite incidental to the purpose for which one would normally be doing this thing. One marries for reasons of expediency when one marries for money, but not when in hope of finding happiness. Hobbes said that 'men never act except with a view to some good to themselves'. This would be quite different from saying that 'they never act except with a view to what is expedient'.

There is also this difference between the prudent and the expedient: one can speak of 'rules of prudence', but less well of 'rules of expediency'. The expedient is what happens to serve. It is not therefore easily bottled in rules.

The word 'prudence' is used too freely in still one more context. When one wishes to justify the social virtues to people, a traditional and inviting move is to refer them, among other things at least, to their own good. 'You ought to hold the peace, be honest, share with others.' 'Why?' 'Because an order in which such practices were universal is of vital concern to you; and your one hope of helping to make such an order is in doing your share.' The classical formulation of this standard move is Hooker's, quoted with approval by Locke: 'If I cannot but wish to receive good . . . how should I look to have any part of my desire herein satisfied, unless I myself be careful to satisfy the like desire: my desire therefore to be loved of my equals in nature, as much as possible may be, imposes upon me a *natural duty* of bearing to themward fully the like affection.'

Now, it is said again, 'So defended, the social duties come to no more than precepts of prudence'; and this goes with the veiled suggestion that it is morally improper to use this defence. But, even if so defended, the social duties are not necessarily reduced purely to precepts of prudence. For they may be recommended in this way either as mere *rules* or as *principles* of self-protection; and as principles they would be misdescribed as mere precepts of prudence. The distinction is this: When one says, 'People ought to practise the social virtues, if only for their own benefit,' one may be saying, 'They ought to practise them for this reason as a *rule*, i.e., normally, as much as each time this is likely to be for their own good.' Or one may be saying, 'They ought to practise them for this reason not merely as a rule but as a *matter of principle*, i.e., every time, whether at that time this is likely to be for their good or not.' And one might defend the adoption of this *principle* by saying, 'Because your best, even if slim, hope of contributing to a society fit for you to live in lies in adding to the number of principled people who will do their share each time, without special regard for their good at that time.'

Now this seems to me a precept of courage rather than one of prudence. The game of attempting by one's actions to make society a place fit for one to live in is a gamble worth the risk only because of the known price of not attempting it. This gamble is a root condition of social living. One is sure to give hostages to fortune, but again, what other hope has one got? Hence, if a man practised the social virtues, thinking that he ought to as a matter of principle, and on these grounds, one will praise him for his *wisdom*, his firm grasp of vital issues, his steadfastness, his courage. But one will not necessarily congratulate him on his prudence. For many times the prudent course might have been otherwise. It may be wise to persist in being honest with cheats, or forbearing with the aggressive, or helpful to those slow to require helpfulness; but it might have been more prudent to persist for no longer than there was requital, or not even to start before requital was assured.

Now would it be a moral precept or not that, if only out of proper care for oneself, one ought to act on principles of wisdom and courage? That one ought to risk life in order to gain it? And, assuming a society of men acting fixedly on these principles but no others, would it or would it not contain men of moral virtue? One might as well ask, 'Is a ski an article of footwear?' There is no more of a straight answer here than there. One may say, 'Not quite'; and the point of saying this needs going into. But it would be more misleading to say, 'Not at all'. For it is part of the meaning of 'moral precept' that it prescribes what a man would do in his wisdom—if he were to consider things widely, looking past the immediate concerns of self and giving essentials due weight before incidentals. As it is also part of what is meant by one's moral capacities that one can live by such considerations, it becomes fruitless after a time to press the point whether such precepts are properly called moral.

There are then varieties of the personal ought, differing in the considerations on which they are based and the qualities needed to follow them; and they all seem at least akin to a 'moral' ought in their action-guiding force and function. But I grant that one does not want to speak of more than a kinship, and the point of this needs considering. One's hesitancy derives from various sources which have to be traced one by one.

Some of the hesitancy comes from contexts where one can say disparagingly, 'He did this *only* for reasons of prudence, *only* for reasons of expediency, *only* for himself.' This plainly applies sometimes, but it does not apply always. One would hardly say of someone without dependents, 'He thought that he ought to save, but *only* for reasons of prudence'; or of someone, 'He thought that he ought to have the carpenter in along with the plumber, but *only* for reasons of expediency or convenience'; or 'He thought that he ought to become a doctor, but *only* because the career would suit him.' 'Only' has no point here. Why else should a man without dependents save, except to be prudent? Why else should anyone have the carpenter in along with the plumber, except for convenience? What better reason is there normally for choosing a career than that it will suit one? On the other hand, there is point in saying, 'He held the peace only because it was prudent', 'He saved only because it was convenient', 'He practises the social virtues only for self-protection'. It is plain why 'only' applies here and is disparaging. One says 'only' because something is done for the wrong or for not quite the right reason—done for *one* reason where there is *another* and nearer reason for doing it anyway. Personal reasons are often in this position, and then they are disparaged as inferior. One saves 'only' because it is expedient, if one ought to have saved anyway for reasons of prudence. One holds the peace 'only' because it was prudent when one ought to have done so anyway as a matter of principle and even if it had not been prudent. And one practises the social virtues 'only' for self-protection when one does not *also* practise them for the general good.

The last case is different from the others. Plainly, one ought to practise the social virtues as principles of general good. But on none but perhaps pure Christian principles would it hold, or necessarily hold, that one ought to practise them on this ground unconditionally, however great the provocation to oneself. The case for the social virtues is weakened when the social environment becomes hostile and intractable by peaceable means; it is correspondingly strengthened where they can also be justified as wise principles of self-protection. That someone practises forbearance 'only' as a wise principle of self-protection is not therefore to say that he practises it for a reason which is neither here nor there; but rather for a reason which falls short of all the reason there is. This was, in effect, the view of the old Natural Law moralists—Hooker, Grotius, Puffendorf: the social virtues derive joint support from our natural concern for our own good and for that of society. Hobbes streamlined this account by denying the second, which provoked subsequent moralists to deny the first. Both Hobbes's sophistical toughness and the well-bred innocence of the academic moralists since are distorted visions which are less convincing than the unsqueamish common sense of the philosophers and divines of earlier times.

X

THE SENSE OF JUSTICE

JOHN RAWLS

I

IN *Emile* Rousseau asserts that the sense of justice is no mere moral conception formed by the understanding alone, but a true sentiment of the heart enlightened by reason, the natural outcome of our primitive affections.[1] In the first part of this paper I set out a psychological construction to illustrate the way in which Rousseau's thesis might be true. In the second part I use several of the ideas elaborated in formulating this construction to consider two questions which arise in the systematic analysis of the concept of justice.

These two questions are: first, to whom is the obligation of justice owed?—that is, in regard to whom must one regulate one's conduct as the principles of justice require?—and second, what accounts for men's doing what justice requires? Very briefly, the answers to these questions are as follows: to the first, the duty of justice is owed to those who are capable of a sense of justice; and to the second, if men did not do what justice requires, not only would they not regard themselves as bound by the principles of justice, but they would be incapable of feeling resentment and indignation, and they would be without ties of friendship and mutual trust. They would lack certain essential elements of humanity.

Throughout, I think of a sense of justice as something which persons have. One refers to it when one says, for example, that cruel and unusual punishments offend one's sense of justice. It may be aroused or assuaged, and it is connected not only with such moral feelings as resentment and indignation but also, as I shall argue, with such natural attitudes as mutual trust and affection. The psychological construction is designed to

From *Philosophical Review*, Vol. 72 (1963), pp. 281-305. Reprinted by permission of the *Philosophical Review* and the author.

[1] Bk. iv, the first part. In the Everyman Edition (London, 1911), see pp. 172–215, in particular pp. 196, 215.

show how the sense of justice may be viewed as the result of a certain natural development; it will be useful in understanding why the capacity for a sense of justice is the fundamental aspect of moral personality in the theory of justice.

II

Before setting out the psychological construction I should like to consider the background of the two questions. The main problem in giving a systematic analysis of the concept of justice is to derive and to arrange the principles associated with the concept.[1] These principles are those which account for the considered judgements of competent persons concerning the justice of political and social institutions. Institutions are understood as those publicly recognized systems of rules which are generally acted upon and which, by defining offices and positions, rights and duties, give political and social activity its form and structure. Now the family of principles associated with the concept of justice can be characterized as those principles which rational persons would acknowledge when the constraints of morality are imposed upon them in circumstances which give rise to questions of justice. These circumstances are those in which persons make conflicting demands on their common institutions and in which they regard themselves as representing or possessing legitimate interests the claims of which they are prepared to press on one another. Questions of justice and fairness arise when free persons, who have no authority over one another, are participating in their common institutions and among themselves settling or acknowledging the rules which define them and which determine the resulting shares in their benefits and burdens. An institution is just or fair, then, when it satisfies the principles which those who participate in it could propose to one another for mutual acceptance from an original position of equal liberty. To derive the familiar principles of justice is to show how they would be mutually acknowledged; and to arrange these principles is to determine their respective priorities, given the nature of the cases to which they apply.

When the concept of justice is applied to the basic structure of the political and social system, the principles associated with the concept are the following: (i) each person participating in it or affected by it has an equal right to the most extensive liberty compatible with a like liberty

---

[1] For an attempt to lay the basis for such an analysis, see my paper, 'Justice as Fairness', *Philosophical Review*, LXVII (1958), 164–94. I begin this section by sketching the parts of this paper which are needed in the following discussion.

for all; and (ii) inequalities (as defined and permitted by the pattern of distribution of rights and duties) are arbitrary unless it is reasonable to expect that they will work out for everyone's advantage, and provided that the positions and offices to which they attach, or from which they may be gained, are open to all. (I state these principles here and sketch their derivation as they are used in the formulation of the psychological construction. The idea underlying this derivation I shall call the conception of justice as fairness.)

The derivation of these principles is indicated by the following analytic construction. Imagine a number of rational and mutually self-interested persons situated in an initial position of equal liberty. Assume that they are to propose and acknowledge before one another general principles applicable to their common institutions as standards by which their complaints against these institutions are to be judged. They do not begin by registering complaints; instead they try to agree to criteria by which a complaint is to be counted as legitimate. Their procedure for this is that each person is allowed to propose the principles upon which he wishes his own complaints to be tried, this privilege being subject to three conditions. It is understood (i) that if the principles one proposes are accepted, the complaints of others will be similarly tried; (ii) that no one's complaints will be heard until everyone is roughly of one mind as to how complaints are to be judged; and (iii) that the principles proposed and acknowledged on any one occasion are binding, failing special circumstances, on all future occasions. The main idea of the procedure is that everyone should be required to make in advance a firm commitment, which others also may reasonably be expected to make, and that no one be given the opportunity to tailor the canons of a legitimate complaint to fit his own special condition and then to discard them when they no longer suit his purpose. The principles accepted will express the standards in accordance with which each person is willing to have his interests limited on the supposition that the interests of others will be limited in the same way. The restrictions which would so arise may be thought of as those which a person would keep in mind if he were designing a social system in which his enemy were to assign him his place. The two principles of justice previously mentioned are those which would be acknowledged given the conditions of this analytic construction; they constitute the principles of justice in this fundamental case.[1]

Now one can distinguish three instances in which the concept of equality applies. The first is to institutions as part of their definition. The

[1] I have tried to show this in an essay, 'Constitutional Liberty and the Concept of Justice', to appear in *Nomos*, Vol. vi.

notion of an institution involves the concept of equality in that the notion of an activity in accordance with rules implies that similar cases, as defined by these rules, are to be treated similarly. Next, the concept of equality applies to the structure of an institution, or of a social system. What equality requires, in the case of the fundamental constitution of society, is included in the two principles of justice. In general, an institution satisfies the demands of equality if it is in accordance with the principles which would be acknowledged by rational and mutually self-interested persons from an original position of equal liberty. Finally, the concept of equality applies to the original position itself, giving rise to the first question: namely, what qualifies a person as holding an original position so that in one's dealings with him one is required to conduct oneself in accordance with principles that could be acknowledged by everyone from an initial position of equality? The answer to this question, I shall argue below, is that it is necessary and sufficient that he be capable, to a certain minimum degree, of a sense of justice.

The second question—namely, what accounts for men's doing what justice requires—arises in the following manner. If the argument of the analytic construction is correct, the concept of justice has associated with it a certain family of principles. The concept of morality, when imposed upon rational and self-interested persons, gives rise to certain definite constraints. A person who has a morality not only accepts general and universal principles as limiting the pursuit of his own interests as well as those of others, but these principles must state certain specific restrictions. Among rational persons a morality without certain familiar principles of justice is impossible. The argument of the analytic construction does not show, however, that rational persons as participants in a scheme of co-operation will do what justice requires in particular cases.[1] The aim of the analytic construction is to derive

---

[1] As typical of what justice requires in particular cases, one may take the prima facie duty of fair play. If the participants in an institution (or practice) accept its rules as just or fair, and so have no complaint to lodge against it, there arises a prima facie duty of the parties to each other to act in accordance with its rules when it falls upon them to comply. When any number of persons engage in an institution, or conduct a joint undertaking according to rules, and thus restrict their liberty, those who have submitted to these restrictions when required have the right to a similar acquiescence on the part of those who have benefited by their submission. These conditions obtain if an institution is correctly acknowledged to be just or fair, for in this case all who participate benefit from it. Thus a tax-dodger violates a duty of fair play: he accepts the benefits of government but will not do his part in releasing resources to it. For the definition of this prima facie duty, I am indebted to H. L. A. Hart. See his paper, 'Are There Any Natural Rights', *Philosophical Review*, LXIV (1955), 185 f.

the principles of justice which apply to institutions. How persons will act in the particular circumstances when, as the rules specify, it is their turn to do their part is a different question altogether. Those engaged in an institution will indeed normally do their part if they feel bound to act on the principles which they would acknowledge under the conditions of the analytic construction. But their feeling bound in this way is not itself accounted for by this construction, and it cannot be accounted for as long as the parties are described solely by the concept of rationality.

In the psychological construction to follow, the stages of a development are described by which the sense of justice might arise from our primitive natural attitudes. This construction may be regarded as purely hypothetical. I do not claim that it represents what actually takes place. Nevertheless, I have tried to make it reasonably plausible and to include in it only those psychological principles which are compatible with our conception of ourselves as moral beings. I shall use several of the ideas elaborated in stating this construction to answer the two questions.

III

The psychological construction by which the sense of justice might develop consists of three parts representing the development of three forms of guilt feelings in this order: authority guilt, association guilt, and principle guilt.[1] There are other forms of guilt feelings, and in other connections it would be essential to discuss them; but for the moment, these other forms may be left aside. The central place given to the feeling of guilt is a matter of convenience and simply a way of arranging what is said about the moral feelings.[2]

To characterize authority guilt, let us suppose an institutional situation in which certain persons are subject to the general precepts or to the particular injunctions of others. The specific case to be taken is the relation of parents and their children. Assume that those subject—the

[1] This construction draws upon Jean Piaget's work, *The Moral Judgment of the Child* (London, 1932). It follows the main lines of his account of the development of the sense of justice and incorporates his distinction between the morality of authority and the morality of mutual respect.

[2] In Section vi I shall discuss briefly some of the defining features of the moral feelings, but I do not propose a formal definition of these feelings. For the purpose of the argument it is sufficient to consider them as given by enumeration; and thus as being, for example, the feelings of guilt and remorse, resentment and indignation, and certain forms of shame and contempt.

children—love, trust, and have faith in those in authority, the parents. Let us suppose also that those subject are not in a position to question the general precepts or particular injunctions which they are expected to obey, either because they do not have sufficient knowledge and understanding or because they lack the concept of justification, both being the case with children. Suppose, further, to avoid needless complications, that the precepts and injunctions given are reasonable, so that the attitudes of love, trust, and faith are not misplaced. Given these conditions, which involve the natural attitudes of love, trust, and faith within a certain institutional background, it follows that those subject will manifest what I shall call authority guilt when they violate the precepts set to them.[1] Their action will be recognized and experienced as a breach of the relation of love and trust with the authoritative person. An absence of guilt feelings would betray an absence of love and trust. Guilt feelings are shown (among other ways) in the inclination to confess and to ask forgiveness in order to restore the previous relation; they are part of what defines a relation as one of love and trust.

These remarks require further elaboration. Assume that this psychological law holds: the child, moved by certain instincts and regulated only (if at all) by rational self-love, comes to love, and to recognize the love of, the parent if the parent manifestly loves the child.[2] The parents' love of the child involves an evident intention to care for the child, to do for him as his rational self-love inclines; it involves taking joy in his presence, the support of his sense of competence, and manifest pleasure at his success. One may suppose that in time the love of the parent will foster in the child an equal love for the parent, and that while the capacity for love is innate it requires special circumstances for its development. The parents' love for the child, then, may explain a child's love for his parents; his love for them does not have—indeed, cannot have—a rational explanation in terms of his antecedent instincts and desires. He does not love them in order to insure, say, his security, although he could seem to love them for this reason. That his love of them does not have a rational explanation follows from the concept of

---

[1] The natural attitudes may also be taken as given by enumeration, and thus as being, for example, love and affection, faith and mutual trust. When it is claimed, then, that affection, say, implies a liability to feelings of guilt, this claim depends on the concepts of affection and of guilt feelings. It does not require a definition of a natural attitude and of a moral feeling.

[2] The formulation of this psychological law is drawn from Rousseau's *Emile* (see p. 174). Rousseau says that while we love from the start what contributes to our preservation, this attachment is quite unconscious and instinctive. What transforms this instinctive liking for others into love is their 'evident intention of helping us'.

love: to love another is to care for him for his own sake as his rational self-love would incline. The child's love of his parents has an explanation —namely, that they first loved him—but not a rational explanation by reference to his original self-love.

If, then, one accepts this psychological principle and assumes that the child's love is an ordered structure of dispositions, or a sentiment, how will it show itself? Here it is necessary to keep in mind the peculiar feature of the authority situation: namely, that the child does not have his own standards of criticism. He is not in a position rationally to reject parental injunctions, so that, if he loves and trusts them, he will accept their precepts. He will also strive to live up to them as worthy objects of esteem, and he will accept their way of judging him. He will impose on himself the standards they embody, and he will judge himself as they would when he violates their precepts. The child will do these things, given his peculiar position in the authority situation, if he does, as we assume, love and trust his parents. At the same time, the child is tempted to transgress the parental precepts. He may wish to rebel against their authority which, in so far as the parents succeed in giving him self-esteem, is a humiliating reminder of his dependence. His own desires may exceed the limits of what is permitted, so that the precepts are experienced as unbearable constraints. The child will have feelings of hatred for the parents, but if he loves them, then once he has given in to temptation and violated their injunctions, he will in part take up their attitude towards himself. He will be disposed to reveal his fault by confession and to seek reconcilation. One who is ashamed redeems himself by successful achievement, but one subject to authority guilt wants to be forgiven and to have the previous relation restored. In these various inclinations and their expression are shown the feelings of guilt. Their absence would manifest an absence of love and trust.

IV

The second part of the psychological construction describes the generation of association guilt. The setting of this form of guilt involves the participation in a joint activity of those who regard themselves as associates. These joint activities may take various forms from social institutions proper to games. I assume it is known to all the participants that the rules defining the scheme of co-operation do in fact satisfy the two principles of justice, and I also suppose that the derivation of these principles, as given in the analytic construction, is understood.[1] This knowledge may be more or less intuitive, but I assume that these facts are nevertheless known.

Now let us suppose that, given a system of joint activity meeting these conditions—perhaps some scheme of economic co-operation—the participants are bound by ties of friendship and mutual trust, and rely on one another to do their part. I suppose that these feelings have been generated in any given person by his participating in the activity itself. I assume as a second psychological law that if a person's capacity for fellow-feeling has been realized in accordance with the first law, then, where another, engaged with him in a joint activity known to satisfy the two principles, with evident intention lives up to his duty of fair play, friendly feelings towards him develop as well as feelings of trust and mutual confidence. (One may suppose the participants introduced into the scheme one by one over a period of time, and in this way acquiring these feelings as the others fulfil their duty of fair play.) So if participants in a joint enterprise regularly act with evident intention in accordance with their duty of fair play, they will tend to acquire ties of friendship and mutual trust.

Now given these feelings and relations against the background of a scheme of co-operation known to satisfy the stated conditions, if a person fails to do his part he will experience feelings of association guilt. These feelings will show themselves in various ways: in the inclination to make good the loss to others (reparation) and to admit what one has done and to apologize; in the inclination to ask for reinstatement and to acknowledge and to accept reproofs and penalties; and in a diminished ability to be angry with others should they likewise fail to do their part. The absence of such inclinations would betray the absence of ties of friendship and relations of mutual trust. It would manifest a capacity to associate with others in disregard of those principles which one knows would be mutually acknowledged. It would show that one had no qualms about the losses inflicted on others (or gains taken from them) as a consequence of one's own acts, and that one was not troubled by the breaches of mutual confidence by which others are deceived. If there are ties of friendship and mutual trust, there exist these various inhibitions and reactions to failing to do one's part. If these inhibitions and reactions are lacking, one has at best

[1] The satisfaction of these principles is strictly necessary only in the case of the fundamental structure of the social system in which each begins; but no essential generality is lost by taking these principles as satisfied. This assumption has the advantage of making the argument less abstract and of illustrating the way in which principles of justice enter into the formulation of the psychological laws of the construction.

only a show of fellow-feeling and mutual trust.

It may be observed that the effect of the second psychological law and the attitudes generated by it play an important part in maintaining schemes of co-operation known to satisfy the two principles of justice (stated in Section II). For such schemes are liable to at least two types of instability. Instability of the first kind is present when, if any one person knows that the others will do their part, it will be worth his while not to do his: the consequences of one person's not doing his part if others do theirs may go unnoticed, or may have no ostensible effect, so that an alternative use of one's time and effort is a personal gain. Such a system of co-operation is unstable: each is tempted to depart from it if he thinks others will keep it going. Since each is aware of another's temptation, mutual trust is in danger of breaking down. Instability of the second kind is present when it is the case that if any one person knows or reasonably supposes that others will not do their part, it will be worth his while to be the first, or among the first, not to do his, or even dangerous for him not to be. These two kinds of instability are related in that if the first kind obtains, then one may think that others will not do their part, and this may bring about instability of the second kind. Where both kinds are present the scheme of co-operation is fragile and participants are moved to withdraw, or even to be afraid not to. (Disarmament schemes are subject to instability of both kinds.) Hobbes seems to have been the first to place the problem of such unstable situations at the centre of the question of political obligation. One way of interpreting the Hobbesian sovereign is as an agency added to unstable systems of co-operation in such a way that it is no longer to anyone's advantage not to do his part given that others will do theirs. By keeping watch and enforcing sanctions, the sovereign acts to inhibit violations and to restore the system when violations occur; and the belief in the sovereign's efficacy removes instability of both kinds.[1]

Now relations of friendship and mutual trust have a similar effect. Once a system of co-operation satisfying the stated conditions is set up and a period of uncertainty survived, the passage of time renders it more stable, given an evident intention on the part of all to do their part. The generation of feelings of friendship and mutual trust tends to reinforce the scheme of co-operation. A greater temptation is required and, should violations occur, the feelings of guilt, shown in

[1] On this topic, see W. J. Baumol, *Welfare Economics and the Theory of the State* (London, 1952). Illuminating also is the discussion in R. D. Luce and H. Raiffa, *Games and Decisions* (New York, 1957), ch. v.

wishing to make reparation and the like, will tend to restore the broken relations. Thus not only may such a system of co-operation be stable in the sense that when each man thinks the others will do their part there is no tendency for him not to do his; it may be inherently stable in the sense that the persistence of the scheme generates, in accordance with the second psychological law, inclinations which further support it. The effect, then, of relations of friendship and mutual trust is analogous to the role of the sovereign; only in this case it is the consequence of a certain psychological principle of human nature in such systems, and of the implications of the generated attitudes.

V

The third part of the psychological construction concerns principle guilt. In both the previous forms of guilt I have supposed it to be connected with an actual natural attitude towards certain particular persons: with authority guilt these persons are parents, and in association guilt they are fellow-associates. Very often, however, we feel guilty for doing something when those injured or put at a disadvantage are not persons with whom we are tied by any form of particular fellow-feeling. To account for feelings of guilt of this kind—principle guilt—I assume a third psychological law as follows: given that the attitudes of love and trust, friendly feelings and mutual respect, have been generated in accordance with the two previous psychological laws, then, if a person (and his associates) are the beneficiaries of a successful and enduring institution or scheme of co-operation known to satisfy the two principles of justice, he will acquire a sense of justice. This will show itself in at least two ways: first, in an acceptance of those particular institutions which are just (as defined by the two principles) and from which he and his associates have benefited. This acceptance of particular institutions shows itself in feeling guilty for infractions which harm other persons even though these persons are not the objects of any particular fellow-feelings. It may be that they have not yet had sufficient opportunity to show an evident intention of doing their part, and so are not yet the object of such feelings by the second law. Or it may be that the institution is too large to allow occasion for such particular ties to be established. The sense of justice will manifest itself second in a willingness to work for (or at least not to oppose) the setting up of just institutions, or for the reform of existing ones where justice requires it. Guilt feelings associated with the sense of justice are characterized as principle guilt feelings since in their explanation reference is made to principles, in this case to principles of justice. These principle guilt feelings spring from breaches of institutions accepted as satisfying the principles of justice, or from resistance to reforms which these principles are seen to require.

Principle guilt is, then, connected with the acceptance of the principles of justice. It represents a step beyond the understanding of their derivation which is all that is presupposed by association guilt. One might say that principle guilt is guilt proper. It is, as the two previous forms of guilt were not, a complete moral feeling. For this reason authority and association guilt should be spoken of with the prefixed adjective. They are not, as defined, complete moral feelings although they include many of the characteristic aspects of moral feelings. Once the full development to principle guilt has taken place, however, and the principles of justice which specify the conditions of association guilt are accepted, then the infractions which gave rise to association guilt will be guilt proper; for now the reference to the accepted principle is given in a person's explanation of his feeling. Furthermore, where the ties of natural attitudes are present in the form of friendship and mutual trust, the feelings of guilt will be greater than where they are absent. The transmuted association guilt will reinforce principle guilt. If one assumes that an appropriate guilt feeling—that is, one based on true beliefs concerning what one has done—implies a fault, and that a greater feeling of guilt implies a greater fault, one can infer that conduct giving rise to association guilt feelings is wrong. Thus all the violations of the natural attitudes generated by association—in particular friendship, affection, and mutual trust—are wrong.

The sense of justice helps to maintain schemes of co-operation just as the natural attitudes of friendship and trust do. The acceptance of the principles of justice implies, failing a special explanation, an avoidance of their violation and a recognition that advantages gained in conflict with them are without value; and should such violations nevertheless occur, in cases of temptation, feelings of guilt will tend to restore joint activity. To grasp this fact, one has only to consider the variety of inclinations and inhibitions in which these feelings are expressed. A system in which each person has, and is known by everyone to have, a sense of justice is inherently stable. Other things being equal, the forces making for its stability increase as time passes. (It may nevertheless break down at a later time if outside elements make for increasingly greater temptations.) This inherent stability is a direct consequence of the reciprocal relation between the second and third psychological laws. The psychological construction as a whole is consistent and self-reinforcing: it is intrinsically stable. To explain this properly one would have to bring the institutions constituting the setting for authority guilt under the regulation of the principles of justice, but there is no insuperable difficulty in this.

VI

It is evident that the foregoing psychological construction relies heavily on the concept of a moral feeling. It will prove useful to make a brief digression and to discuss the main features of this concept. These features may be given by considering the chief questions which must be asked in examining the concept of the various moral feelings.[1]

There are, first, such questions as: (*a*) What are the various linguistic expressions which are used to give voice to the having of a particular moral feeling, and the significant variations, if any, between the expressions for different feelings? (*b*) What are the characteristic behavioural manifestations of a particular moral feeling, and what are the ways in which a person characteristically betrays how he feels? (*c*) What are the characteristic sensations and kinesthetic feelings, if any, which go with a given moral feeling? When a person is angry, for example, he may feel hot; he may tremble and feel a tightening in his stomach; he may be unable to talk without his voice shaking; or he may be unable to suppress certain gestures. But if there are such characteristic sensations and behavioural manifestations for at least some moral feelings, these will not be, in any case, guilt, or shame, or whatever the feeling is. Such characteristic sensations and manifestations are neither necessary nor sufficient in particular instances for someone to feel guilty or ashamed. This is not to deny that some characteristic sensations and behavioural manifestations of disturbance may be necessary if one is overwhelmed by feelings of guilt, or if one is intensely ashamed. To feel guilty or ashamed it is often sufficient, however, that a person sincerely say that he feels guilty or ashamed, provided that he has the concept of guilt or shame and that he is prepared to give an appropriate explanation of why he feels as he does.

This fact introduces perhaps the main question in examining the moral feelings, namely: (*d*) what is the definitive type of explanation

[1] These questions are, I think, the direct consequence of applying to the concepts of the moral feelings the forms of analysis used by Wittgenstein in the *Philosophical Investigations* (Oxford, 1953). See also, for example, what G. E. M. Anscombe says about anger in 'Pretending', *Proceedings of the Aristotelian Society*, Supp. Vol. XXXII (1958), 285–9, and what Philippa Foot says about pride and fear in 'Moral Beliefs', *Proceedings of the Aristotelian Society*, LIX (1958–9), 86–9.

required for having a given moral feeling, and how do these explanations differ from one feeling to another? Thus, when someone says that he feels guilty, what sort of explanation do we expect and within what limits? Certainly not any account is acceptable. Even such a pheno-menon as neurotic guilt feelings, which is recognized as a deviation from the definitive case, is accepted as a kind of guilt feeling only because of the special kind of explanation accepted for these departures from the norm, and because it is supposed that a fuller psychological investigation will reveal the similarity with other guilt feelings. In general, it is a necessary condition and a defining feature of moral feelings that the person's explanation invokes a moral concept and its associated principle(s) and thereby makes a reference to an acknowledged right or a wrong.[1] For example, a person feels guilty because he knows that he has taken more than his share and treated others unfairly, or a person feels ashamed because he has been cowardly and not spoken out. What distinguishes the different moral feelings is the principles and faults which their explanations typically invoke. The same act may give rise to both guilt and shame, say, if the person regards the action, as it is often possible to do, as each feeling requires. One who cheats may feel both guilty and ashamed: guilty because he has violated a trust and unfairly advanced himself, ashamed because by resorting to such means he admits his lack of ability and has given in to weakness. It may be remarked here that for a person to have a moral feeling it is not necessary that everything asserted in his explanation be true. A person may be in error, for example, in thinking that he has taken more than his share. He may not be guilty. But his explanation is in order since it is of the right sort and the beliefs it expresses are sincere.

Next, there is a group of questions concerning the bearing of the moral feelings on action. Thus, (e) what are the characteristic intentions, endeavours, and inclinations of a person having the feeling; what are the sorts of things he feels like doing, or feels unable to do? An angry person characteristically tries to strike back or to block the purposes of the person at whom he is angry. One who is plagued by authority

[1] Those who question this proposition are likely to offer various forms of guilt feelings as counter-examples. This is easy to understand since the earliest forms of guilt feelings are those of authority guilt, and we are unlikely to grow up without having what one may call residue-guilt feelings. For example, a person raised in a strict religious sect may have been taught that going to the theatre is wrong. While he no longer believes this, he tells us that he still feels guilty when attending the theatre. But these are not proper guilt feelings, since he is not about to apologize to anyone, or to resolve not to attend again, and so on. Indeed, he should say rather that he has certain sensations and feelings of uneasiness, and the like, which resemble those which he has when he feels guilty.

guilt is disposed to reveal his fault and to attempt to set matters right by confession and reconciliation, whereas one who suffers from association guilt is inclined to admit what he has done and to ask for reinstatement, to acknowledge and to accept reproofs and penalties, and also he finds himself less able to be angry with others when they behave wrongly. Again, one can ask: (f) What feelings and responses does a person having the feeling expect on the part of other persons, and how does he anticipate that they will act towards him, as this is shown, say, in various characteristic distortions in his interpretation of others' conduct towards him? Also, (g) what are the characteristic temptations to actions giving rise to the given feeling and how characteristically is the feeling resolved or gotten rid of? Some such connections with action are also, in addition to an appropriate explanation, a necessary condition for having a moral feeling. (The last two questions have played little part in the construction which sets out the forms of guilt feeling, but they would be important, for example, in distinguishing feelings of guilt from feelings of shame.)

Finally, a question which I have emphasized is: (h) what, if any, is the natural basis of a moral feeling? There are two distinct kinds of questions involved here. One is: if a person, given his circumstances, fails to have a certain moral feeling, is there a natural attitude which would thereby be shown to be absent? The other is: if a person, given his circumstances, has a moral feeling, is there a natural attitude which would thereby be shown to be present? In presenting the psychological construction I have been concerned solely with the first kind of question. This construction provides a background for the second kind also, but I have left it entirely aside. Thus I have held that, in the context of the authority situation, the existence of love and trust for those in authority implies feelings of guilt for violating authoritative injunctions, and that the absence of such guilt feelings implies the absence of the natural attitudes of love and trust. Similarly, in the context of associative arrangements, the natural attitudes of friendship, affection, and mutual trust imply feelings of guilt for recognized violations of duties of fair play, and the absence of such guilt feelings implies an absence of the natural attitudes of friendship, affection, and mutual trust. These propositions are not, then, to be confused with their converses, which raise different problems altogether.

The thought here is that, by definition, a natural attitude and a moral feeling are both orderings of certain characteristic dispositions, and that the dispositions connected with the natural attitudes and those connected with the moral feelings are related, in such a way that the

absence of certain moral feelings implies the absence of certain natural
attitudes; or, alternatively, that the presence of certain natural
attitudes implies a liability to certain moral feelings. These propositions are necessary truths: they hold in virtue of the relations
between the concepts of the moral feelings and the natural attitudes.
How this is so may be grasped from an example. If *A* loves *B*, then,
failing a special explanation, *A* is afraid for *B* when *B* is threatened
and tries to ward off the danger; and when *C* attacks *B*, *A* is angry
with *C* and strives to prevent his attack from succeeding. Unless there
are special circumstances, *A* is joyful when together with *B*, and
when *B* suffers injury or dies, *A* is stricken with grief; and so on. Love
is a sentiment—that is, among other things, a set of dispositions to
experience and to manifest these primary emotions in a certain way.[1]
Now the necessary truths of the form mentioned above simply assert
that the disposition to feel guilty in certain circumstances is just as much
a defining feature of the natural attitude of love as the disposition to
be joyful in the other's presence or to be sorrowful at his hurt.

For the argument to follow, the essential points about the moral
feelings are these: (*a*) these feelings are not to be identified with
characteristic sensations and behavioural manifestations, even if those
exist, but must be understood as essentially including certain types
of explanation and certain connections with conduct and natural attitudes; (*b*) these feelings presuppose the acceptance of certain moral
principles which are invoked in their explanation, and in part what
distinguish different feelings are the different principles occurring in
these explanations; and (*c*) these feelings have necessary connections
with certain natural attitudes such as love, affection, and mutual trust,
and were a liability to these feelings completely absent there would
be an absence also of these natural attitudes.

VII

Consider now the second question: namely, what accounts for men's
acting on their duty of justice in particular cases? When they have
a sense of justice, an answer is that they accept the principles of
justice and regard themselves bound to act in accordance with schemes
of co-operation which satisfy these principles when it comes their turn.
This explanation is perfectly satisfactory. Moreover, it is often a sufficient
reason for one's doing one's part that the principles of justice require

---

[1] On this point, see A. F. Shand, *The Foundations of Character*, 2nd ed. (London,
1920), pp. 55 f.

it; or, more generally, that doing so is in accordance with principles which would be acknowledged in an original position of equal liberty. I should like, however, to view the second question in another way. I want to consider what follows from the assumption that certain persons would never act in accordance with their duty of justice except as reasons of self-interest and expediency dictate.

From what was said about association guilt it would follow that between any two such persons participating in a scheme of co-operation there are no ties of friendship and mutual trust. If such ties existed they would accept reasons other than those of expediency and self-interest for their acting fairly. This consequence is relatively obvious. But it also follows that, barring self-deception, these persons are incapable of feeling resentment and indignation towards another's actions as being unjust. If one of them cheats and deceives another, and this is found out, none of them has a ground for complaint. The injured cannot feel resentment; the others cannot feel indignation. They do not accept the principles of justice, and they experience no inhibitions from principle guilt feelings for breaches of their duty of fair play. Resentment and indignation are moral feelings. Resentment is our reaction to the injuries and harms which the wrongs of others inflict upon us, and indignation is our reaction to the injuries which the wrongs of others inflict on others. Both resentment and indignation require, then, an explanation which invokes a moral concept, say the concept of justice, and its associated principles(s) and so makes a reference to a right or a wrong. In order to experience resentment and indignation one must accept the principles which specify these rights and wrongs. By hypothesis the members of this scheme neither accept these principles nor experience any inhibition from principle guilt feelings. Now to deny that these persons are incapable of resentment and indignation is not to say that they might not be angry or annoyed with one another. A person without a sense of justice may be enraged at someone who fails to act fairly. But anger and annoyance are distinct from resentment and indignation; they are not, as resentment and indignation are, moral feelings. No doubt there are many behavioural similarities between these feelings: the emotional display in expression and gesture may sometimes be indistinguishable. Still, the explanation of the feeling will normally enable us to tell them apart.

One may say, then, that a person who lacks a sense of justice and who would never act as justice requires except as self-interest and expediency prompt, not only is without ties of friendship, affection, and mutual trust, but is incapable of experiencing resentment and indignation. Thus a person who lacks a sense of justice is also without certain natural attitudes and certain moral feelings of a particularly elementary kind. Put another way, one who lacks a sense of justice lacks certain fundamental attitudes and capacities included under the notion of humanity. Now the moral feelings are admittedly unpleasant, in some extended sense of unpleasant; but there is no way for us to avoid a liability to them without disfiguring ourselves. This liability is the price of love and trust, of friendship and affection, and of a devotion to institutions and traditions from which we have benefited and which serve the general interests of mankind. Moreover, as long as men are possessed of interests and aspirations of their own, as long as they are prepared in the pursuit of their own ends and ideals to press their claims on one another—that is, so long as the conditions giving rise to questions of justice obtain among them—it is inevitable that, given temptation and passion, this liability will be realized. (Since being moved by ends and ideals of excellence implies a liability to humiliation and shame, and an absence of a liability to humiliation and shame implies a lack of such ends and ideals, one can say of shame and humiliation also that they are a part of the notion of humanity.) Now the fact that one who lacks a sense of justice, and thereby a liability to guilt, lacks thereby certain fundamental attitudes and capacities included under the notion of humanity is not to be taken as a reason for acting as justice dictates. But this fact is an important truth. By understanding what it would be like not to have a sense of justice— that it would be to lack part of our humanity, too—we are led to understand our having this sense.

VIII

Consider now the first question: namely, to whom is the obligation of justice owed, that is, in regard to beings of what kind must we regulate our conduct by the principles of justice? Put another way, what qualifies a being as entitled to hold an initial position of equal liberty, so that in our dealings with him we are required to conduct ourselves in accordance with principles which could be acknowledged in such a position? The answer to this question is that it is necessary and sufficient that the being is capable of a sense of justice. This answer requires some explanation.

First I shall try to show that the capacity for a sense of justice is sufficient. The capacity for a sense of justice includes these capacities: to understand, at least in an intuitive way, the meaning and content of the principles of justice and their application to particular institutions; to understand, at least in an intuitive way, the derivation of these principles as indicated in the analytic construction; and to have the capacities of feeling, attitude, and conduct, mentioned in the three laws of the psychological construction. None of these capacities imposes conditions which are at all stringent, and I assume that they are satisfied to the required degree by the vast majority of mankind. Now the thought behind taking the capacity for a sense of justice as sufficient is that the principles of justice are characterized as those principles which persons could propose to one another for mutual acceptance in an original position of equal liberty. In this position it is assumed that there is an absence of information; in particular, it is assumed that the parties do not know their social position, nor do they know their peculiar talents and abilities—that is, their native assets. Briefly, they do not know how they have fared in the natural lottery. Nevertheless, in the original position, knowing the possibility (or allowing for it) of different native endowments, it is rational for them to acknowledge the two principles of justice. These principles require that any special benefits for those more fortunate in the natural lottery must be gained in ways which at the same time improve the condition of the less fortunate. The parties in the original positions are assumed to be moral persons abstracted from certain kinds of knowledge of themselves and their situation. Yet they have the capacity to understand and to give the undertaking which the analytic construction describes, and then to act on it: that is, they have the capacity expressed by the sense of justice. To say that the sense of justice is sufficient is to say, then, that the duty of justice is owed to those who could participate in the contractual situation of the original position and act on it. And, indeed, this is sufficient, for in the conception of justice of the analytic construction the consequences of the natural lottery are irrelevant in the original position. The unknown distribution of talents and abilities may, however, be exploited in accordance with principles which everyone in the original position would acknowledge.

Moreover, the capacity for a sense of justice need be possessed only to the extent required for participation in the original position. Certainly some persons have a greater capacity for a sense of justice than others. These persons may properly be placed in positions where the judicial virtues are especially fitting, but their superior capacity should be regarded as any other advantage in the natural lottery, the benefits from it being subject to the principles of justice. A special capacity for a sense of justice may qualify a man for certain offices, then, but assuming that a certain minimum is satisfied, these peculiar gifts are not a proper ground for establishing different grades of citizenship The minimum is sufficient to share in the position of equal citizenship in a constitutional democracy.[1]

To show that a capacity for a sense of justice is necessary is perhaps more difficult. One has a reluctance, moreover, to admit that this capacity is necessary, for one is averse to granting that any human being might not be owed the duty of justice. Yet if one holds that a capacity for a sense of justice is necessary and that a human being may lack this capacity, one allows for this possibility. But perhaps this reluctance is merely the aversion to admitting that any human being is incapable of a sense of justice. In any case, it seems almost certain that at least the vast majority of mankind have a capacity for a sense of justice and that, for all practical purposes, one may safely assume that all men originally possess it. It is plausible to suppose that any being capable of language is capable of the intellectual performances required to have a sense of justice; and, given these intellectual powers, the capacity for the natural attitudes of love and affection, faith and mutual trust, appears to be universal. There seems to be no doubt then that the minimum requisites for the development of a sense of justice are possessed by men as part of their original natural capacity, and it is this original capacity which is said to be necessary. It is another question entirely whether the duty of justice is owed to persons who, although they possessed the capacity originally, have lost it through no fault of their own: through illness or accident, or from experiencing such a deprivation of affection in childhood that their capacity for the natural attitudes has not developed properly.

The following considerations may show that a capacity for a sense of justice is necessary. First, it does not follow from a person's not being owed the duty of justice that he may be treated in any way that one pleases. We do not normally think of ourselves as owing the duty of justice to animals, but it is certainly wrong to be cruel to them. Their capacity for feeling pleasure and pain, for some form of happiness, is enough to establish this. To deny that this capacity is sufficient is not, then, to licence everything. Other faults will still be possible, since the principles of humanity and liberality are more extensive in their application. On the other hand, something must account for animals not being owed the duty of justice, and a plausible explanation is their

---

[1] The manner in which the conception of justice as fairness requires such a position I have tried to show in the essay mentioned in footnote 1, p. 122.

lack of the capacity for a sense of justice and the other capacities which this sense presupposes.

Again one might say that the duty of justice is owed only to those who can complain of not being justly treated. Since, as previously argued, a person lacking a sense of justice cannot himself complain nor feel resentment if others do not act in regard to him as the principles of justice require, the duty of justice, it might be held, is not owed to him. This suggestion follows from the idea that if a person has a right to something, it must be that he can claim it and protest its not being given him. This idea is not incompatible with there being persons who claim rights for others in certain types of situations. For example, one thinks of guardians for children and of trustees for others' rights in special cases. In the instance of children, one supposes that the capacity for a sense of justice is there and only awaits development. Guardians must secure this development and they must decide for their wards in view of what a person is presumed to want and to claim once he reaches the age of reason. The case at hand, however, supposes that there never was nor will there ever be the capacity. If it is said that others might nevertheless complain, one could say that the duty, if there is one, is owed to them. In any case, the analytic construction excludes this possibility *qua* the initial position, so that accepting this basis of the necessity of a sense of justice would accord with that construction.

Finally, one may follow Kant in holding that a good will or, in the present case, a sense of justice is a necessary condition of the worthiness to be happy.[1] One may hold that the sense of justice is a necessary part of the dignity of the person, and that it is this dignity which puts a value upon the person distinct from and logically prior to his capacity for enjoyment and his ability to contribute to the enjoyment of others through the development of his talents. It is because of this dignity that the conception of justice as fairness is correct in viewing each person as an individual sovereign, as it were, none of whose interests are to be sacrificed for the sake of a greater net balance of happiness but rather only in accordance with principles which all could acknowledge in an initial position of equal liberty.[2] In the absence of a sense of justice on everyone's part, there would be, it might be said, no objection to the utilitarianism principle. In the absence of this capacity, the liability to pleasure and pain, to joy and sorrow, might be taken

---

[1] See *Grundlegung zur Metaphysik der Sitten, Gesammelte Schriften*, ed. by the Royal Prussian Academy (Berlin, 1903), IV, 393, 434–6.

[2] This conception of justice may be said to express the sense of Kant's thought that persons must never be treated as means simply but always at the same time as an end. See *Grundlegung*, 427–31.

as alone relevant, and the greatest happiness principle would be entirely natural. Certainly in the absence of the capacity for a sense of justice no one could complain if the utilitarian principle were applied, and so the possession of a sense of justice is necessary for the conception of justice as fairness to hold. But lack of a sense of justice would undermine our capacity to identify ourselves with and to care about a society of such persons, if such a society could exist. We would not be moved by its injustices, since what they cannot resent and be indignant about among themselves we cannot resent and be indignant about for them. This is not to say that we might not be moved by the cruelties of such a society, but from the standpoint of justice, it would not be a society which aroused our moral feelings.

The capacity for a sense of justice is, then, necessary and sufficient for the duty of justice to be owed to a person—that is, for a person to be regarded as holding an initial position of equal liberty. This means that one's conduct in relation to him must be regulated by the principles of justice or, more generally, by the principles which rational and self-interested persons could acknowledge before one another in such a position. This conclusion may be contrasted with two other possible views. It is distinct from classical utilitarianism which holds that a capacity for pleasure and pain, for joy and sorrow, is sufficient for being a full subject of rights. The conclusion is also distinct from an aristocratic ethic which takes as necessary certain attributes and capacities such as strength, beauty, and superior intelligence, and which would impose the requirement of initial equality only within the same rank and allow original inequalities between superior and lower ranks. Such an aristocratic doctrine can only be maintained, I think, if one assumes a specific obligation on the parties in the original position: namely, the obligation to develop human persons of a certain style and aesthetic grace, or the obligation to the pursuit of knowledge and the cultivation of the arts, or both. I cannot discuss here the propriety of this assumption, or whether if it were accepted it would justify the inequalities commonly associated with aristocracy. It suffices to say that in the analytic construction no such obligation is assumed. The sole constraints imposed are those expressed in the formal elements of the concept of morality, and the only circumstances assumed are those exhibiting the conflicts of claims which give rise to questions of justice. The natural consequence of this construction is that the capacity for the sense of justice is the fundamental aspect of moral personality in the theory of justice.

XI

HUMAN WORTH, MERIT, AND EQUALITY

Gregory Vlastos

LET ME begin with the first on my list of maxims of distributive justice:
'To each according to his need.' Since needs are often unequal, this
looks like a precept of unequal distribution. But this is wrong. It is
in fact *the most perfect form of equal distribution*. To explain this
let me take one of the best established rights in the natural law tradition:
the right to the security of life and person. Believing that this is an
equal right, what do we feel this means in cases of special need?

Suppose, for instance, New Yorker X gets a note from Murder, Inc.,
that looks like business. To allocate several policemen and plain clothes
men to guard him over the next few weeks at a cost a hundred times
greater than the per capita cost of security services to other citizens
during the same period, is surely *not* to make an exception to the equal
distribution required by the equal right of all citizens to the security
of their life and person; it is not done on the assumption that X has
a greater right to security or a right to greater security. If the visitor
from Mars drew this conclusion from the behaviour of the police,
he would be told that he was just mistaken. The greater allocation of
community resources in X's favour, we would have to explain, is made
precisely *because* X's security rights are equal to those of other people
in New York. This means that X is entitled to the same level of police-
made security as is maintained for other New Yorkers. Hence in these
special circumstances, where his security level would drop to zero without extra support, he should be given this to bring his security level
nearer the normal. I say 'nearer', not 'up to' the normal, because I am
talking of New York as of 1961. If I were thinking of New York with
an ideal municipal government, ideally supplied with police resources,
I *would* say 'up to the normal', because that is what equality of right
would ideally mean. But as things are, perhaps the best that can be
done for X without disrupting the general level of security maintained
for all the other New Yorkers is to decrease his chances of being

Part II of 'Justice and Equality', by Gregory Vlastos, from *Social Justice*, ed.
Richard B. Brandt, © 1962 (Prentice-Hall, 1962), pp. 41–53. Reprinted by permission
of Prentice-Hall, Inc., Englewood Cliffs, New Jersey, U.S.A.

bumped off in a given week to, say, one to ten thousand, while those of ordinary citizens, with ordinary protection are, say, one to ten million—no small difference.[1] Now if New York were more affluent, it would be able to buy more equality[2] of security for its citizens (as well as more security): by getting more, and perhaps also better paid, policemen, it would be able to close the gap between security maintained for people in ordinary circumstances and that supplied in cases of special need, like that of X in his present jam. Here we stumble on something of considerable interest: that approximation to the goal of completely equal security benefits for all citizens is a function of two variables: first, and quite obviously, of the pattern of distribution of the resources; second, and less obviously, of their size. If the distributable resources are so meagre that they are all used up to maintain a general level barely sufficient for ordinary needs, their reallocation to meet exceptional need will look too much like robbing Peter to pay Paul. In such conditions there is likely to be little, if any, provision for extremity of need and, what is more, the failure to meet the extremity will not be felt as a social injustice but as a calamity of fate. And since humanity has lived most of its life under conditions of general indigence, we can understand why it has been so slow to connect provision for special need with the notion of justice, and has so often made it a matter of charity; and why 'to each according to his need' did not become popularized as a precept of justice until the first giant increase in the productive resources, and then only by men like Blanc and Marx, who projected an image of a superaffluent, machine-run society on the grid of an austerely equalitarian conception of justice.[3]

So we can see why distribution according to personal need, far from conflicting with the equality of distribution required by a human right, is so linked with its very meaning that under ideal conditions equality

---

[1] These figures, needless to say, are 'pulled out of a hat'.

[2] This point was first suggested to me by Professor Kenneth Boulding's striking remark that 'only a rich society can afford to be equalitarian', *The Economics of Peace* (Englewood Cliffs, N.J.: Prentice-Hall, 1945), p. 111. The more guarded form in which I am stating the point will protect it against apparent counter-examples to Boulding's remark, e.g., the astonishing equalitarianism that was still practised by the Eskimos of the Coronation Gulf and the Mackenzie River early in this century (see V. Stefansson's essay in *Freedom*, Ruth N. Anshen, ed., [New York: Harcourt, Brace and World, 1940]).

[3] The well-known maxim, 'from each according to his ability, to each according to his need' (Karl Marx, *Critique of the Gotha Programme*, 1875), echoes, without acknowledgment, a remark in the 9th edition of Louis Blanc's *L'Organization du travail* (Paris, 1850) that 'true equality' is that 'which apportions work to ability and recompense to needs' (cited in D. O. Wagner, *Social Reformers* [New York: The Macmillan Co., 1946], p. 218).

of right would coincide with distribution according to personal need. Our visitor misunderstood the sudden mobilization of New York policemen in favour of Mr. X, because he failed to understand that it is benefits to persons, not allocation of resources as such, that are meant to be made equal; for then he would have seen at once that unequal distribution of resources would be required to equalize benefits in cases of unequal need. But if he saw this he might then ask, 'But why do you want this sort of equality?' My answer would have to be: Because the human worth of all persons is equal, however unequal may be their merit. To the explanation of this proposition I shall devote the balance of this Section.

By 'merit' I shall refer throughout this essay to all the kinds of valuable qualities or performances in respect of which persons may be graded.[1] The concept will not be restricted to moral actions or dispositions.[2] Thus wit, grace of manner and technical skill count as meritorious qualities fully as much as sincerity, generosity, or courage. Any valuable human characteristic, or cluster of characteristics, will qualify, provided only it is 'acquired', i.e., represents what its possessor has himself made of his natural endowments and environmental opportunities. Given the immense variety of individual differences, it will be commonly the case that of any two persons either may excel the other in respect of different kinds or sub-kinds of merit. Thus if A and B are both clever and brave men, A may be much the cleverer as a business man, B as a literary critic, and A may excel in physical, B in moral, courage. It should be clear from just this that to speak of 'a person's merit' will be strictly senseless except in so far as this is an elliptical way of referring to that person's merits, i.e., to those specifiable qualities or activities in which he rates well. So if there is a value attaching to the person himself as an integral and unique individual, *this* value will not fall under merit or be reducible to it. For it is of the essence of merit, as here defined, to be a grading concept; and there is no way of grading individuals as such. We can only grade them with respect to their qualities, hence only by abstracting from their individuality. If A is valued for some meritorious quality, m, his individuality does not enter into the valuation. As an individual he is

---

[1] This is only one of the senses recognized by the dictionary (*The Shorter Oxford English Dictionary*, s.v., 4 and 6): 'Excellence', 'An Excellence', the latter being illustrated by 'Would you ask for his merits? Alas! he has none' (from Goldsmith). In the other senses listed by the dictionary the word either *means* 'desert' or at least includes this in its meaning. On the present use of 'merit' the connection with 'desert' is synthetic.

[2] As is done by some philosophical moralists, e.g., Sir David Ross, op. cit., pp. 135 ff., where 'merit' and (moral) 'virtue' are co-extensive.

then dispensable; his place could be taken without loss of value by any other individual with as good an *m*-rating. Nor would matters change by multiplying and diversifying the meritorious qualities with which *A* is endowed. No matter how enviable a package of well-rounded excellence *A* may represent, it would still follow that, if he is valued only for his merit, he is not being valued as an individual. To be sure individuals *may* be valued only for their merits. This happens all too commonly. *A* might be valued in just this way by *P*, the president of his company, for whom *A*, highly successful vice-president in charge of sales, amusing dinner-guest, and fine asset to the golf club, is simply high-grade equipment in various complexes of social machinery which *P* controls or patronizes. On the other hand, it is possible that, much as *P* prizes this conjunct of qualities (*M*), he values *A* also as an individual. *A* may be his son, and he may be genuinely fond of him. If so, his affection will be for *A*, not for his *M*-qualities. The latter *P* approves, admires, takes pride in, and the like. But his affection and good will are for *A*, and *not only because*, or *in so far as*, *A* has the *M*-qualities. For *P* may be equally fond of another son who rates well below *A* in *P*'s scoring system. Moreover, *P*'s affection for *A*, as distinct from his approval or admiration of him, need not fluctuate with the ups and downs in *A*'s achievements. Perhaps *A* had some bad years after graduating from college, and it looked then as though his brilliant gifts would be wasted. It does not follow that *P*'s love for *A* then lapsed or even ebbed. Constancy of affection in the face of variations of merit is one of the surest tests of whether or not a parent does love a child. If he feels fond of it only when it performs well, and turns coldly indifferent or hostile when its achievements slump, then his feeling for the child can scarcely be called *love*. There are many relations in which one's liking or esteem for a person are strictly conditional on his measuring up to certain standards. But convincing evidence that the relation is of this type is no evidence that the relation is one of parental love or any other kind of love. It does nothing to show that one has this feeling, or any feeling, for an *individual*, rather than for a place-holder of qualities one likes to see instantiated by somebody or other close about one.

Now if this concept of value attaching to a person's individual exist-ence, over and above his merit—'individual worth',[1] let me call it—

---

[1] That this is *intrinsic* worth goes without saying. But I do not put this term into my label, since I want to distinguish this kind of value as sharply as possible from that of merit, and I include under 'merit' not only extrinsically, but also intrinsically, valuable qualities.

were applicable *only* in relations of personal love, it would be irrelevant for the analysis of justice. To serve our purpose its range of application must be co-extensive with that of justice. It must hold in all human relations, including (or rather, especially in) the most impersonal of all, those to total strangers, fellow-citizens or fellow-men. I must show that the concept of individual worth does meet this condition.

Consider its role in our political community, taking the prescriptions of our laws for the treatment of persons as the index to our valuations. For merit (among other reasons) persons may be appointed or elected to public office or given employment by state agencies. For demerit they may lose licences, jobs, offices; they may be fined, jailed, or even put to death. But in a large variety of law-regulated actions directed to individuals, either by private persons or by organs of the state, the question of merit and demerit does not arise. The 'equal protection of the laws' is due to persons not to meritorious ones, or to them in some degree above others.[1] So too for the right to vote. One does not have it for being intelligent and public-spirited, or lose it for being lazy, ignorant, or viciously selfish. One is entitled to exercise it as long as, having registered, one manages to keep out of jail. This kind of arrangement would look like whimsy or worse, like sheer immoralism, if the only values recognized in our political community were those of merit. For obviously there is nothing compulsory about our political system; we could certainly devise, if we so wished, workable alternatives which would condition fundamental rights on certain kinds of merit. For example, we might have three categories of citizenship. The top one might be for those who meet high educational qualifications and give definite evidence of responsible civic interest, e.g., by active participation in political functions, tenure of public office, record of leadership in civic organizations and support to them, and the like. People in this *A*-category might have multiple votes in all elections and exclusive eligibility for the more important political offices; they might also be entitled to a higher level of protection by the police and to a variety of other privileges and immunities. At the other end there would be a *C*-category, disfranchised and legally underprivileged, for those who do not meet some lower educational test or have had a record of law-infraction or have been on the relief rolls for over three months. In

[1] A modicum of merit by way of self-help and law-obedience is generally presupposed. But it would be a mistake to think of the protection of the laws as a reward for good behaviour. Thus many legal protections are due as much to those who will not look out for themselves as to those who do, and to law-breakers as much as to law-observers.

between would be the *B*'s with ordinary suffrage and intermediate legal status.

This '*M*-system' would be more complicated and cumbersome than ours. But something like it could certainly be made to work if we were enamoured of its peculiar scheme of values. Putting aside the question of efficiency, it gives us a picture of a community whose political valuations, conceived entirely in terms of merit, would never be grounded on individual worth, so that this notion would there be politically useless.[1] For us, on the other hand, it is indispensable.[2] We have to appeal to it when we try to make sense of the fact that our legal system accords to all citizens an identical status, carrying with it rights such as the *M*-system reserves to the *B*'s or the *A*'s, and some of which (like suffrage or freedom of speech) have been denied even to the nobility in some caste-systems of the past. This last comparison is worth pressing: it brings out the illuminating fact that in one fundamental respect our society is much more like a caste society (with a *unique* caste) than like the *M*-system. The latter has no place for a rank of dignity which descends on an individual by the purely existential circumstance (the 'accident') of birth and remains his unalterably for life. To reproduce this feature of our system we would have to look not only to caste-societies, but to extremely rigid ones, since most of them make some provision for elevation in rank for rare merit or degradation for extreme demerit. In our legal system no such thing can happen: even a criminal may not be sentenced to second-class citizenship.[3] And the fact that first-class citizenship, having been made common, is no longer a mark of distinction does not trivialize the privileges it entails. It is the simple truth, not declamation, to speak of it, as I have done, as a 'rank of dignity' in some ways comparable to that enjoyed by hereditary nobilities of the past. To see this one need only think of the position of groups in our society who have been cheated out of this status by the subversion of their constitutional rights. The difference in social position between Negroes and whites described in Dollard's classic[4] is not smaller than

---

[1] Though it might have uses in the family or other relations.

[2] Even where a purely pragmatic justification is offered for democracy (e.g., Pendleton Herring, *Politics of Democracy* [New York: W. W. Norton & Co., 1940]) equality of worth must still be acknowledged, if only as a popular 'myth' or 'dogma'.

[3] No one, I trust, will confuse second-class citizenship with extreme punishments, such as the death-penalty or a life-sentence, or, for that matter, with *any* legal punishment in a democratic society. Second-class citizens are those deprived of rights without any presumption of legal guilt.

[4] John Dollard, *Caste and Class in a Southern Town* (New Haven: Yale University Press, 1937).

that between, say, bourgeoisie and aristocracy in the *ancien régime* of France. It might well be greater.

Consider finally the role of the same value in the moral community. Here differences of merit are so conspicuous and pervasive that we might even be tempted to *define* the moral response to a person in terms of moral approval or disapproval of his acts or disposition, i.e., in terms of the response to his moral merit. But there are many kinds of moral response for which a person's merit is as irrelevant as is that of New Yorker *X* when he appeals to the police for help. If I see someone in danger of drowning I will not need to satisfy myself about his moral character before going to his aid. I owe assistance to any man in such circumstances, not merely to good men. Nor is it only in rare and exceptional cases, as this example might suggest, that my obligations to others are independent of their moral merit. To be sincere, reliable, fair, kind, tolerant, unintrusive, modest in my relations with my fellows is not due them because they have made brilliant or even passing moral grades, but simply because they happen to be fellow-members of the moral community. It is not necessary to add, 'members in good standing'. The moral community is not a club from which members may be dropped for delinquency. Our morality does not provide for moral outcasts or half-castes. It does provide for punishment. But this takes place *within* the moral community and under its rules. It is for this reason that, for example, one has no right to be cruel to a cruel person. His offence against the moral law has not put him outside the law. He is still protected by its prohibition of cruelty—as much so as are kind persons. The pain inflicted on him as punishment for his offence does not close the reserve of good will on the part of all others which is his birthright as a human being; it is a limited withdrawal from it. Capital punishment, if we believe in it, is no exception. The fact that a man has been condemned to death does not licence his jailors to beat him or virtuous citizens to lynch him.

Here, then, as in the single-status political community, we acknowledge personal rights which are not proportioned to merit and could not be justified by merit. Their only justification could be the value which persons have simply because they are persons: their 'intrinsic value as individual human beings', as Frankena calls it; the 'infinite value' or the 'sacredness' of their individuality, as others have called it. I shall speak of it as 'individual human worth'; or 'human worth', for short. What these expressions stand for is also expressed by saying that men are 'ends in themselves'. This latter concept is Kant's. Some of the kinks in his formulation of it[1] can be straightened out by explaining it as follows: Everything other than a person can only have a value *for* a person. This applies not only to physical objects, natural or man-made, which have only instrumental value, but also to those products of the human spirit which have also intrinsic, no less than extrinsic value: an epic poem, a scientific theory, a legal system, a moral disposition. Even such things as these will have value only because they can be (*a*) experienced or felt to be valuable by human beings and (*b*) chosen by them from competing alternatives. Thus of everything without exception it will be true to say: if *x* is valuable and is not a person, then *x* will have value for some individual other than itself. Hence even a musical composition or a courageous deed, valued for their own sake, as 'ends' not as means to anything else, will still fall into an entirely different category from that of the *valuers*, who do not need to be valued as 'ends' by someone else[2] in order to have value. In just this sense persons, and only persons, are 'ends in themselves'.

The two factors in terms of which I have described the value of the valuer—the capacities answering to (*a*) and (*b*) above—may not be exhaustive. But their conjunction offers a translation of 'individual human worth' whose usefulness for working purposes will speak for itself. To (*a*) I might refer as 'happiness', if I could use this term as Plato and Aristotle used *eudaimonia*, i.e., without the exclusively hedonistic connotations which have since been clamped on it. It will be less misleading to use 'well-being' or 'welfare' for what I intend here; that is, the enjoyment of value in all the forms in which it can be experienced by human beings. To (*b*) I shall refer as 'freedom', bringing under this term not only conscious choices and deliberate decisions but also those subtler modulations and more spontaneous expressions of individual preference which could scarcely be called 'choices' or 'decisions' without some forcing of language. So understood, a person's well-being and free-

---

[1] See, e.g., H. Sidgwick, *Methods of Ethics* (London, 1874), p. 363. For a parallel objection see the next note. Still another is that Kant, using the notion of *intrinsic worth* (*Würde* in contrast to *Preis*) to define *end in itself*, and hence as its sufficient condition, tends to conflate the value of *persons* as ends in themselves with that of their *moral merit*. Thus, though he says that 'Respect [the attitude due to a being which is an end in itself] always applies to persons only' (*Critique of Practical Reason*, trans. L. W. Beck [New York, 1956], p. 79) he illustrates by respect for a person's 'righteousness' (*l.c.*) and remarks: 'Respect is a tribute we cannot refuse to pay to merit . . .' (p. 80).

[2] Though, of course, they may be (if they are loved or respected as persons). In that case it will not be, strictly, the persons, but their welfare or freedom, which will be the 'end' of those who so love or respect them: since only that which can be realized by action can be an end, to speak of another *person* as my end is bad logical grammar.

dom are aspects of his individual existence as unique and unrepeatable as is that existence itself: If *A* and *B* are listening to the same symphony with similar tastes and dispositions, we may speak of their enjoying the 'same' good, or having the 'same' enjoyment, and say that each has made the 'same' choice for this way of spending his time and money. But here 'same' will mean no more than 'very similar'; the two enjoyments and choices, occurring in the consciousness of *A* and *B* respectively, are absolutely unique. So in translating '*A*'s human worth' into 'the worth of *A*'s well-being and freedom' we are certainly meeting the condition that the former expression is to stand for whatever it is about *A* which, unlike his merit, has *individual* worth.

We are also meeting another condition: that the equality of human worth be justification, or ground, of equal human rights. I can best bring this out by reverting to the visitor from Mars who had asked a little earlier why we want equalization of security benefits. Let us conjure up circumstances in which his question would spring, not from idle curiosity, but from a strong conviction that this, or any other, right entailing such undiscriminating equality of benefits, would be entirely *un*reasonable. Suppose then that he hails from a strict meritarian community, which maintains the *M*-system in its political life and analogous patterns in other associations. And to make things simpler, let us also suppose that he is shown nothing in New York or elsewhere that is out of line with our formal professions of equality, so that he imagines us purer, more strenuous, equalitarians than we happen to be. The pattern of valuation he ascribes to us then seems to him fantastically topsy-turvy. He can hardly bring himself to believe that rational human beings should want equal personal rights, legal and moral, for their 'riff-raff' and their élites. Yet neither can he explain away our conduct as pure automatism, a mere fugue of social habit. 'These people, or some of them,' he will be saying to himself, 'must have some reason for this incredible code. What could these be?' If we volunteered an answer couched in terms of human worth, he might find it hard to understand us. Such an answer, unglossed, would convey to him no more than that we recognize something which is highly and equally valuable in all persons, but has nothing to do with their merit, and constitutes the ground of their equal rights. But this might start him hunting—snark-hunting—for some special quality named by 'human worth' as honesty is named by 'honesty' and kindness by 'kindness', wondering all the while how it could have happened that he and all his tribe have had no inkling of it, if all of them have always had it.[1]

[1] Cf. Melden, *Rights and Right Conduct*, p. 80.

But now suppose that we avail ourselves of the aforesaid translation. We could then tell him: 'To understand our code you should take into account how very different from yours is our own estimate of the relative worth of the welfare and freedom of different individuals. We agree with you that not all persons are capable of experiencing the same values. But there is a wide variety of cases in which persons are capable of this. Thus, to take a perfectly clear case, no matter how A and B might differ in taste and style of life, they would both crave relief from acute physical pain. In that case we would put the same value on giving this to either of them, regardless of the fact that A might be a talented, brilliantly successful person, B "a mere nobody". On this we would disagree sharply. You would weigh the welfare of members of the élite more highly than that of "riff-raff", as you call them. We would not. If A were a statesman, and giving him relief from pain enabled him to conclude an agreement that would benefit millions, while B, an unskilled labourer, was himself the sole beneficiary of the like relief, we would, of course, agree that the *instrumental* value of the two experiences would be vastly different—but not their *intrinsic* value. In all cases where human beings are capable of enjoying the same goods, we feel that the intrinsic value of their enjoyment is the same. In just this sense we hold that (1) *one man's well-being is as valuable as any other's*. And there is a parallel difference in our feeling for freedom. You value it only when exercised by good persons for good ends. We put no such strings on its value. We feel that choosing for oneself what one will do, believe, approve, say, see, read, worship, has its own intrinsic value, the same for all persons, and quite independently of the value of the things they happen to choose. Naturally, we hope that all of them will make the best possible use of their freedom of choice. But we value their exercise of that freedom, regardless of the outcome; and we value it equally for all. For us (2) *one man's freedom is as valuable as any other's?*

This sort of explanation, I submit, would put him in a position to resolve his dilemma. For just suppose that, taking this homily at face-value, he came to think of us as believing (1) and (2).[1] No matter how unreasonable he might think of us he would feel it entirely reasonable that, since we do believe in equal *value* of human well-being and freedom, we should also believe in the prima facie equality of men's *right* to well-being and to freedom. He would see the former as a good reason for the latter; or, more formally, he could think of (1) and (2) respectively as the crucial premises in justification arguments whose respective con-

---

[1] I am bypassing the factual question of the extent to which (1) and (2) are generally believed.

clusions would be: (3) One man's (prima facie) right to well-being is equal to that of any other, and (4) One man's (prima facie) right to freedom is equal to that of any other. Then, given (4), he could see how this would serve as the basis for a great variety of rights to specific kinds of freedom: freedom of movement, of association, of suffrage, of speech, of thought, of worship, of choice of employment, and the like. For each of these can be regarded as simply a specification of the general right to freedom, and would thus be covered by the justification of the latter. Moreover, given (3), he could see in it the basis for various welfare-rights, such as the right to education, medical care, work under decent conditions, relief in periods of unemployment, leisure, housing, etc.[1] Thus to give him (1) and (2) as justification for (3) and (4) would be to give him a basis for every one of the rights which are mentioned in the most complete of currently authoritative declarations of human rights, that passed by the Assembly of the United Nations in 1948. Hence to tell him that we believe in the equal worth of individual freedom and happiness would be to answer, in terms he can understand, his question 'What is your reason for your equalitarian code?'[2]

Nowhere in this defence of the translation of 'equal human worth' into 'equal worth of human well-being and freedom' have I claimed that the

[1] I am well aware of the incompleteness of this highly schematic account. It does not pretend to give the full argument for the justification of (3) and (4) (and see next note) or of their specifications). Among other omissions, it fails to make allowance for the fact that the complex inter-relations of these various rights would affect the justification of each.

[2] On p. 19 [of Social Justice, ed. Richard B. Brandt, 1962. Ed.] Frankena writes as though his own answer to the same question would be, 'because "all men are similarly capable of enjoying a good life" '; this, he says, is what 'justifies the prima facie requirement that they be treated as equals'. But that A and B are similarly capable of enjoying respectively good lives G(A) and G(B) is not a compelling reason for saying that A and B have equal right respectively to G(A) and G(B). The Brahmin who held (Sir Henry Maine, Early History of Institutions [New York, 1875], p. 399) that 'a Brahmin was entitled to 20 times as much happiness as anyone else' need not have held that the Brahmin's capacity for happiness (or, for 'enjoying a good life') differs in the same ratio from that of others. All he would have to deny would be the equal value of the happiness of Brahmins and of others. It is some such premise as this that Frankena must affirm to bring off his justification-argument. I might add that I am not objecting to listing capacity among the premises. The only reason I did not is that I was only citing the 'crucial' premise, the one that would be normally decisive for the acceptance or rejection of the justificandum. A reference to capacity would also be necessary, and I would follow Frankena in conceding that 'men may well be different in such a way that the best life of which one is capable simply is not as good as that of which another is capable' (p. 20), adding a like concession in the case of freedom. A's and B's prima facie equal rights to well-being and to freedom are in effect equal rights to that well-being and freedom of which A and B are equally capable. Thus where the capacity for freedom is severely limited (e.g., that of an idiot or anyone else in the non compos mentis class), the right to freedom would be correspondingly limited.

former can be *reduced* to the latter. I offered individual well-being and freedom simply as two things which do satisfy the conditions defined by individual human worth. Are there others? For the purposes of this essay this may be left an open question. For if there are, they would provide, at most, additional grounds for human rights. The ones I have specified are grounds enough. They are all I need for the analysis of equalitarian justice as, I trust, will appear directly.

XII

THE IDEA OF EQUALITY

Bernard Williams

The idea of equality is used in political discussion both in statements of fact, or what purport to be statements of fact—that men *are* equal—and in statements of political principles or aims—that men *should be* equal, as at present they are not. The two can be, and often are, combined: the aim is then described as that of securing a state of affairs in which men are treated as the equal beings which they in fact already are, but are not already treated as being. In both these uses, the idea of equality notoriously encounters the same difficulty: that on one kind of interpretation the statements in which it figures are much too strong, and on another kind much too weak, and it is hard to find a satisfactory interpretation that lies between the two.[1]

To take first the supposed statement of fact: it has only too often been pointed out that to say that all men are equal in all those characteristics in respect of which it makes sense to say that men are equal or unequal, is a patent falsehood; and even if some more restricted selection is made of these characteristics, the statement does not look much better. Faced with this obvious objection, the defender of the claim that all men are equal is likely to offer a weaker interpretation. It is not, he may say, in their skill, intelligence, strength, or virtue that men are equal, but merely in their being men: it is their common humanity that constitutes their equality. On this interpretation, we should not seek for some special characteristics in respect of which men are equal, but merely remind ourselves that they are all men. Now to this it might be objected that being men is not a respect in which men can strictly speaking be said to be *equal*; but, leaving that aside, there is the more immediate objection that if all that the statement does is to remind us that men

From *Philosophy, Politics and Society* (Second Series), ed. Laslett and Runciman (Blackwell, 1962), pp. 110–31. Reprinted by permission of the author.
[1] For an illuminating discussion of this and related questions, see R. Wollheim and I. Berlin, 'Equality', *Proceedings of the Aristotelian Society*, Vol. LVI (1955–6), p. 281 seq.

are men, it does not do very much, and in particular does less than its proponents in political argument have wanted it to do. What looked like a paradox has turned into a platitude.

I shall suggest in a moment that even in this weak form the statement is not so vacuous as this objection makes it seem; but it must be admitted that when the statement of equality ceases to claim more than is warranted, it rather rapidly reaches the point where it claims less than is interesting. A similar discomfiture tends to overcome the practical maxim of equality. It cannot be the aim of this maxim that all men should be treated alike in all circumstances, or even that they should be treated alike as much as possible. Granted that, however, there is no obvious stopping point before the interpretation which makes the maxim claim only that men should be treated alike in similar circumstances; and since 'circumstances' here must clearly include reference to what a man is, as well as to his purely external situation, this comes very much to saying that for every difference in the way men are treated, some general reason or principle of differentiation must be given. This may well be an important principle; some indeed have seen in it, or in something very like it, an essential element of morality itself.[1] But it can hardly be enough to constitute the principle that was advanced in the name of *equality*. It would be in accordance with this principle, for example, to treat black men differently from others just because they were black, or poor men differently just because they were poor, and this cannot accord with anyone's idea of equality.

In what follows I shall try to advance a number of considerations that can help to save the political notion of equality from these extremes of absurdity and of triviality. These considerations are in fact often employed in political argument, but are usually bundled together into an unanalysed notion of equality in a manner confusing to the advocates, and encouraging to the enemies, of that ideal. These considerations will not enable us to define a distinct third interpretation of the statements which use the notion of equality; it is rather that they enable us, starting with the weak interpretations, to build up something that in practice can have something of the solidity aspired to by the strong interpretations. In this discussion, it will not be necessary all the time to treat separately the supposedly factual application of the notion of equality, and its application in the maxim of action. Though it is sometimes important to distinguish them, and there are clear grounds for doing so, similar considerations often apply to both. The two go significantly together: on

[1] For instance, R. M. Hare: see his *Language of Morals* (Oxford: The Clarendon Press, 1952).

the one hand, the point of the supposedly factual assertion is to back up social ideals and programmes of political action; on the other hand—a rather less obvious point, perhaps—those political proposals have their force because they are regarded not as gratuitously egalitarian, aiming at equal treatment for reasons, for instance, of simplicity or tidiness, but as affirming an equality which is believed in some sense already to exist, and to be obscured or neglected by actual social arrangements.

1. *Common humanity*. The factual statement of men's equality was seen, when pressed, to retreat in the direction of merely asserting the equality of men as men; and this was thought to be trivial. It is certainly insufficient, but not, after all, trivial. That all men are human is, if a tautology, a useful one, serving as a reminder that those who belong anatomically to the species *homo sapiens*, and can speak a language, use tools, live in societies, can interbreed despite racial differences, etc., are also alike in certain other respects more likely to be forgotten. These respects are notably the capacity to feel pain, both from immediate physical causes and from various situations represented in perception and in thought; and the capacity to feel affection for others, and the consequences of this, connected with the frustration of this affection, loss of its objects, etc. The assertion that men are alike in the possession of these characteristics is, while indisputable and (it may be) even necessarily true, not trivial. For it is certain that there are political and social arrangements that systematically neglect these characteristics in the case of some groups of men, while being fully aware of them in the case of others; that is to say, they treat certain men as though they did not possess these characteristics, and neglect moral claims that arise from these characteristics and which would be admitted to arise from them.

Here it may be objected that the mere fact that ruling groups in certain societies treat other groups in this way does not mean that they neglect or overlook the characteristics in question. For, it may be suggested, they may well recognize the presence of these characteristics in the worse-treated group, but claim that in the case of that group, the characteristics do not give rise to any moral claim; the group being distinguished from other members of society in virtue of some further characteristic (for instance, by being black), this may be cited as the ground of treating them differently, whether they feel pain, affection, etc., or not.

This objection rests on the assumption, common to much moral philosophy that makes a sharp distinction between fact and value, that the question whether a certain consideration is *relevant* to a moral issue is an evaluative question: to state that a consideration is relevant or irrelevant to a certain moral question is, on this view, itself to commit oneself to a certain kind of moral principle or outlook. Thus, in the case under discussion, to say (as one would naturally say) that the fact that a man is black is, by itself, quite irrelevant to the issue of how he should be treated in respect of welfare, etc., would, on this view, be to commit to oneself to a certain sort of moral principle. This view, taken generally, seems to me quite certainly false. The principle that men should be differentially treated in respect of welfare merely on grounds of their colour is not a special sort of moral principle, but (if anything) a purely arbitrary assertion of will, like that of some Caligulan ruler who decided to execute everyone whose name contained three 'R's.

This point is in fact conceded by those who practise such things as colour discrimination. Few can be found who will explain their practice merely by saying, 'But they're black: and it is my moral principle to treat black men differently from others'. If any reasons are given at all, they will be reasons that seek to correlate the fact of blackness with certain other considerations which are at least candidates for relevance to the question of how a man should be treated: such as insensitivity, brute stupidity, ineducable irresponsibility, etc. Now these reasons are very often rationalizations, and the correlations claimed are either not really believed, or quite irrationally believed, by those who claim them. But this is a different point; the argument concerns what counts as a moral reason, and the rationalizer broadly agrees with others about what counts as such—the trouble with him is that his reasons are dictated by his policies, and not conversely. The Nazis' 'anthropologists' who tried to construct theories of Aryanism were paying, in very poor coin, the homage of irrationality to reason.

The question of relevance in moral reasons will arise again, in a different connection, in this paper. For the moment its importance is that it gives a force to saying that those who neglect the moral claims of certain men that arise from their human capacity to feel pain, etc., are *overlooking* or *disregarding* those capacities; and are not just operating with a special moral principle, conceding the capacities to these men, but denying the moral claim. Very often, indeed, they have just persuaded themselves that the men in question have those capacities in a lesser degree. Here it is certainly to the point to assert the apparent platitude that these men are also human.

I have discussed this point in connection with very obvious human characteristics of feeling pain and desiring affection. There are, however, other and less easily definable characteristics universal to humanity, which may all the more be neglected in political and social arrangements. For instance, there seems to be a characteristic which might be called 'a desire for self-respect'; this phrase is perhaps not too happy, in suggesting a particular culturally-limited, bourgeois value, but I mean by it a certain human desire to be identified with what one is doing, to be able to realize purposes of one's own, and not to be the instrument of another's will unless one has willingly accepted such a role. This is a very inadequate and in some ways rather empty specification of a human desire; to a better specification, both philosophical reflection and the evidences of psychology and anthropology would be relevant. Such investigations enable us to understand more deeply, in respect of the desire I have gestured towards and of similar characteristics, what it is to be human; and of what it is to be human, the apparently trivial statement of men's equality as men can serve as a reminder.

2. *Moral capacities.* So far we have considered respects in which men can be counted as all alike, which respects are, in a sense, negative: they concern the capacity to suffer, and certain needs that men have, and these involve men in moral relations as the recipients of certain kinds of treatment. It has certainly been a part, however, of the thought of those who asserted that men were equal, that there were more positive respects in which men were alike; that they were equal in certain things that they could do or achieve, as well as in things that they needed and could suffer. In respect of a whole range of abilities, from weight-lifting to the calculus, the assertion is, as was noted at the beginning, not plausible, and has not often been supposed to be. It has been held, however, that there are certain other abilities, both less open to empirical test and more essential in moral connections, for which it is true that men are equal. These are certain sorts of moral ability or capacity, the capacity for virtue or achievement of the highest kind of moral worth.

The difficulty with this notion is that of identifying any purely moral capacities. Some human capacities are more relevant to the achievement of a virtuous life than others: intelligence, a capacity for sympathetic understanding, and a measure of resoluteness would generally be agreed to be so. But these capacities can all be displayed in non-moral connections as well, and in such connections would naturally be thought to differ from man to man like other natural capacities. That this is the fact of the matter has been accepted by many thinkers, notably, for instance, by Aristotle. But against this acceptance, there is a powerful strain of thought that centres on a feeling of ultimate and outrageous absurdity in the idea that the achievement of the highest kind of moral worth should depend on natural capacities, unequally and fortuitously distributed as they are; and this feeling is backed up by the observation that these natural capacities are not themselves the bearers of the moral worth, since those that have them are as gifted for vice as for virtue.

This strain of thought has found many types of religious expression; but in philosophy it is to be found in its purest form in Kant. Kant's view not only carries to the limit the notion that moral worth cannot depend on contingencies, but also emphasizes, in its picture of the Kingdom of Ends, the idea of *respect* which is owed to each man as a rational moral agent—and, since men are equally such agents, is owed equally to all, unlike admiration and similar attitudes, which are commanded unequally by men in proportion to their unequal possession of different kinds of natural excellence. These ideas are intimately connected in Kant, and it is not possible to understand his moral theory unless as much weight is given to what he says about the Kingdom of Ends as is always given to what he says about duty.

The very considerable consistency of Kant's view is bought at what would generally be agreed to be a very high price. The detachment of moral worth from all contingencies is achieved only by making man's characteristic as a moral or rational agent a transcendental characteristic; man's capacity to will freely as a rational agent is not dependent on any empirical capacities he may have—and, in particular, is not dependent on empirical capacities which men may possess unequally—because, in the Kantian view, the capacity to be a rational agent is not itself an empirical capacity at all. Accordingly, the respect owed equally to each man as a member of the Kingdom of Ends is not owed to him in respect of any empirical characteristics that he may possess, but solely in respect of the transcendental characteristic of being a free and rational will. The ground of the respect owed to each man thus emerges in the Kantian theory as a kind of secular analogue of the Christian conception of the respect owed to all men as equally children of God. Though secular, it is equally metaphysical: in neither case is it anything empirical *about* men that constitutes the ground of equal respect.

This transcendental, Kantian conception cannot provide any solid foundation for the notions of equality among men, or of equality of respect owed to them. Apart from the general difficulties of such transcendental conceptions, there is the obstinate fact that the concept of 'moral agent', and the concepts allied to it such as that of responsibility, do and must have an empirical basis. It seems empty to say that all men are equal as moral agents, when the question, for instance, of men's responsibility for their actions is one to which empirical considerations are clearly relevant, and one which moreover receives answers in terms of different degrees of responsibility and different degrees of rational control over action. To hold a man responsible for his actions is presumably the central case of treating him as a moral agent, and if men are not treated as equally responsible, there is not much left to their equality as moral agents.

If, without its transcendental basis, there is not much left to men's equality as moral agents, is there anything left to the notion of the *respect* owed to all men? This notion of 'respect' is both complex and unclear, and I think it needs, and would repay, a good deal of investigation. Some content can, however, be attached to it; even if it is some way away from the ideas of moral agency. There certainly is a distinction, for instance, between regarding a man's life, actions or character from an aesthetic or technical point of view, and regarding them from a point of view which is concerned primarily with what it is *for him* to live that life and do those actions in that character. Thus from the technological point of view, a man who has spent his life in trying to make a certain machine which could not possibly work is merely a failed inventor, and in compiling a catalogue of those whose efforts have contributed to the sum of technical achievement, one must 'write him off': the fact that he devoted himself to this useless task with constant effort and so on, is merely irrelevant. But from a human point of view, it is clearly not irrelevant: we are concerned with him, not merely as 'a failed inventor', but as a man who wanted to be a successful inventor. Again, in professional relations and the world of work, a man operates, and his activities come up for criticism, under a variety of professional or technical titles, such as 'miner' or 'agricultural labourer' or 'junior executive'. The technical or professional attitude is that which regards the man solely under that title, the human approach that which regards him as *a man who has* that title (among others), willingly, unwillingly, through lack of alternatives, with pride, etc.

That men should be regarded from the human point of view, and not merely under these sorts of titles, is part of the content that might be attached to Kant's celebrated injunction 'treat each man as an end in himself, and never as a means only'. But I do not think that this is all that should be seen in this injunction, or all that is concerned in the notion of 'respect'. What is involved in the examples just given could be explained by saying that each man is owed an effort at identification: that he should not be regarded as the surface to which a certain label can be applied, but one should try to see the world (including the label) from his point of view. This injunction will be based on, though not of course fully explained by, the notion that men are conscious beings who necessarily have intentions and purposes and see what they are doing in a certain light. But there seem to be further injunctions connected with the Kantian maxim, and with the notion of 'respect', that go beyond these considerations. There are forms of exploiting men or degrading them which would be thought to be excluded by these notions, but which cannot be excluded merely by considering how the exploited or degraded men see the situation. For it is precisely a mark of extreme exploitation or degradation that those who suffer it do *not* see themselves differently from the way they are seen by the exploiters; either they do not see themselves as anything at all, or they acquiesce passively in the role for which they have been cast. Here we evidently need something more than the precept that one should respect and try to understand another man's consciousness of his own activities; it is also that one may not suppress or destroy that consciousness.

All these I must confess to be vague and inconclusive considerations, but we are dealing with a vague notion: one, however, that we possess, and attach value to. To try to put these matters properly in order would be itself to try to reach conclusions about several fundamental questions of moral philosophy. What we must ask here is what these ideas have to do with equality. We started with the notion of men's equality as moral agents. This notion appeared unsatisfactory, for different reasons, in both an empirical and a transcendental interpretation. We then moved, *via* the idea of 'respect', to the different notion of regarding men not merely under professional, social, or technical titles, but with consideration of their own views and purposes. This notion has at least this much to do with equality: that the titles which it urges us to look behind are the conspicuous bearers of social, political, and technical *inequality*, whether they refer to achievement (as in the example of the inventor), or to social roles (as in the example of work titles). It enjoins us not to let our fundamental attitudes to men be dictated by the criteria of technical success of social position, and not to take them at the value carried by these titles and by the structures in which these titles place them. This does not mean, of course, that the more fundamental view that should be taken of men is in the case of every man the same: on the contrary. But it does mean that each man is owed the effort of understanding, and that in achieving it, each man is to be (as it were) abstracted from certain conspicuous structures of inequality in which we find him.

These injunctions are based on the proposition that men are beings who are necessarily to some extent conscious of themselves and of the world they live in. (I omit here, as throughout the discussion, the clinical cases of people who are mad or mentally defective, who always constitute special exceptions to what is in general true of men.) This proposition does not assert that men are equally conscious of themselves and of their situation. It was precisely one element in the notion of exploitation considered above that such consciousness can be decreased by social action and the environment; we may add that it can similarly be increased. But men are at least potentially conscious, to an indeterminate degree, of their situation and of what I have called their 'titles', are capable of reflectively standing back from the roles and positions in which they are cast; and this reflective consciousness may be enhanced or diminished by their social condition.

It is this last point that gives these considerations a particular relevance to the political aims of egalitarianism. The mere idea of regarding men from 'the human point of view', while it has a good deal to do with politics, and a certain amount to do with equality, has nothing specially to do with political equality. One could, I think, accept this as an ideal, and yet favour, for instance, some kind of hierarchical society, so long as the hierarchy maintained itself without compulsion, and there was human understanding between the orders. In such a society, each man would indeed have a very conspicuous title which related him to the social structure; but it might be that most people were aware of the human beings behind the titles, and found each other for the most part content, or even proud, to have the titles that they had. I do not know whether anything like this has been true of historical hierarchical societies; but I can see no inconsistency in someone's espousing it as an ideal, as some (influenced in many cases by a sentimental picture of the Middle Ages) have done. Such a person would be one who accepted the notion of 'the human view', the view of each man as something more than his title, as a valuable ideal, but rejected the ideals of political equality.

Once, however, one accepts the further notion that the degree of man's consciousness about such things as his role in society is itself in some part the product of social arrangements, and that it can be increased, this ideal of a stable hierarchy must, I think, disappear. For what keeps stable hierarchies together is the idea of necessity, that it is somehow foreordained or inevitable that there should be these orders; and this idea of necessity must be eventually undermined by the growth of people's reflective consciousness about their role, still more when it is combined with the thought that what they and the others have always thought about their roles in the social system was the product of the social system itself.

It might be suggested that a certain man who admitted that people's consciousness of their roles was conditioned in this way might nevertheless believe in the hierarchical ideal: but that in order to preserve the society of his ideal, he would have to make sure that the idea of the conditioning of consciousness did not get around to too many people, and that their consciousness about their roles did not increase too much. But such a view is really a very different thing from its naïve predecessor. Such a man, no longer himself 'immersed' in the system, is beginning to think in terms of compulsion, the deliberate *prevention* of the growth of consciousness, which is a poisonous element absent from the original ideal. Moreover, his attitude (or that of rulers similar to himself) towards the other people in the ideal society must now contain an element of condescension or contempt, since he will be aware that their acceptance of what they suppose to be necessity is a delusion. This is alien to the spirit of human understanding on which the original ideal was based. The hierarchical idealist cannot escape the fact that certain things which can be done decently without self-consciousness can, with self-consciousness, be done only hypocritically. This is why even the rather hazy and very general notions that I have tried to bring together in this section contain some of the grounds of the ideal of political equality.

3. *Equality in unequal circumstances*. The notion of equality is invoked not only in connections where men are claimed in some sense all to be equal, but in connections where they are agreed to be unequal, and the question arises of the distribution of, or access to, certain goods to which their inequalities are relevant. It may be objected that the notion of equality is in fact misapplied in these connections, and that the appropriate ideas are those of fairness or justice, in the sense of what Aristotle called 'distributive justice', where (as Aristotle argued) there is no question of regarding or treating everyone as equal, but solely a question of distributing certain goods in proportion to men's recognized inequalities.

I think it is reasonable to say against this objection that there is some foothold for the notion of equality even in these cases. It is useful here to make a rough distinction between two different types of inequality, inequality of *need* and inequality of *merit*, with a corresponding distinction between goods—on the one hand, goods demanded by the need, and on the other, goods that can be earned by the merit. In the case of needs, such as the need for medical treatment in case of illness, it can be presumed for practical purposes that the persons who have the need actually desire the goods in question, and so the question can indeed be regarded as one of distribution in a simple sense, the satisfaction of an existing desire. In the case of merit, such as for instance the possession of abilities to profit from a university education, there is not the same presumption that everyone who has the merit has the desire for the goods in question, though it may, of course, be the case. Moreover, the good of a university education may be legitimately, even if hopelessly, desired by those who do not possess the merit; while medical treatment or unemployment benefit are either not desired, or not legitimately desired, by those who are not ill or unemployed, i.e. do not have the appropriate need. Hence the distribution of goods in accordance with merit has a competitive aspect lacking in the case of distribution according to need. For these reasons, it is appropriate to speak, in the case of merit, not only of the distribution of the good, but of the distribution of the opportunity of achieving the good. But this, unlike the good itself, can be said to be distributed equally to everybody, and so one does encounter a notion of *general* equality, much vaunted in our society today, the notion of equality of opportunity.

Before considering this notion further, it is worth noticing certain resemblances and differences between the cases of need and of merit. In both cases, we encounter the matter (mentioned before in this paper) of the relevance of reasons. Leaving aside preventive medicine, the proper ground of distribution of medical care is ill health: this is a necessary truth. Now in very many societies, while ill health may work as a necessary condition of receiving treatment, it does not work as a sufficient condition, since such treatment costs money, and not all who are ill have the money; hence the possession of sufficient money becomes in fact an additional necessary condition of actually receiving treatment. Yet more extravagantly, money may work as a sufficient condition by itself, without any medical need, in which case the reasons that actually operate for the receipt of this good are just totally irrelevant to its nature; however, since only a few hypochrondriacs desire treatment when they do not need it, this is, in this case, a marginal phenomenon.

When we have the situation in which, for instance, wealth is a further necessary condition of the receipt of medical treatment, we can once more apply the notions of equality and inequality: not now in connection with the inequality between the well and the ill, but in connection with the inequality between the rich ill and the poor ill, since we have straightforwardly the situation of those whose needs are the same not receiving the same treatment, though the needs are the ground of the treatment. This is an irrational state of affairs.

It may be objected that I have neglected an important distinction here. For, it may be said, I have treated the ill health and the possession of money as though they were regarded on the same level, as 'reasons for receiving medical treatment', and this is a muddle. The ill health is, at most, a ground of the *right* to receive medical treatment; whereas the money is, in certain circumstances, the causally necessary condition of securing the right, which is a different thing. There is something in the distinction that this objection suggests: there is a distinction between a man's rights, the reasons why he should be treated in a certain way, and his power to secure those rights, the reasons why he can in fact get what he deserves. But this objection does not make it inappropriate to call the situation of inequality an 'irrational' situation: it just makes it clearer what is meant by so calling it. What is meant is that it is a situation in which reasons are insufficiently *operative*; it is a situation insufficiently controlled by reasons—and hence by reason itself. The same point arises with another form of equality and equal rights, equality before the law. It may be said that in a certain society, men have equal rights to a fair trial, to seek redress from the law for wrongs committed against them, etc. But if a fair trial or redress from the law can be secured in that society only by moneyed and educated persons, to insist that everyone *has* this right, though only these particular persons can *secure* it, rings hollow to the point of cynicism: we are concerned not with the abstract existence of rights, but with the extent to which those rights govern what actually happens.

Thus when we combine the notions of the *relevance* of reasons, and the *operativeness* of reasons, we have a genuine moral weapon, which can be applied in cases of what is appropriately called unequal treatment, even where one is not concerned with the equality of people as a whole. This represents a strengthening of the very weak principle mentioned at the beginning of this paper, that for every difference in the way men are treated, a reason should be given: when one requires further that the reasons should be relevant, and that they should be socially operative, this really says something.

Similar considerations will apply to cases of merit. There is, however, an important difference between the cases of need and merit, in respect of the relevance of reasons. It is a matter of logic that particular sorts of needs constitute a reason for receiving particular sorts of good. It is, however, in general a much more disputable question whether certain sorts of merit constitute a reason for receiving certain sorts of good. For instance, let it be agreed, for the sake of argument, that the public school system provides a superior type of education, which it is a good thing to receive. It is then objected that access to this type of education is unequally distributed, because of its cost: among boys of equal promise or intelligence, only those from wealthy homes will receive it, and, indeed, boys of little promise or intelligence will receive it, if from wealthy homes; and this, the objection continues, is irrational.

The defender of the public school system might give two quite different sorts of answer to this objection; besides, that is, the obvious type of answer which merely disputes the facts alleged by the objector. One is the sort of answer already discussed in the case of need : that we may agree, perhaps, that boys of promise and intelligence have a right to a superior education, but in actual economic circumstances, this right cannot always be secured, etc. The other is more radical : this would dispute the premise of the objection that intelligence and promise are, at least by themselves, the grounds for receiving this superior type of education. While perhaps not asserting that wealth itself constitutes the ground, the defender of the system may claim that other characteristics significantly correlated with wealth are such grounds; or, again, that it is the purpose of this sort of school to maintain a tradition of leadership, and the best sort of people to maintain this will be people whose fathers were at such schools. We need not try to pursue such arguments here. The important point is that, while there can indeed be genuine disagreements about what constitutes the relevant sort of merit in such cases, such disagreements must also be disagreements about the nature of the good to be distributed. As such, the disagreements do not occur in a vacuum, nor are they logically free from restrictions. There is only a limited number of reasons for which education could be regarded as a good, and a limited number of purposes which education could rationally be said to serve; and to the limitations on this question, there correspond limitations on the sorts of merit or personal characteristic which could be rationally cited as grounds of access to this good. Here again we encounter a genuine strengthening of the very weak principle that, for differences in the way that people are treated, reasons should be given.

We may return now to the notion of equality of opportunity; understanding this in the normal political sense of equality of opportunity for *everyone in society* to secure certain goods. This notion is introduced into political discussion when there is question of the access to certain goods which, first, even if they are not desired by everyone in society, are desired by large numbers of people in all sections of society (either for themselves, or, as in the case of education, for their children), or would be desired by people in all sections of society if they knew about the goods in question and thought it possible for them to attain them; second, are goods which people may be said to earn or achieve; and third, are goods which not all the people who desire them can have. This third condition covers at least three different cases, however, which it is worth distinguishing. Some desired goods, like positions of prestige, management, etc., are *by their very nature* limited : whenever there are some people who are in command or prestigious positions, there are necessarily others who are not. Other goods are *contingently* limited, in the sense that there are certain conditions of access to them which in fact not everyone satisfies, but there is no intrinsic limit to the numbers who might gain access to it by satisfying the conditions: university education is usually regarded in this light nowadays, as something which requires certain conditions of admission to it which in fact not everyone satisfies, but which an indefinite proportion of people might satisfy. Third, there are goods which are *fortuitously* limited, in the sense that although everyone or large numbers of people satisfy the conditions of access to them, there is just not enough of them to go round; so some more stringent conditions or system of rationing have to be imposed, to govern access in an imperfect situation. A good can, of course, be both contingently and fortuitously limited at once: when, due to shortage of supply, not even the people who are qualified to have it, limited in numbers though they are, can in every case have it. It is particularly worth distinguishing those kinds of limitation, as there can be significant differences of view about the way in which a certain good is limited. While most would now agree that high education is contingently limited, a Platonic view would regard it as necessarily limited.

Now the notion of equality of opportunity might be said to be the notion that a limited good shall in fact be allocated on grounds which do not *a priori* exclude any section of those that desire it. But this formulation is not really very clear. For suppose grammar school education (a good perhaps contingently, and certainly fortuitously, limited) is allocated on grounds of ability as tested at the age of 11; this would normally be advanced as an example of equality of opportunity, as opposed to a system of allocation on grounds of parents' wealth. But does not the criterion of ability exclude *a priori* a certain section of people, viz. those that are not able—just as the other excludes *a priori* those who are not wealthy? Here it will obviously be said that this was not what was meant by *a priori* exclusion: the present argument just equates this with exclusion of anybody, i.e. with the mere existence of some condition that has to be satisfied. What then is *a priori* exclusion? It must mean exclusion on grounds *other* than those appropriate or rational for the good in question. But this still will not do as it stands. For it would follow from this that so long as those allocating grammar school education on grounds of wealth thought that such grounds were appropriate or rational (as they might in one of the ways discussed above in connection with public schools), they could sincerely describe their system as one of equality of opportunity—which is absurd.

Hence it seems that the notion of equality of opportunity is more complex than it first appeared. It requires not merely that there should be no exclusion from access on grounds other than those appropriate or rational for the good in question, but that the grounds considered appropriate for the good should themselves be such that people from all sections of society have an equal chance of satisfying them. What now is a 'section of society'? Clearly we cannot include under this term sections of the populace identified just by the characteristics which figure in the grounds for allocating the good—since, once more, any grounds at all must exclude some section of the populace. But what about sections identified by characteristics which are *correlated* with the grounds of exclusion? There are important difficulties here: to illustrate this, it may help first to take an imaginary example.

Suppose that in a certain society great prestige is attached to membership of a warrior class, the duties of which require great physical strength. This class has in the past been recruited from certain wealthy families only; but egalitarian reformers achieve a change in the rules, by which warriors are recruited from all sections of the society, on the results of a suitable competition. The effect of this, however, is that the wealthy families still provide virtually all the warriors, because the rest of the populace is so under-nourished by reason of poverty that their physical strength is inferior to that of the wealthy and well nourished. The reformers protest that equality of opportunity has not really been achieved; the wealthy reply that in fact it has, and that the poor now have the opportunity of becoming warriors—it is just bad luck that their characteristics are such that they do not pass the test. 'We are not,' they might say, 'excluding anyone *for* being poor; we exclude people for being weak, and it is unfortunate that those who are poor are also weak.'

This answer would seem to most people feeble, and even cynical. This is for reasons similar to those discussed before in connection with equality before the law; that the supposed equality of opportunity is quite empty—indeed, one may say that it does not really exist—unless it is made more effective than this. For one knows that it could be made more effective; one knows that there is a causal connection between being poor and being undernourished, and between being undernourished and being physically weak. One supposes further that something could be done—subject to whatever economic conditions obtain in the imagined society—to alter the distribution of wealth. All this being so, the appeal by the wealthy to the 'bad luck' of the poor must appear as disingenuous.

It seems then that a system of allocation will fall short of equality of opportunity if the allocation of the good in question in fact works out unequally or disproportionately between different sections of society, if the unsuccessful sections are under a disadvantage which could be removed by further reform or social action. This was very clear in the imaginary example that was given, because the causal connections involved are simple and well known. In actual fact, however, the situations of this type that arise are more complicated, and it is easier to overlook the causal connections involved. This is particularly so in the case of educational selection, where such slippery concepts as 'intellectual ability' are involved. It is a known fact that the system of selection for grammar schools by the '11 +' examination favours children in direct proportion to their social class, the children of professional homes having proportionately greater success than those from working-class homes. We have every reason to suppose that these results are the product, in good part, of environmental factors; and we further know that imaginative social reform, both of the primary educational system and of living conditions, would favourably effect those environmental factors. In these circumstances, this system of educational selection falls short of equality of opportunity.[1]

This line of thought points to a connection between the idea of equality of opportunity, and the idea of equality of persons, which is stronger than might at first be suspected. We have seen that one is not really offering equality of opportunity to Smith and Jones if one contents oneself with applying the same criteria to Smith and Jones at, say, the age of 11; what one is doing there is to apply the same criteria to Smith as affected by favourable conditions and to Jones as affected by unfavourable but curable conditions. Here there is a necessary pressure to equal up the conditions: to give *Smith* and *Jones* equality of opportunity involves regarding their conditions, where curable, as themselves part of what is done to Smith and Jones, and not part of Smith and Jones themselves. Their identity, for these purposes, does not include their curable environment, which is itself unequal and a contributor of inequality. This abstraction of persons in themselves from unequal environments is a way, if not of regarding them as equal, at least of moving recognizably in that direction; and is itself involved in equality of opportunity.

One might speculate about how far this movement of thought might go. The most conservative user of the notion of equality of opportunity is, if sincere, prepared to abstract the individual from some effects of his environment. We have seen that there is good reason to press this further, and to allow that the individuals whose opportunities are to be

[1] See on this C. A. R. Crosland, 'Public Schools and English Education', *Encounter* (July 1961).

equal should be abstracted from more features of social and family background. Where should this stop? Should it even stop at the boundaries of heredity? Suppose it were discovered that when all curable environmental disadvantages had been dealt with, there was a residual genetic difference in brain constitution, for instance, which was correlated with differences in desired types of ability; but that the brain constitution could in fact be changed by an operation.[1] Suppose further that the wealthier classes could afford such an operation for their children, so that they always came out top of the educational system; would we then think that poorer children did not have equality of opportunity, because they had no opportunity to get rid of their genetic disadvantages?

Here we might think that our notion of personal identity itself was beginning to give way; we might well wonder *who were* the people whose advantages and disadvantages were being discussed in this way. But it would be wrong, I think, to try to solve this problem simply by saying that in the supposed circumstances our notion of personal identity would have collapsed in such a way that we could no longer speak of the individuals involved—in the end, we could still pick out the individuals by spatio-temporal criteria, if no more. Our objections against the system suggested in this fantasy must, I think, be moral rather than metaphysical. They need not concern us here. What is interesting about the fantasy, perhaps, is that if one reached this state of affairs, the individuals would be regarded as in all respects equal in themselves—for in themselves they would be, as it were, pure subjects or bearers of predicates, everything else about them, including their genetic inheritance, being regarded as a fortuitous and changeable characteristic. In these circumstances, where everything about a person is controllable, equality of opportunity and absolute equality seem to coincide; and this itself illustrates something about the notion of equality of opportunity.

I said that we need not discuss here the moral objections to the kind of world suggested in this fantasy. There is, however, one such point that is relevant to the different aspects of equality that have been discussed in this paper as a whole. One objection that we should instinctively feel about the fantasy world is that far too much emphasis was being placed on achieving high ability; that the children were just being regarded as locations of abilities. I think we should still feel this even if everybody (with results hard to imagine) was treated in this way; when not everybody was so treated, the able would also be more successful

---

[1] A yet more radical situation—but one more likely to come about—would be that in which an individual's characteristics could be *pre-arranged* by interference with the genetic material. The dizzying consequences of this I shall not try to explore.

than others, and those very concerned with producing the ability would probably also be over-concerned with success. The moral objections to the excessive concern with such aims are, interestingly, not unconnected with the ideal of equality itself; they are connected with equality in the sense discussed in the earlier sections of this paper, the equality of human beings despite ther differences, and in particular with the complex of notions considered in the second section under the heading of 'respect'.

This conflict within the ideals of equality arises even without resort to the fantasy world. It exists today in the feeling that a thorough-going emphasis on equality of opportunity must destroy a certain sense of common humanity which is itself an ideal of equality.[1] The ideals that are felt to be in conflict with equality of opportunity are not necessarily other ideals of equality—there may be an independent appeal to the values of community life, or to the moral worth of a more integrated and less competitive society. Nevertheless, the idea of equality itself is often invoked in this connection, and not, I think, inappropriately.

If the idea of equality ranges as widely as I have suggested, this type of conflict is bound to arise with it. It is an idea which, on the one hand, is invoked in connection with the distribution of certain goods, some at least of which are bound to confer on their possessors some preferred status or prestige. On the other hand, the idea of equality of respect is one which urges us to give less consideration to those structures in which people enjoy status or prestige, and to consider people independently of those goods, on the distribution of which equality of opportunity precisely focuses our, and their, attention. There is perhaps nothing formally incompatible in these two applications of the idea of equality: one might hope for a society in which there existed both a fair, rational, and appropriate distribution of these goods, and no contempt, condescension, or lack of human communication between persons who were more and less successful recipients of the distribution. Yet in actual fact, there are deep psychological and social obstacles to the realization of this hope; as things are, the competitiveness and considerations of prestige that surround the first application of equality certainly militate against the second. How far this situation is inevitable, and how far in an economically developed and dynamic society, in which certain skills and talents are necessarily at a premium, the obstacles to a wider realization of equality might be overcome, I do not think that we know: these are in good part questions of psychology and sociology, to which we do not have the answers.

[1] See, for example, Michael Young, *The Rise of the Meritocracy* (London: Thames and Hudson. 1958).

When one is faced with the spectacle of the various elements of the idea of equality pulling in these different directions, there is a strong temptation, if one does not abandon the idea altogether, to abandon some of its elements: to claim, for instance, that equality of opportunity is the only ideal that is at all practicable, and equality of respect a vague and perhaps nostalgic illusion; or, alternatively, that equality of respect is genuine equality, and equality of opportunity an inegalitarian betrayal of the ideal—all the more so if it were thoroughly pursued, as now it is not. To succumb to either of these simplifying formulae would, I think, be a mistake. Certainly, a highly rational and efficient application of the ideas of equal opportunity, unmitigated by the other considerations, could lead to a quite inhuman society (if it worked—which, granted a well-known desire of parents to secure a position for their children at least as good as their own, is unlikely). On the other hand, an ideal of equality of respect that made no contact with such things as the economic needs of society for certain skills, and human desire for some sorts of prestige, would be condemned to a futile Utopianism, and to having no rational effect on the distribution of goods, position, and power that would inevitably proceed. If, moreover, as I have suggested, it is not really known how far, by new forms of social structure and of education, these conflicting claims might be reconciled, it is all the more obvious that we should not throw one set of claims out of the window; but should rather seek, in each situation, the best way of eating and having as much cake as possible. It is an uncomfortable situation, but the discomfort is just that of genuine political thought. It is no greater with equality than it is with liberty, or any other noble and substantial political ideal.

NOTES ON THE CONTRIBUTORS

GILBERT RYLE was Wayneflete Professor of Metaphysical Philosophy at Oxford from 1945 to 1968. His influential book *The Concept of Mind* appeared in 1949, *Dilemmas* in 1954, and he has published over the years a large number of important papers and articles.

R. M. HARE is White's Professor of Moral Philosophy at Oxford, and was formerly a Fellow of Balliol there. His most important publications are *The Language of Morals* (1952) and *Freedom and Reason* (1963).

ANTHONY KENNY is a Fellow of Balliol College, Oxford. His book *Action, Emotion and Will* was published in 1963.

C. H. WHITELEY is a member of the Department of Philosophy at the University of Birmingham. Among his publications is *An Introduction to Metaphysics* (1950).

J. O. URMSON is a Fellow of Corpus Christi College, Oxford, and was formerly Professor of Philosophy at Dundee. His book *Philosophical Analysis* was published in 1958, and he edited the late J. L. Austin's William James lectures, *How to Do Things with Words* (1962).

C. D. BROAD was Knightbridge Professor of Moral Philosophy at Cambridge from 1933 to 1953. Among his very numerous publications are *Scientific Thought* (1923), *The Mind and its Place in Nature* (1925), and *An Examination of McTaggart's Philosophy* (1933–8). *The Philosophy of C. D. Broad*, edited by P. A. Schilpp, appeared in 1959.

A. CAMPBELL GARNETT retired some years ago from the Department of Philosophy at the University of Wisconsin. His publications range from *Reality and Value* (1937) to *The Perceptual Process* (1965).

DONALD DAVIDSON, formerly at Stanford, is now a member of the Department of Philosophy at Princeton. He is the co-author (with P. Suppes) of *Decision Making* (1957).

W. D. FALK, formerly at the University of Melbourne, Wayne State University, and the University of Syracuse, is now at the University of North Carolina. He has published important articles on questions in ethical theory.

John Rawls, formerly at Cornell University and the Massachusetts Institute of Technology, is now at Harvard. His writings on ethical theory have been widely influential.

Gregory Vlastos is a member of the Department of Philosophy at Princeton. He has published valuable articles on ancient philosophy and political theory as well as on ethics.

Bernard Williams was Professor of Philosophy at Bedford College, London from 1964 to 1967, and is now Knightbridge Professor of Philosophy at Cambridge. He edited, with A. C. Montefiore, *British Analytical Philosophy*, published in 1966.

BIBLIOGRAPHY

I. PLEASURE AND PAIN

ALSTON, WILLIAM P., 'Pleasure', in Paul Edwards (ed.), *Encyclopedia of Philosophy* (New York: The Macmillan Co. & The Free Press, 1967), pp. 341–9.

ARISTOTLE, *Nichomachean Ethics*, Bks. VIIB and XA.

BAIER, KURT, *The Moral Point of View* (Ithaca, N.Y.: Cornell University Press, 1958), pp. 266–77.

BAIN, ALEXANDER, *Mental and Moral Sciences*, Second Edn. (London: Longmans, Green & Co., 1868), appendix C.

BEDFORD, ERROL, 'Pleasure and Belief', *Proceedings of the Aristotelian Society*, Supp. Vol. 33 (1959), pp. 281–304.

BENTHAM, JEREMY, *An Introduction to the Principles of Morals and Legislation* (London: 1789), chaps. 3–5.

GALLIE, W. B., 'Pleasure', *Proceedings of the Aristotelian Society*, Supp. Vol. 28 (1954), pp. 147–64.

GALLOP, DAVID, 'True and False Pleasures', *Philosophical Quarterly*, Vol. 10 (1960), pp. 331–42.

GARDINER, P. L., 'Pain and Evil', *Proceedings of the Aristotelian Society*, Supp. Vol. 38 (1964), pp. 107–24.

HART, H. L. A., 'Bentham', *Proceedings of the British Academy*, Vol. 48 (1962), pp. 297–320.

ISENBERG, A., 'Pleasure and Falsity', *American Philosophical Quarterly*, Vol. 1 (1964), pp. 96–100.

KENNICK, W., 'Pleasure and Falsity', *American Philosophical Quarterly*, Vol. 1 (1964), pp. 92–5.

KENNY, ANTHONY, *Action, Emotion, and Will* (London: Routledge and Kegan Paul, 1963), chap. 6.

MACINTYRE, ALISDAIR, 'Pleasure As a Reason for Action', *The Monist*, Vol. 49 (1965), pp. 215–33.

MANSER, A. R., 'Pleasure', *Proceedings of the Aristotelian Society*, Vol. 61 (1960–1), pp. 223–38.

McNAUGHTON, R. M., 'A Metrical Concept of Happiness', *Philos. and Phenom. Research*, Vol. 14 (1953), pp. 172–83.

NOWELL-SMITH, P. H., *Ethics* (Harmondsworth: Penguin Books, 1954), chap. 10.

PENELHUM, TERENCE, 'The Logic of Pleasure', *Philos. and Phenom. Research*, Vol. 17 (1957), pp. 488–503.

PENELHUM, TERENCE, 'Pleasure and Falsity', *American Philosophical Quarterly*, Vol. 1 (1964), pp. 81–91.

PERRY, DAVID, *The Concept of Pleasure* (The Hague: Mouton & Co., 1967).

PERRY, B. B., *General Theory of Value* (New York: Longmans, Green & Co., 1926), chap. 21.

PLATO, *Philebus*.

RYLE, GILBERT, *The Concept of Mind* (London: Hutchinson, and New York: Barnes and Noble, 1949), pp. 107–9.

RYLE, GILBERT, *Dilemmas* (Cambridge: Cambridge University Press, 1954), chap. 4.

SIDGWICK, HENRY, *The Methods of Ethics* (London: Macmillan, 1907), Bk. 1, chap. 4, Bk. 11, chaps. 2, 3.

TAYLOR, C. C. W., 'Pleasure', *Analysis, Supplement*, 1962, pp. 1–19.

THALBERG, IRVING, 'False Pleasures', *Journal of Philosophy*, Vol. 59 (1962), pp. 65–74.

VON WRIGHT, GEORG, *The Varieties of Goodness* (London: Routledge and Kegan Paul, 1963), chap. 4.

WILLIAMS, B. A. O., 'Pleasure and Belief', *Proceedings of the Aristotelian Society*, Supp. Vol. 33 (1959), pp. 57–72.

II. HAPPINESS AND THE IDEA OF A SUPREME GOOD

ANSCOMBE, ELIZABETH, *Intention* (Oxford: Blackwell, and Ithaca, N.Y.: Cornell University Press, 1957), pp. 33 ff.

AQUINAS, ST. THOMAS, *Summa Theologica* (London: Burns, Oates, and Washbourne, Ltd., 1920), Part 11, First Part, QQ1–v—'Treatise on the Last End'.

ARISTOTLE, *Nichomachean Ethics*, Bks. 1 and x.

BRANDT, R. B., 'The Concept of Welfare', in *The Structure of Economic Science*, ed. S. R. Krupp (Englewood Cliffs: Prentice-Hall, 1966), pp. 257–76.

HARDIE, W. F. R., 'The Final Good in Aristotle's Ethics', *Philosophy*, Vol. 40 (1965), pp. 277–95.

HARE, R. M., *Freedom and Reason* (Oxford: Clarendon Press, 1963), pp. 125–9.

MILL, J. S., *Utilitarianism*, esp. chap. 2.

RUSSELL, BERTRAND, *The Conquest of Happiness* (London: Allen and Unwin, and New York: Liveright, 1930).

SIEGLER, FREDERICK, 'Reason, Happiness and Goodness', in J. J. Walsh and H. L. Shapiro (eds.), *Aristotle's Ethics* (Belmont, Calif.: Wadsworth Publ. Co., 1967), pp. 30–46.

VON WRIGHT, G. H., *The Varieties of Goodness* (London: Routledge and Kegan Paul, 1963), chap. 5.

WILLIAMS, B. A. O., 'Aristotle on the Good', *Philosophical Quarterly*, Vol. 12 (1962), pp. 289–96.

III. DUTY AND OBLIGATION

BAIER, KURT, *The Moral Point of View* (Ithaca: Cornell University Press, 1958), chap. 9.

BRADLEY, F. H., 'My Station and its Duties', *Ethical Studies*, Second Edn. (Oxford University Press, 1962).

BRANDT, R. B., 'The Concepts of Obligation and Duty', *Mind*, Vol. 73 (1964), pp. 374–93.

CHISHOLM, RODERICK, 'The Ethics of Requirement', *American Philosophical Quarterly*, Vol. 1 (1964), pp. 147–53.

CICERO, *De Officiis*.

EPICTETUS, *The Enchiridion*.

FEINBERG, JOEL, 'Duties, Rights, and Claims', *American Philosophical Quarterly*, Vol. 3 (1966), pp. 137–44.

HART, H. L. A., 'Legal and Moral Obligation', in A. I. Melden (ed.), *Essays in Moral Philosophy* (Seattle: University of Washington Press, 1958), pp. 82–102.

HART, H. L. A., *The Concept of Law* (Oxford: Clarendon Press, 1961), pp. 27–40, 79–88.

HOBBES, THOMAS, *The Leviathan*, chaps. 13–21.

KANT, IMMANUEL, *Fundamental Principles of the Metaphysic of Morals*, Sections I and II.

LEMMON, E. J., 'Moral Dilemmas', *Philosophical Review*, Vol. 86 (1962), pp. 139–58.

MELDEN, A. I., 'Promising', *Mind*, Vol. 65 (1956), pp. 49–66.

ROSS, W. D., *The Right and the Good* (Oxford: Clarendon Press, 1930).

ROSS, W. D., *Foundations of Ethics* (Oxford: Clarendon Press, 1939).

WARRENDER, HOWARD, *Hobbes's Theory of Obligation* (Oxford: Clarendon Press, 1957).

IV. SUPEREROGATION

AQUINAS, ST. THOMAS, *Summa Theologica* (London: Burns, Oates, and

Washbourne, Ltd., 1920), Part II, First Part, Qu. 108, Art. 4, and Qu. 184, Art. 3.

BARNES, ARTHUR S., 'Counsels, Evangelical' in *The Catholic Encyclopedia* (New York: Encyclopedia Press, 1908), Vol. IV, pp. 435–6.

CHISHOLM, RODERICK, 'The Ethics of Requirement', *American Philosophical Quarterly*, Vol. 1 (1964), pp. 147–53.

CHISHOLM, RODERICK, 'Supererogation and Offense: A Conceptual Scheme for Ethics', *Ratio*, Vol. 5 (1963), pp. 1–14.

CHOPPA, YOGENDRA, 'Professor Urmson on "Saints and Heroes"', *Philosophy*, Vol. 38 (1963), pp. 160–6.

COOPER, NEIL, 'Rules and Morality', *Proceedings of the Aristotelian Society*, Supp. Vol. 33 (1959), pp. 159–72.

EDGERLY, R., 'Rules and Morality', *Proceedings of the Aristotelian Society*, Supp. Vol. 33 (1959), pp. 173–94.

FEINBERG, JOEL, 'Supererogation and Rules', *Ethics*, Vol. 71 (1961), pp. 276–88.

FULLER, LON L., *The Morality of Law* (New Haven: Yale University Press, 1964), chap. 1.

HANNAY, JAMES O., 'Counsels and Precepts' in James Hastings (ed.), *Encyclopedia of Religion and Ethics* (New York: Chas. Scribner's Sons, 1955), Vol. 4, pp. 203–5.

LADD, JOHN, *The Structure of a Moral Code* (Cambridge, Mass.: Harvard University Press, 1957), pp. 125–30.

MAYO, BERNARD, *Ethics and the Moral Life* (London: Macmillan and Co., 1958), chap. 11 ('Negative and Positive Morality').

SEEBERG, R., 'Supererogation, Works of', in Samuel Macauley Jackson (ed.), *The New Schaff-Herzog Encyclopedia of Religious Knowledge* (Grand Rapids, Michigan: Baker Book House, 1949).

THIEME, KARL, 'Consilia Evangelica' in S. M. Jackson (ed.), *The New Schaff-Herzog Encyclopedia of Religious Knowledge* (Grand Rapids, Michigan: Baker Book House, 1949).

V. CONSCIENCE AND CONSCIENTIOUSNESS

BEISWANGER, G., 'The Logic of Conscience', *Journal of Philosophy*, Vol. 47 (1950), pp. 225–34.

BROAD, C. D., 'Ought We to Fight for Our Country in the Next War?' in *Ethics and the History of Philosophy* (London: Routledge and Kegan Paul, 1952), pp. 232–43.

BUTLER, JOSEPH, *Fifteen Sermons Preached at Rolls Chapel* (London: 1729).

DUNCAN-JONES, A., *Butler's Moral Philosophy* (Harmondsworth : Penguin Books, 1952).

DUNCAN-JONES, A., 'The Notion of Conscience', *Philosophy*, Vol. 30 (1955), pp. 131–40.

FEINBERG, JOEL, 'On Being "Morally Speaking a Murderer"', *Journal of Philosophy*, Vol. 61 (1964), pp. 158–72.

FOTION, N. G., 'On "Conscience"', *Analysis*, Vol. 20 (1959), pp. 41–4.

FROMM, ERICH, *Man For Himself* (London : Routledge and Kegan Paul, 1949, and New York : Holt, Rinehart and Winston, 1947), pp. 92–107.

FUSS, PETER, 'Conscience', *Ethics*, Vol. 74 (1964), pp. 111–20.

KANT, IMMANUEL, *Fundamental Principles of the Metaphysic of Morals*, esp. Section 1.

KOLNAI, A., 'Erroneous Conscience', *Proceedings of the Aristotelian Society*, Vol. 63 (1957–8), pp. 171–99.

LEWIS, H. D., 'Obedience to Conscience', *Mind*, Vol. 54 (1945), pp. 227–53.

LLEWELYN, JOHN E., 'Conscientiousness', *Australasian Journal of Philosophy*, Vol. 38 (1960), pp. 218–24.

McGUIRE, M. C., 'On Conscience', *Journal of Philosophy*, Vol. 60 (1963), pp. 253–63.

NOWELL-SMITH, P. H., *Ethics* (Harmondsworth : Penguin Books, 1954, chaps. 17 ('Conscientiousness') and 18 ('Conscience').

THOMAS, D. O., 'Obedience to Conscience', *Proceedings of the Aristotelian Society*, Vol. 64 (1963–4), pp. 243–59.

WAND, BERNARD, 'The Content and Function of Conscience', *Journal of Philosophy*, Vol. 58 (1961), pp. 765–73.

WAYLAND, FRANCIS, *The Elements of Moral Science*, ed. J. L. Blau (Cambridge, Mass. : Harvard University Press, 1963), chap. 2, pp. 42–75.

VI. INCONTINENCE

ARISTOTLE, *Nichomachean Ethics*, Bk. VII, A.

AQUINAS, ST. THOMAS, *Summa Theologica* (London : Burns, Oates, and Washbourne, Ltd., 1920), Part II, Second Part, Questions 155 ('Continence') and 156 ('Incontinence').

DAVIDSON, DONALD, 'Actions, Reasons, and Causes', *Journal of Philosophy*, Vol. 60 (1963), pp. 685–700.

EWING, A. C., *Second Thoughts in Moral Philosophy* (London : Routledge and Kegan Paul, 1959), chap. 1.

FALK, W. D., '"Ought" and Motivation', *Proceedings of the Aristotelian Society*, Vol. 48 (1947–8), pp. 111–38.

FRANKENA, W. K., 'Obligation and Motivation in Recent Moral Philosophy', in A. I. Melden (ed.), *Essays in Moral Philosophy* (Seattle: University of Washington Press, 1958), pp. 40–81.

HARE, R. M., *Freedom and Reason* (Oxford: Clarendon Press, 1963), pp. 67–85.

GARDINER, P. L., 'On Assenting to a Moral Principle', *Proceedings of the Aristotelian Society*, Vol. 55 (1954–5), pp. 23–44.

GRANT, C. K., 'Akrasia and the Criteria of Assent to Practical Principles', *Mind*, Vol. 65 (1956), pp. 400–7.

LEMMON, E. J., 'Moral Dilemmas', *Philosophical Review*, Vol. 86 (1962), pp. 139–58.

MAYO, BERNARD, *Ethics and the Moral Life* (London: Macmillan, 1958), chap. 7.

NOWELL-SMITH, P. H., *Ethics* (Harmondsworth: Penguin Books, 1954), pp. 265–9.

PLATO, *Republic* and *Protagoras*.

PRICHARD, H. A., *Duty and Interest* (Oxford: Clarendon Press, 1928).

SANTAS, G., 'The Socratic Paradoxes', *Philosophical Review*, Vol. 73 (1964), pp. 147–64.

SANTAS, G., 'Plato's *Protagoras* and Explanations of Weakness', *Philosophical Review*, Vol. 75 (1966), pp. 3–33.

WALSH, J. J., *Aristotle's Conception of Moral Weakness* (New York: Columbia University Press, 1963).

VII. SELF-REGARDING VIRTUES

ARISTOTLE, *Nichomachean Ethics*, Bks. III–V *et passim*.

BAIER, KURT, *The Moral Point of View* (Ithaca, N.Y.: Cornell University Press, 1958), pp. 107–17, 188–90, 214–30.

FALK, W. D., 'Morality, Self, and Others', in H. Castañeda and G. Nakhnikian (eds.) *Morality and the Language of Conduct* (Detroit: Wayne State University, 1963), pp. 25–68.

FOTION, N., 'Can We Have Moral Obligations to Ourselves?', *Australasian Journal of Philosophy*, Vol. 43 (1965), pp. 27–34.

HORSBURGH, H. J. N., 'Prudence', *Proceedings of the Aristotelian Society*, Supp. Vol. 36 (1962), pp. 65–76.

KADING, D., 'Are There Really No Duties to Oneself?', *Ethics*, Vol. 70 (1960).

KANT, IMMANUEL, *Fundamental Principles of the Metaphysic of Morals*, esp. Section II.

Knight, F., 'I, Me, My Self, and My Duties', *Ethics*, Vol. 71 (1961), pp. 209–12.

Mabbott, J. D., 'Prudence', *Proceedings of the Aristotelian Society*, Supp. Vol. 36 (1962), pp. 51–64.

Mothersill, Mary, 'Professor Wick on Duties to Oneself', *Ethics*, Vol. 71 (1961), pp. 205–8.

Plato, *Republic*.

Prichard, H. A., *Duty and Interest* (Oxford: Oxford University Press, 1928).

Singer, M., 'On Duties to Oneself', *Ethics*, Vol. 69 (1959), pp. 202–5.

von Wright, Georg, *The Varieties of Goodness* (London: Routledge and Kegan Paul, 1963), chap. 7, esp. pp. 149–54.

Wick, W., 'More About Duties to Oneself', *Ethics*, Vol. 70 (1960), pp. 158–63.

Wick, W., 'Still More About Duties to Oneself', *Ethics*, Vol. 71 (1961), pp. 213–17.

VIII. JUSTICE AND MORAL EQUALITY

Aristotle, *Nichomachean Ethics*, Bk. v.

Berlin, Isaiah, 'Equality', *Proceedings of the Aristotelian Society*, Vol. 56 (1955–6), pp. 301–26.

Brandt, R. B. (ed.), *Social Justice* (Englewood Cliffs: Prentice-Hall, 1962).

Beardsley, E. L., 'Determinism and Moral Perspectives', *Philosophy and Phenomenological Research*, Vol. 21 (1960), pp. 1–20.

Chapman, John, 'Justice and Fairness', in C. J. Friedrich and J. W. Chapman (eds.), *Nomos VI: Justice* (New York: Atherton Press, 1963), pp. 147–69.

Feinberg, Joel, 'Justice and Personal Desert', in C. J. Friedrich and J. W. Chapman (eds.), *Nomos VI: Justice* (New York: Atherton Press, 1963), pp. 68–97.

Findlay, J. N., 'The Structure of the Kingdom of Ends', *Proceedings of the British Academy*, Vol. 43 (1957), pp. 97–115.

Foot, Philippa, 'Moral Beliefs', *Proceedings of the Aristotelian Society*, Vol. 59, pp. 83–104.

Frankena, W. K., 'Some Beliefs About Justice', The Lindley Lecture (1966), published by the Department of Philosophy, University of Kansas.

Fried, Charles, 'Justice and Liberty' in C. J. Friedrich and J. W. Chapman (eds.), *Nomos VI: Justice* (New York: Atherton Press, 1963), pp. 126–46.

Hook, Sidney (ed.), *Law and Philosophy* (New York: New York University Press, 1964).

Hume, David, *Enquiry Concerning the Principles of Morals*, Section III.

Kant, Immanuel, *Fundamental Principles of the Metaphysic of Morals*, esp. Section II.

Margolis, Joseph, 'That All Men Are Created Equal', *Journal of Philosophy*, Vol. 52 (1955), pp. 337–46.

Melden, A. I., *Rights and Right Conduct* (Oxford: B. Blackwell, 1959).

Piaget, Jean, *The Moral Judgement of the Child* (London: Routledge & Kegan Paul, 1960).

Pennock, J. R. and Chapman, C. H. (eds.), *Nomos IX: Equality* (New York: Atherton Press, 1967).

Raphael, D. D., 'Equality and Equity', *Philosophy*, Vol. 22 (1946), pp. 118–32.

Raphael, D. D., 'Justice and Liberty', *Proceedings of the Aristotelian Society*, Vol. 51 (1950–1), pp. 167–96.

Raphael, D. D., 'Conservative and Prosthetic Justice', *Political Studies*, Vol. 12 (1964), pp. 149–62.

Rousseau, J. J., *Emile* (London: Everyman, 1911), pp. 172–215

Runciman, W. G., 'Social Equality', *Philosophical Quarterly*, Vol. 17 (1967), pp. 221–30.

Rawls, J., 'Justice as Fairness', *Philosophical Review*, Vol. 68 (1958), pp. 164–94.

Rawls, J., 'Constitutional Liberty and the Concept of Justice', in C. J. Friedrich and J. W. Chapman (eds.), *Nomos VI: Justice* (New York: Atherton Press, 1963), pp. 98–125.

Rawls, J., 'Legal Obligation and the Duty of Fair Play, in Sidney Hook (ed.), *Law and Philosophy* (New York: New York University Press, 1964), pp. 3–18.

Von Leyden, W., 'On Justifying Inequality', *Political Studies*, Vol. 11 (1963), pp. 56–70.

Wolff, Robert P., 'A Refutation of Rawls's Theorem on Justice', *Journal of Philosophy*, Vol. 63 (1966), pp. 179–90.

Wollheim, Richard, 'Equality', *Proceedings of the Aristotelian Society*, Vol. 56 (1955–6), pp. 281–300.

Young, Michael, *The Rise of the Meritocracy* (London: Thames and Hudson, 1958).

INDEX OF NAMES

(not including authors mentioned only in the Bibliography)